THE COOKING DOC'S
KIDNEY-HEALTHY
COOKING

A MODERN 10-STEP GUIDE TO PREVENTING & MANAGING KIDNEY DISEASE

BLAKE SHUSTERMAN, MD

DELICIOUS RECIPES,
MOTIVATIONAL STORIES &
THE LATEST SCIENCE!

"I always tell my patients that what they eat is 100-fold more important than the pills I give them. The Cooking Doc provides the details you need to create a healthier lifestyle and better self-management of kidney disease. Outside the United States, many people with kidney disease do not take as many medications for their blood pressure or to lower phosphate levels because they do not eat processed foods. Cooking healthy will make you healthier and this book will open the door to a new way of life."

—Holly Kramer, MD, MPH.
Nephrologist and President, National Kidney Foundation

"The Cooking Doc's book is a must-read for anyone who wants to slow progression of kidney disease, or who wants to eat more healthfully! Dr. Blake translates the most up-to-date nutrition science into actionable lifestyle changes. This book is filled with delicious recipes to help you #ChangeYourBuds and start cooking for kidney health. His recipes are not complicated, so even people with minimal cooking skills can make them. I recommend this book to anyone who wants to eat right to protect their kidneys."

—Melanie Betz, MS, RD, CSR, CSG.
The Kidney Dietitian, www.thekidneydietitian.org

THE COOKING DOC'S KIDNEY-HEALTHY COOKING

A Modern 10-Step Guide to Preventing & Managing Kidney Disease

Blake Shusterman, MD

For more information, go to: www.thecookingdoc.co.

First edition October 2020

Book design by Danielle Foster
Photography by Andrew Meade
Food and prop styling by Claire Perez
Images @ Shutterstock/Natalia Hubbert pp. 2, 3, 16, 26, 32, 37, 39, 49, 68, 72, 76, 84, 86, 102, 104, 105, 106, 112, 113, 118, 127, 252; Shutterstock/masha.an p. 18; Shutterstock/runLenarun p. 22; Shutterstock/Rina Shee p. 33; Shutterstock/R_lion_O p. 46; Shutterstock/Maltiase p. 48; Shutterstock/2NatS p. 102; Shutterstock/Tefi p. 120

Library of Congress Cataloging-in-Publication Data is on file at the Library of Congress.

ISBN: 978-1-7356793-0-3 (paperback)
ISBN: 978-1-7356793-1-0 (e-book)
ISBN: 978-1-7356793-2-7 (Adobe PDF version)

DISCLAIMER

This book is intended as a reference only, not as a medical manual. The information provided here is designed to help you make informed decisions about your diet and health. It is not intended as a substitute for the medical advice of physicians or for any treatment that may have been prescribed by your doctor. You should consult a physician regularly in all matters relating to your health. If you suspect that you have a medical condition, I urge you to seek competent medical help. Please consult with your own physician or healthcare specialist regarding the suggestions and recommendations made in this book. The use of this book implies your acceptance of this disclaimer.

Mention of specific products, companies, organizations, or authorities in this book does not imply endorsement by the author or publisher, nor does mention of specific products, companies, organizations, or authorities imply that they endorse or are affiliated in any way with this book, its author, or the publisher.

The personal examples in this book are compilations of individual stories and experiences often combined into one story to make a more specific point. All names and identifying details regarding the basis for these examples have been changed to protect the privacy of individuals.

TABLE OF CONTENTS

INTRODUCTION   1

PART I
10 STEPS

STEP 1
UNDERSTAND YOUR KIDNEYS   17

STEP 2
CHOOSE YOUR BEVERAGES WISELY   25
    SWEET TEA SUBSTITUTE   33
    BERRY-BANANA HEMP SMOOTHIE   40
    PUMPKIN PIE SMOOTHIE   41

STEP 3
UNCOVER HIDDEN SALT &
#CHANGEYOURBUDS   43

STEP 4
EMBRACE PLANT-BASED EATING   61
    ROASTED SWEET POTATOES   66

STEP 5
GET POTASSIUM RIGHT   67
    FIVE-MINUTE SPINACH   73
    BRAISED PURPLE CABBAGE   78

STEP 6
AVOID HIGH-PROTEIN PITFALLS   81

STEP 7
DISCOVER ALKALINE-RICH FOODS   89
    KALE & GOLDEN RAISIN SALAD   94
    SAUTEED RAINBOW CHARD & APPLES   97

STEP 8
IDENTIFY & ELIMINATE SNEAKY
PHOSPHORUS   99

STEP 9
INTEGRATE THE DASH, MEDITERRANEAN
& DIABETIC DIETS INTO YOUR ROUTINE   107
    ROASTED BEET, GOAT CHEESE & WALNUT SALAD
    WITH BLUEBERRY VINAIGRETTE   116

STEP 10
KEEP AN OPEN MIND IF YOU
START DIALYSIS   123

PART II
RECIPES

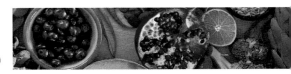

SOUPS 133

NO-SODIUM CHICKEN STOCK — 134
NO-SODIUM VEGETABLE STOCK — 136
GRANDMA JULIE'S CHICKEN SOUP — 137
HEARTY LENTIL VEGETABLE SOUP — 139
LEEK & YELLOW SQUASH SOUP — 141

SPREADS, SNACKS & SAUCES 143

DEVILED EGGS WITH PICKLED RED ONION — 144
QUICK PICKLED RED ONIONS — 145
CRISPY CHICKPEAS — 146
SMOKY EGGPLANT SPREAD — 148
ROASTED RED PEPPER & WHITE BEAN HUMMUS — 149
SALSA FRESCA — 150
EDAMAME DIP — 152
BUTTER BEAN DIP — 153
TZATZIKI SAUCE — 154
AVOCADO LIME CREMA — 155

BREAKFAST 157

MAPLE CINNAMON CHIA PUDDING — 158
SLOW-COOKED STEEL-CUT OATS — 160
SPICED APRICOT WALNUT MUFFINS — 161
EGG MUFFINS WITH SPINACH & ARTICHOKE HEARTS — 162
SUNFLOWER BUTTER & BLUEBERRY TOAST — 164
AVOCADO TOAST WITH CHILE FLAKES — 165

PLANT BASED 167

STUFFED ZUCCHINI BOATS — 168
CORN & BLACK BEAN QUESADILLA — 170
CURRIED SWEET POTATOES & CHICKPEAS — 173
CRANBERRY, PEPITA & BROCCOLI SALAD — 175
VEGAN BOLOGNESE SAUCE — 176
MEDITERRANEAN CHOPPED SALAD — 178

CHICKEN 181

SHEET PAN LEMON-LIME CHICKEN & POTATOES — 182
ZA'ATAR CHICKEN SALAD — 185
CHICKEN FARRO BOWLS — 187
CREOLE CHICKEN BURGERS — 189
SPICED CHICKEN, ORANGE & AVOCADO SALAD — 191
SEARED CAJUN CHICKEN THIGHS — 193
BAKED CHICKEN BREASTS — 194

SEAFOOD 197

LEMON CAPER ROASTED SALMON — 198
TUNA, CANNELLINI & DILL SALAD — 200
SEARED SALMON WITH TZATZIKI SAUCE — 203
SALMON BURGER — 205
THAI SHRIMP SALAD — 206

BEANS, GRAINS & PASTA — 209

SOUTHWEST QUINOA SALAD — 210

LIGHT MACARONI & CHEESE WITH PEAS — 212

CHICKEN, KALE & FARRO CASSEROLE — 214

ROASTED TOMATO & ZUCCHINI SPAGHETTI WITH VEGAN BASIL-CASHEW PESTO — 216

ROASTED CARROTS, CRANBERRIES & COUSCOUS — 219

LEMON HERB COUSCOUS SALAD — 221

VEGETARIAN SUMMER PASTA SALAD — 222

VEGETABLE SIDES — 225

BROCCOLI-CAULIFLOWER MASH WITH ROASTED GARLIC — 226

ROASTED GARLIC — 227

SAUTEED BROCCOLINI & GARLIC — 228

LEMONY CAULIFLOWER RICE — 229

BALSAMIC ROASTED VEGETABLES — 230

BABY BOK CHOY WITH GINGER & GARLIC — 232

ROASTED BRUSSELS SPROUTS — 233

SWEETS — 235

PEACH-RASPBERRY SKILLET BAKE — 236

HEALTHIER RICE PUDDING — 238

STEWED CINNAMON APPLES — 239

ALMOND-PUMPKIN SEED CHOCOLATE BARK — 240

DRESSINGS & SPICE BLENDS — 243

MEDITERRANEAN VINAIGRETTE — 244

DIJON VINAIGRETTE — 244

LEMON SHALLOT VINAIGRETTE — 245

BALSAMIC VINAIGRETTE — 245

BLUEBERRY VINAIGRETTE — 246

RED WINE VINAIGRETTE — 248

SHERRY VINAIGRETTE — 248

CUMIN LIME VINAIGRETTE — 249

NO-SODIUM ALL-PURPOSE SEASONING — 250

NO-SODIUM CAJUN SEASONING — 251

ENDNOTES — 253

ACKNOWLEDGMENTS — 256

RECIPE INDEX — 257

INDEX — 260

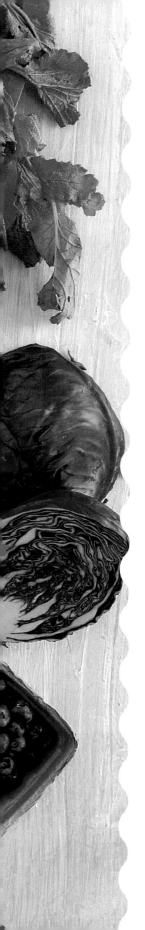

INTRODUCTION

My family knows me as Blake. My patients know me as Dr. Shusterman. The online world knows me as The Cooking Doc. Before we begin, I'll share the background of all three of my identities to help you fully appreciate and understand this book.

I'm a nephrologist, which means that I specialize in the branch of medicine that deals with the kidneys. Also known as nephrology, this specialty covers all aspects of kidney health and kidney disease, including high blood pressure, dialysis, and kidney transplants, among many others. My nine years of medical training taught me exactly how the kidneys work, down to the microscopic level, the mechanisms in the body that produce chronic kidney disease (CKD), and how to provide cutting-edge, life-saving care for hospitalized people with failing kidneys.

Once I finished my extensive education, I decided to join a practice in upstate South Carolina.

Despite all my training, I was unprepared for what awaited me. Upon arrival in a state that perennially ranks among the top 10 in rates of diabetes, obesity, and high blood pressure, I found myself buried in a complex pile of kidney disease risk factors, including poverty, genetics, and dietary ignorance. Neither my medical school, my residency, nor my fellowship had taught me how to best help these patients. Now that I was out in the real world, I had hundreds of people counting on me to care for them in their battles with high blood pressure, progressive kidney disease, and obesity. Many were also struggling to afford medications, find and keep jobs, care for elderly or sick family members, and figure out what foods to buy and eat.

I knew all the science I needed to be a kidney doctor. I knew the medications that my patients would need. I knew the ins and outs of dialysis. I also knew that being an excellent doctor required more than that. How could I enter this community and find a way to make a difference in these people's lives? Where would I find my calling in the field of kidney disease, and how could I help real people manage their very real kidney disease in South Carolina?

The first few weeks of my practice pointed me toward that calling. On my first day at my new job, I was set to see patients at a dialysis center in a rural town. I arrived early (8 a.m.) to tour the facility while waiting for my new partner to arrive. The last stop in my self-guided tour was the lobby—and there, two large, rectangular glass-front machines caught my eye.

They weren't the latest and greatest dialysis machines. Instead, they contained food: snacks and soda. On one side, Doritos, Cheetos, and Oreos, and on the other side, Coca-Cola, Mountain Dew, and Orange Crush; the same foods that likely contributed to many patients' kidney failure were presented as food options in the lobby of the health-care facility providing them with lifesaving treatment! I was stunned. What kind of example were we setting for our patients? Why would a dialysis center agree to put these foods front and center in their lobby?

No one else had given it a second thought. When I suggested that the dialysis unit should remove the machines or provide healthier food options inside them, the nurses, patients, technicians, and other doctors looked at me like I was crazy. The machines stayed.

Individual meetings with my patients over the next few months provided further enlightenment. I'd often ask what they'd eaten for breakfast that day.

"A bacon, egg, and cheese biscuit."

"Grits with butter and orange juice."

"Waffles and sausage."

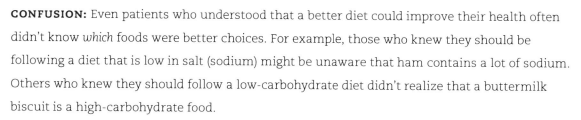

When I asked if they knew that some of these foods may make their diseases more difficult to manage—sending blood pressure higher or diabetes out of control—I heard a few common refrains:

SURPRISE: Many didn't realize that diet had such a significant effect on their medical conditions.

CONFUSION: Even patients who understood that a better diet could improve their health often didn't know *which* foods were better choices. For example, those who knew they should be following a diet that is low in salt (sodium) might be unaware that ham contains a lot of sodium. Others who knew they should follow a low-carbohydrate diet didn't realize that a buttermilk biscuit is a high-carbohydrate food.

LACK OF CONTROL: Husbands told me that their wives did "all the shopping and cooking." Elderly patients often lived with their children or grandchildren and therefore couldn't choose the foods they ate.

MONEY WORRIES: Many patients told me that they were on a very limited income and therefore couldn't afford fresh, healthy food.

TIME PRESSURE: So many patients recounted that it was difficult to shop for and prepare healthy food given their busy lives, considering that they worked multiple jobs or cared for children or ailing family members.

THE YUCK FACTOR: Almost everyone told me that healthy food didn't "taste good" and didn't "fill me up." I can't tell you how many times I heard that I was crazy to suggest that someone eat oatmeal with berries instead of grits with butter and salt. Or how many patients told me that they'd tried the salads at McDonalds, but they weren't filling—and tasted awful, to boot.

Perhaps you have personally shared some of the same thoughts as my patients.

Other than my obvious concern about my patients' health, I had a more personal reason to focus on what my patients were eating: I love food, I love eating, and I love cooking. From the time when I was very young, our family activities always revolved around food: "What's for dinner?" "Where are we going to dinner?" The second we'd sit down to eat a meal, we'd start planning the next one. Family dinners defined my childhood, and cooking and sharing meals together defined my holiday celebrations. We shared our home-cooked meals through good times and bad.

From time to time, I even impress my wife with my cooking. Although my repertoire was very limited at the time I proposed to her, I knew enough to make a shrimp cocktail for her to celebrate the event. Now that I think about it, though, I probably bought precooked shrimp in a little plastic container from the grocery store—but I *definitely* made the cocktail sauce.

As my interest grew in figuring out how to improve kidney health through food, I realized I had to come up with an encouraging and inspiring way to reach out to my patients. When I was growing up, I learned to cook by watching *Every Day with Rachael Ray*, *Top Chef*, and Food Network shows, so I decided to follow in their footsteps: I'd teach patients with kidney disease by making cooking videos. I developed an online persona, The Cooking Doc®, and I created videos that showcased how to cook healthy food in delicious ways.

My approach didn't catch on right away in my neck of the woods, South Carolina. I quickly realized that most people around there didn't believe that healthy cooking could taste good. Their taste buds were so conditioned to traditional Southern food and fast food that they couldn't appreciate the unfamiliar flavors of freshly cooked and differently seasoned meals.

I saw it every day in my practice. For example, many of my patients grew up eating heavily salted food. So when I suggested that they try vegetables seasoned with extra virgin olive oil, vinegar, and a tiny pinch of salt, they said it tasted like someone had forgotten to season them. Those who had quenched their thirst with Coca-Cola or Mountain Dew every day since they were young didn't take kindly to my suggestion to drink mostly water, calling it "tasteless" and "gross." Many patients were accustomed to gathering with family and friends each Sunday after church for a meal of fried chicken, macaroni and cheese, and potato salad. Imagine their horror when I suggested baked chicken with a quinoa or chickpea salad instead.

These are the circumstances that led me to develop my Change Your Buds philosophy and the #ChangeYourBuds hashtag. "Changing your buds" means retraining—in a slow and deliberate manner—your taste buds to appreciate and enjoy healthier foods. This book shows you how, in detail. As you get ready to learn, consider these broad guidelines:

* Incorporate healthier foods and cooking techniques into your diet over the course of a few years, instead of all at once.

* Learn to cook with new seasonings and practice cooking techniques that highlight the natural flavors and textures of vegetables, grains, leaner meats, and beans.

* Be flexible.

* Pay attention to how your body feels when you cut down on soda and fast food. Spoiler alert: you'll feel better over time.

* Understand that some healthy foods will not satisfy your taste buds in the same way as the foods you may be used to eating. For me, nothing can come close to the hot, crunchy, salty first bite of a fistful of McDonald's French fries or the rich decadence of chocolate cake. These foods aren't inherently "bad," and they can fit into a healthy diet if they're consumed only on occasion. I still eat these foods on special occasions—not more than once every couple of months. The rest of the time, I'll substitute baked French fries or pieces of dark chocolate instead.

* Gather the support of your family.

* Restock your pantry and refrigerator with healthy options.

* Shop frequently.

* Try new foods.

* Find a few healthy breakfast recipes that you enjoy and stick to them.

* Learning to change your taste buds won't happen if you don't commit to cooking at home. This takes dedication, support, and time. If you are transitioning from a lifestyle of dining out every day to one where you're cooking at home each day, you need to add an hour to your daily schedule to account for the time you'll spend shopping, cooking, and cleaning up. If you don't think you have a spare hour each day to dedicate to home cooking, consider what activities you can cut out of your daily life. You may find that extra hour by cutting back on watching TV, waking up half an hour earlier, or limiting your internet/social-media surfing every day.

Focus on *why* you're making this transition. You're choosing to cook at home and eat healthier because your health is important to you and your family. You've decided to learn to enjoy healthier foods because you want to protect your heart, your kidneys, and your brain as much as possible. You've dedicated yourself to changing your buds because you want to support the only body you have for as long as you can.

On my Cooking Doc website (www.thecookingdoc.co), Facebook (www.facebook.com/thecookingdoc) and Instagram (www.instagram.com/thecookingdoc) pages, and YouTube channel (www.youtube.com /user/CarolinaNephrologyTV), you'll find some of the best resources available for healthy cooking and eating. There, you'll see me in my twin roles of chef and doctor. My cooking videos will show you how to create delicious food that will help keep you and your kidneys healthy.

Using This Book

Kidney disease is relentless. Are you? The unrelenting nature of kidney disease can wear down even the strongest person. The best way to challenge this ruthless condition is with your own unwavering persistence. The tips you'll discover in this book will help you be relentless, too. Before we discuss specifics, though, let's figure out where you are in your journey.

When you look in the mirror, who do you see looking back at you? Someone who sits passively on the sidelines, delegating the management of your chronic kidney disease, diabetes, and high blood pressure to doctors? A confused patient who constantly scours the internet for information about the best diets and medications but remains uneasy and discouraged by the conflicting information you find there? Maybe you see a frightened reflection, someone who has heard your doctors' pleas and warnings but who remains in denial about your failing kidneys. Or is there a fighter looking back, determined to keep yourself healthy and well?

It doesn't matter if any or all of these descriptions apply to you; this book will help. Simply by choosing to read it, you've made it clear that you refuse to let kidney disease define you. I've spent the last 10 years searching for the best foods and dietary patterns for preserving kidney health, and I'm ready to share that information with you. When you look at yourself in the mirror, I want you to see a confident, informed person dedicated to making whatever changes are necessary and possible to protect your health. Whether you've just been diagnosed with kidney disease, or you are simply looking to make preventive changes to protect your kidneys' normal health, this book will provide the tools and the information you need to change your diet and make it happen.

MY ROLE

My love for food and cooking, combined with my desire to improve the care of people with kidney disease, provided the inspiration for The Cooking Doc® brand and this book, but that's not the whole story of my beginnings. To fully understand my motivations, I must tell you about one of my greatest failures as a doctor.

Many years ago, I was once fired by a patient, who I'll call Clara. A fiery woman in her sixties, Clara had recently been referred to me after a diagnosis of early-stage kidney disease (Stage 3A chronic kidney disease). I found that Clara's kidney function was nearly normal, but nonetheless, she asked me for guidance on how to help her kidneys stay in good shape through changes in her diet.

And that's where I failed Clara. Instead of providing her with tools to make the dietary changes she sought, I told her that her kidneys were in such good shape that she didn't need to worry about her diet. Clara was inquisitive, dedicated, and ready to take control, and she'd turned to me for advice. In return, I brushed her off with reassurance and platitudes. Before she left the office, she fired me.

For years, I thought Clara was in the wrong. Yet as my understanding of the relationship between food and kidney disease grew, along with my awareness of how important it was for me to inspire my patients to improve their own situations, I realized that the fault entirely was on me. I had not lived up to my responsibility as her doctor. Perhaps Clara didn't need a traditional "renal (remember, renal means kidney related) diet," but I should have explained how she could take control of the situation and protect her kidneys. I learned so much from that experience. That's why I've put everything I know about managing kidney disease through diet into this book, in the hope that I'll never disappoint another patient.

HOW THIS BOOK CAN HELP YOU

This book is the resource I should have been able to provide to Clara. It will help you maintain your kidney function—whether or not you already have kidney disease. It will make you feel better, and it will lower your risk of developing kidney failure—when the only treatments available are dialysis or a transplant.

As patients with kidney disease, diabetes, or high blood pressure go from doctor to doctor, they often accumulate dozens of medications but never acquire knowledge about how to manage these conditions by changing their diet. Eating the right foods just might:

* Allow you to reduce the dosage of or even stop taking some blood pressure and diabetes medications.

* Delay the need for dialysis.

* Improve your kidney function.

* Boost your energy.

* Help you lose weight.

* Promote your gut health.

Adding a regular exercise routine to these changes can lead to more drastic improvements.

In this book, you'll discover how to eat in a way that can benefit your kidneys. You'll learn how to make lifestyle changes that will make a huge difference in your health: eating more fruits and vegetables, limiting your red meat intake, packing your own lunches and snacks when you're on the go, and learning how to cook healthy meals at home instead of going out to restaurants and fast-food joints all the time. You can start adopting these healthy and tasty dietary patterns today, and over time, they will become habit. I want you to be able to eat well, love what you eat, and maintain the important role food plays in your family and traditions. With a little practice, this kind of healthy eating will become second nature.

Although many of the ideas in this book are intended specifically for people with chronic kidney disease (CKD) who are not on dialysis, anyone who wants to improve their diet in a way that helps prevent obesity, diabetes, high blood pressure, and kidney disease can benefit from them.

As you read this book, remember that there is no one-size-fits-all way of eating. Each suggestion or tip does not apply to everyone with kidney disease or to everyone who reads this book. It's probable that you won't like some of the recipes and foods I include. Some of the tips may be hard or impossible for you to follow. There are likely guidelines that I mention that you may not agree with. That's all OK. Use this book as a guide to help you change your eating habits—a jumping-off point for bettering your health that will help you find foods and menus you can stick with in the long term. Let this book inspire you to cook and create delicious food at home. Take the suggestions to your doctor or dietitian and find the ones that apply specifically to wherever you are in your journey with kidney disease.

In each chapter, you'll find specific information on the best foods to eat and the science behind them. If you're not particularly interested in the science, just read the stories and tips, and then skip right to the delicious and easy-to-make recipes.

IMPORTANT NOTE: **Before you make any significant changes to your diet, make sure you check first with a dietitian or a doctor. They can help you avoid many common dietary mistakes, make sure you end up with a diet that's tailored to your stage of kidney disease, and help keep you on the right track.**

JOE AND MARK

I used to have a pair of first cousins, Joe and Mark, as patients. The fathers of both men had ended up on dialysis before they passed away, so the cousins were referred to me to help them manage their own kidney disease and avoid the same fate.

Joe arrived for the first visit with his wife and 14-year-old daughter. Gripped with fears that he was heading in the same direction as his father and resolved to avoid dialysis, Joe and his wife decided to join forces and overhaul their lifestyle together. They struggled, to be sure. Obstacles cropped up frequently along the way, including money worries, family illnesses, and work responsibilities. Nevertheless, they persisted, and as a family, they learned to eat fast food less frequently, cook nutritious meals at home, and exercise together. I last saw Joe five years ago, when he and his family moved out of state. At that point, his kidney function had stabilized, and he remained dedicated to his path of wellness.

Mark took a different route. Shortly after I met him, Mark's mother-in-law became ill, and his wife had to give up her job to care for her. Mark's priorities changed as a result: he had to focus on providing for his family during this difficult time. He worked a 70-hour week driving a truck, which meant that he rarely slept well and ended up eating fast food often.

Most of the time, Mark took his medications, but in some months, he couldn't afford them, and in others, he forgot about them altogether. I saw him only rarely, as he could only come in when he had a weekday off.

You can imagine the result: Mark's kidney function slowly declined. Three years after our first visit, I gave Mark the difficult news that his kidneys had failed. He started dialysis. When talking to Mark, I fully understood the choices that he had made. He prided himself on being able to care for his family. But because he did not have a family support system, a financial cushion, or a governmental backstop to help him through his difficult time, his only option was to sacrifice his personal health and wellness for that of his family. Frankly, this tale says as much or more about the medical and support system in the United States as it does about the benefits of food on kidney health. If Mark had thought his cousin Joe's path was possible for him, he certainly would have taken it. Would Mark's kidneys have remained stable if he had been given the opportunity to follow the same path as Joe? I'm not sure, but he would have had a better chance. This is the chance I want you to have.

SETTING EXPECTATIONS

Consider the following case study: Betty, a spry 78-year-old woman who worked full time at a library, became my patient late in the progression of her kidney disease. When Betty and her daughter Mary came to our first appointment, both were shocked to learn that Betty's kidneys were functioning at only 18 percent of their capacity. Betty's regular doctor was a grade-school classmate of hers—an old-school family doctor who had delivered her children and cared for her husband until his death. Despite their close connection, her doctor had never told her about her kidney disease.

As they absorbed the diagnosis, Betty and Mary asked me about dietary changes that could help improve her kidney function and keep her off dialysis. Over the next three or four visits, I provided the same recommendations described in this book, and both Betty and her daughter agreed to follow my guidance to the letter.

Over time, Betty lost 10 pounds, and Mary lost thirty. Betty's high blood pressure and diabetes numbers were better than they'd been in 15 years. Unfortunately, Betty's kidneys failed despite the measures she'd taken, and she started dialysis about a year later. So even though Betty and Mary had succeeded in improving many aspects of their health, Betty's kidney function did not improve. Perhaps the kidney failure would have happened sooner if she hadn't followed through so well. I like to think so, but it's impossible to know for sure.

Believe it or not, situations like the one Betty found herself in—discovering that she had kidney disease years after her doctor had first recognized it—are very common. Many doctors note abnormal kidney function and then go on to watch their patients' kidneys slowly deteriorate for years without telling them. I see this every day. By withholding this information, doctors rob their patients of the opportunity to change their dietary and health habits before their kidney function gets worse. Learn from this: each time you see your primary care doctor, ask explicitly about your kidney function.

Although this book provides insight into how to manage kidney disease with diet, I must be clear on this: these measures will not cure kidney disease, nor will they fully reverse it. Even if you follow them perfectly, these guidelines may not keep you off dialysis or from needing a kidney transplant in the future. Last, they won't take the place of many of the medications your doctors may recommend to help control your medical problems. That said, this helpful information will hopefully slow or halt the progression of your kidney disease and supply you with tools that can improve many other aspects of your health.

10 STEPS: THE FUNDAMENTALS OF THE COOKING DOC'S KIDNEY DIET

I use a 10-step plan to set my patients on the path to kidney health. Some may take you months to achieve, and that's OK. Even if you slowly incorporate these steps into your diet over the course of years, you're moving toward a lifetime of health and wellness. In this book, I've broken out each of the steps into chapters. Some people may prefer to master a chapter before moving on, and others may choose to jump around a bit and pick bits and pieces from each chapter. Either approach is great! The steps are:

STEP 1: Understand your kidneys.

STEP 2: Choose your beverages wisely. Change your drinking habits and opt for unsweetened options.

STEP 3: Uncover hidden salt and #ChangeYourBuds to prefer less salt. Stock your pantry and refrigerator with ingredients that will allow you to create delicious, reduced-sodium meals from scratch—and then *practice, practice, practice* cooking them.

STEP 4: Embrace plant-based eating.

STEP 5: Get potassium right. Speak to your doctor or dietitian about how much potassium you can safely eat.

STEP 6: Avoid high-protein pitfalls.

STEP 7: Discover alkaline-rich foods.

STEP 8: Identify and eliminate sneaky phosphorus.

STEP 9: Integrate the DASH, Mediterranean, and Diabetic diets into your routine.

STEP 10: If you are starting dialysis, forget most of what you have learned before and start from scratch. If your kidneys fail and you require dialysis, don't despair. Your diet will need to change significantly, but diet can still help manage your health while on dialysis.

These steps are most effective when started during Stage 1–3 CKD. However, if you have Stage 4 or 5 CKD, or are on dialysis, you will find tips and tricks to help you manage and understand the relationship between food and kidney health.

DIETITIANS: A TERRIFIC RESOURCE

If you have access to dietitians in your community, use them. After you read this book, you may be left with many questions about which recipes are right for your stage of kidney disease and how to best make changes into your own diet. Receiving individualized counseling from a registered dietitian on these issues will help you make these changes in a manageable way.

Another benefit: dietitians tailor their recommendations to your specific situation and consider any family dynamics or financial limitations you may be facing. Most hospitals have registered dietitians on staff, and many have dietitians who specialize in kidney disease. Often, their consultations are covered by insurance. Ask your doctor for a referral or recommendation, or you can visit the website for the Academy of Nutrition and Dietetics (www.eatright.org) to find a dietitian in your area.

EXERCISE

During my third year of medical school, my fellow students and I were assigned to take each other's blood pressure. After splitting up into pairs, I took the first practice round. My partner's blood pressures were normal: 130/60, 120/58, 136/64. Then, she and I switched places. She awkwardly placed the cuff on my bicep, placed the bell of her stethoscope on my upper arm, and positioned the earpieces. After two minutes of inexperienced squeezing and releasing, she finally arrived at a shockingly high result: 170/110.

Assuming an error in her technique, I insisted she repeat the reading, and then I had our professor verify the result. The answer was consistent and undeniable: I had hypertension. Shortly thereafter, I started a medication regimen and continued it the next seven years. During that time, my life was hectic: my last two years of medical school, three years of residency, and two years in a fellowship. On top of that, my wife and I had a baby. I didn't have much free time, and I didn't exercise more than once a week.

At the end of that difficult journey, I finally found myself with a manageable schedule. I started to exercise more often and incorporated running into my regular routine. The effect on my blood pressure was downright magical. After two years of regular exercise and working closely with my doctor, I was able to discontinue all my blood pressure medication. Today, I continue to run multiple times a week, and my blood pressure remains excellent. While my results were somewhat atypical, some of my patients have achieved similar results by exercising regularly.

Exercise is the closest thing doctors have to a miracle drug. It can help improve your mood, increase your energy, clear your head, ease joint pain, and help maintain the health of almost every organ system in your body. No pill can do all that. If you don't have any dedicated exercise time built into your routine, find a way to make it happen.

You may have noticed that I didn't mention weight loss as a reason to exercise. Many people find that exercise is not an effective way to lose weight, and by focusing on that aspect of it, they're easily discouraged and stop. You should exercise because it makes you feel better, not because you want to lose weight.

Hundreds of different exercise options are available to you these days. Find one you enjoy and stick with it for as long as you can. If you can't find a group class or exercise routine in your area that you enjoy, search YouTube, Hulu, or Netflix for a routine you can do at home. Or find an app that encourages you to move in a way that feels good for you, whether it's a yoga program or a fitness tracker that motivates you to walk more each day.

Here's the bottom line:

Get moving!

Set a goal to move every day, or for at least 150 minutes each week.

PART I
10 STEPS

STEP 1

UNDERSTAND YOUR KIDNEYS

Don't let the cardiologists and poets fool you: your kidneys are the real heart and soul of your body. (Of course, as a kidney doctor, I'm a little biased.) What if I told you that more than any other organ, your kidneys regulate your blood pressure? What if I told you that your kidneys are the main filters of the blood in your body, keeping it clean and regulated? What if I told you that the inner workings of these tiny little organs are so complicated, we still don't fully understand everything they do? Last, what if I told you that your kidneys are such sensitive little buggers that all sorts of things can cause short- and long-term damage to them, including medications, herbs, infections, and failure of other organ systems, like the liver and heart. If you knew all that about your kidneys, you would want to do everything possible to keep them functioning in tip-top shape.

Even though they do so much more inside the body, let's reduce the kidneys and their function down to a very simplistic idea for a minute: they remind me of the song "Washing Machine," which my brother used to play all the time when he was little.

"The washing machine / the washing machine / the clothes go in dirty / the clothes come out clean."

My version has similar lyrics: "The kidney machine / the kidney machine / the blood goes in dirty / the blood comes out clean."

In the following section, you'll learn what you need to know about your kidneys to protect their long-term health.

The ABCs of Kidney Function and Kidney Disease

A t birth, you have between 700,000 and 1.8 million working filters, known as glomeruli, per kidney. This number slowly decreases as you age.

B lood flows into the kidney through the renal artery, and the filtered blood flows out through the renal vein. About 180 liters (almost 50 gallons) of blood flows through your kidneys each day.

C reatinine is a measure of kidney function. It is produced in your body every day as old muscle cells die, and it floats around in the bloodstream until the kidneys remove it. When working normally, the kidneys keep blood creatinine levels below 1.3 mg/dL for most men and below 1.1 mg/dL for most women. If the kidneys are having difficulty, creatinine levels in the blood will rise. Generally speaking, the higher the creatinine level, the worse the kidney function, but creatinine level is not a perfect marker of how the kidneys are filtering: age, muscle mass, gender, and weight all influence creatinine levels. A young, muscular man and a petite, elderly woman can have the same creatinine levels but completely different kidney function. Still, it is important to know your average creatinine level.

Diet has a significant effect on kidney function.

Dialysis is performed when kidney function is so low that it cannot sustain health and life. It can be performed at home or in a dialysis center. A person on dialysis receives a diagnosis of kidney failure, also known as end-stage kidney disease. In kidney failure, the kidneys are unable to filter toxins well enough or remove enough fluid from your body to keep you alive or to keep you feeling well. Only a dialysis machine or a kidney transplant will enable a person with kidney failure to survive.

Electrolyte balance (meaning phosphorus, potassium, calcium, sodium, magnesium, etc.) is maintained by the kidneys. When your doctor checks your blood, the levels of all these electrolytes are measured. If the kidneys are having difficulty, these electrolyte levels may be abnormal.

Filtration is the process by which the kidneys clean the blood. The kidneys filter out certain things in the blood that the body does not need.

Glomeruli are the tiny structures in the kidneys that do much of the filtering. They are composed of very small blood vessels.

eGFR stands for your estimated glomerular filtration rate. You must know this number if you want to understand your kidney disease. The higher your eGFR, the better your kidneys are functioning, and the lower the eGFR, the worse your kidneys are functioning. Thus, these numbers go in the opposite direction of creatinine. You can think of eGFR as an estimation of the percentage that your kidneys are working; an eGFR of 100 ml/min means that your kidneys are working at 100 percent of capacity, whereas an eGFR of 35 ml/min means that your kidneys are working at only 35 percent of capacity.

Hormones are produced and regulated by the kidneys. Some of these hormones help control blood pressure, which is why patients are sometimes sent to kidney doctors to help manage their blood pressure. The kidneys also produce a hormone called erythropoietin that signals the bones to produce blood cells. If your kidneys are damaged, you may develop anemia (low hemoglobin) if your levels of erythropoietin drop too low.

Intoxication by alcohol does not directly harm the kidneys, but intoxication by other drugs can.

Just having kidney disease doesn't mean you have any symptoms of it. In fact, kidney disease rarely produces symptoms until it reaches the later stages.

Kidneys sit on either side of the spine, just under the ribs, and most people are born with two. The average size of a kidney is 4 to 5 inches (10 to 13 centimeters), or about the size of a fist. The right kidney is usually a little smaller than the left one.

Lots of people have kidney disease: 37 million people in the United States and 850 million people worldwide.

You are not alone!

Medications can affect the kidneys, and the dose of many medications must be adjusted for people with chronic kidney disease.

Numbers to know if you have kidney disease: eGFR, albuminuria or proteinuria, and creatinine.

Nephrologists are the doctors who care for people with kidney disease.

Nephrons are the entire filtration unit of the kidneys; they include both the glomerulus and the tubule.

Older people have fewer functioning filters in their kidneys than younger people because of a process called nephrosclerosis. This process of scarring in the filters of the kidneys occurs during the normal course of aging but can be accelerated by other conditions, including diabetes, high blood pressure, genetic disorders, and many others. Luckily, the kidneys start with many extra filters, so losing some doesn't necessarily cause problems. Even so, the more filters you have, the better.

Potassium and phosphorus are two of the most important electrolytes that are regulated by the kidneys; this book has chapters dedicated to each of them.

Proteinuria refers to excess protein leaking into the urine. If protein is leaking into your urine, you may notice that it is especially bubbly. Your doctor may report this to you as *albuminuria* or *proteinuria*. The exact amount can be determined either through a one-time urine test known as an albumin-to-creatinine or protein-to-creatinine ratio or through a 24-hour urine collection.

It's important to know your number!

Quantify your kidney function by having blood and urine samples drawn at your doctor's office.

Risk factors for kidney disease include diabetes, high blood pressure, family history of kidney disease, obesity, and age greater than 60. If you fall into any of these categories, ask your doctor to screen you for kidney damage.

Stages of chronic kidney disease (CKD) are determined by assessing your glomerular filtration rate (eGFR). As kidney disease progresses, the stage of kidney disease increases. Stage 1 CKD is the least severe, and Stage 5 CKD is the most advanced stage before dialysis.

Screening for kidney disease can diagnose problems in the earlier stages when more can be done to address kidney health. This can be done through two simple tests: a blood test to check serum creatinine and glomerular filtration rate, and a urine test to check for abnormal proteinuria (albuminuria).

Tubules, the most intelligent part of the kidney filtration system, maintain the body in homeostasis—that is, keeping the body in balance. The tubules work tirelessly to regulate electrolytes in the blood, maintaining the balance of the body's salt and water levels and keeping the right amount of electrolytes, including potassium, calcium, and magnesium, in your body. For example, when you drink more water than your body needs, the kidney tubules know exactly how much water to release into the urine. The same goes for potassium and sodium in the foods you eat. After the kidneys process the blood and determine which toxins and electrolytes can be gotten rid of and which substances need to stay in the body, any waste is excreted in the urine.

Transplanted kidneys are placed in the lower abdomen. When a kidney transplant is performed, the diseased kidneys are not removed. Kidney transplants are performed at specialized transplant centers, and a transplanted kidney can come from a living donor or from someone who has passed away.

Uremia is the set of symptoms that develop in patients with advanced kidney disease who are close to needing dialysis. These symptoms usually occur during Stage 5 CKD. Uremic symptoms can include itching, overwhelming fatigue, confusion, shortness of breath, fluid buildup in the legs and abdomen, difficulty sleeping, nausea or vomiting, loss of appetite, a metallic taste in the mouth, etc. These generic symptoms may be associated with several conditions that are unrelated to kidney failure, so it's important to have your blood and urine tested to assess your kidney health.

Ureters carry urine from the kidneys to the bladder.

WHAT ARE THE STAGES OF CHRONIC KIDNEY DISEASE (CKD)?

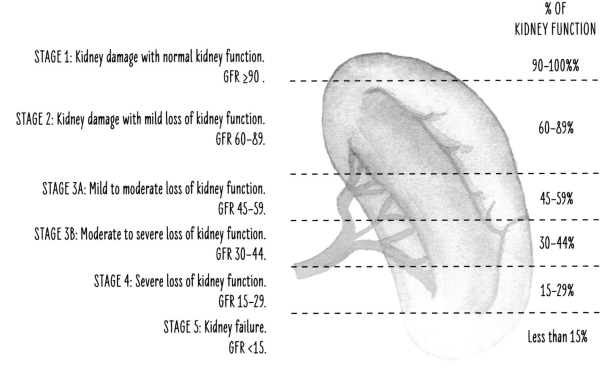

% OF
KIDNEY FUNCTION

STAGE 1: Kidney damage with normal kidney function.
GFR ≥90 .

90–100%%

STAGE 2: Kidney damage with mild loss of kidney function.
GFR 60–89.

60–89%

STAGE 3A: Mild to moderate loss of kidney function.
GFR 45–59.

45–59%

STAGE 3B: Moderate to severe loss of kidney function.
GFR 30–44.

30–44%

STAGE 4: Severe loss of kidney function.
GFR 15–29.

15–29%

STAGE 5: Kidney failure.
GFR <15.

Less than 15%

* Adapted from https://www.kidney.org/atoz/content/gfr

Very few people with CKD progress to kidney failure, the stage in which dialysis or a kidney transplant is required. In fact, kidney disease often stabilizes for many years without producing any symptoms. For a small number of patients, however, kidney disease does progress to a level that requires dialysis or a kidney transplant.

Water is filtered by the kidneys, and any extra water in the body is excreted in the urine.

e**X**amples of diseases that cause kidney problems include diabetes and high blood pressure. These are the most common causes, but many other diseases can lead to kidney damage. Other examples include polycystic kidney disease, being born with only a single kidney or having a kidney removed due to cancer or infection, glomerulonephritis, genetic diseases, and many others.

You can improve your health, even if you have kidney disease. There are many ways to maintain some control over your disease, including taking all your medications as prescribed, starting an exercise program, and improving your eating habits.

Zero symptoms occur with early-stage kidney disease. Most people with Stages 1 through 3 (early stage) CKD don't exhibit any symptoms related to abnormal kidney function. Because kidney disease is usually asymptomatic, it is important to be screened often for kidney disease by having your doctor check your urine and blood.

Ask Your Doctor for These Numbers

Before diving into the recipes and recommendations in this book, you will need a few specific numbers from your doctor. This will help you determine which information applies to you and will help you incorporate these guidelines into your daily life. If you can, bring this book into the office the next time you see your doctor and ask the following questions:

WHAT IS MY eGFR? _____

WHAT IS MY STAGE OF CKD? _____

DO I HAVE HIGH POTASSIUM LEVELS IN MY BLOOD? _____

WHAT IS MY BLOOD POTASSIUM LEVEL? _____

DO I HAVE PROTEIN IN MY URINE? _____

DO I HAVE HIGH BLOOD PRESSURE? _____

DO I HAVE HIGH PHOSPHORUS LEVELS IN MY BLOOD? _____

DO I NEED TO LIMIT THE AMOUNT OF FLUID THAT I DRINK? _____

DO I HAVE DIABETES? _____

Polycystic Kidney Disease

If you have been diagnosed with autosomal dominant polycystic kidney disease (ADPKD), you may be in any of the stages of CKD: from Stage 1 to Stage 5, kidney failure, or kidney transplant. As you use this book, choose the dietary guidelines that fall within your stage of CKD. You can better maintain your kidney health if you control your blood pressure, avoid diabetes, maintain a healthy weight, and stay active. The suggestions in this book will help you achieve these goals, and anyone with ADPKD should start following these dietary guidelines today.

The only difference in the dietary recommendations between ADPKD and other forms of kidney disease is that drinking extra water may slow the growth of the kidney cysts. People with other forms of kidney disease either may have to limit fluid intake or likely won't get any extra benefit from drinking extra water. Human trials are currently underway to help us answer this question about fluid intake for people with ADPKD. In the meantime, follow the fluid advice in Step 2, but sneak in an extra few glasses of water or flavored water each day after discussing with your physician.

STEP 2
CHOOSE YOUR BEVERAGES WISELY

Water and salt are two of the most important words in the languages of both cooking and kidney health. No cook or kidney doctor is worth his or her salt—get it?—without an expert level of knowledge about these two substances. By the time you've finished reading these next two chapters, I want you to be an expert as well. Whether you're navigating your way through a grocery store, a kitchen, or a restaurant menu, you need to know how to best put salt to use and choose beverages in ways that protect the health of your kidneys.

Drink When You're Thirsty, and Drink Mostly Water

When people come to see me for the first time, they're often frightened. They're very concerned that I'll tell them they must go on dialysis as soon as they walk into my office. To help manage some of that first-visit stress, many of my office patients choose to bring a family member with them, and I'm always glad to have them there.

These family members usually have something to say, as family members often do, about the drinking patterns of the patient. I usually hear something to the effect of, "I've told him for years that he doesn't drink enough water," or "I've been giving him cranberry juice every day since I found out about his kidney problems. Do you think that has helped?"

The answer is no. Forcing people to drink water when they're not thirsty or prescribing extra cranberry juice doesn't benefit the kidneys (except for ADPKD and kidney stones—more about that later in this chapter). But knowing which beverages are the best choices and which should be avoided can help you keep your kidneys healthy.

Because I hear these statements so often, I decided to focus an entire chapter on what kinds of beverages are the best choices for patients with kidney disease and how much of them should be consumed. As you'll see, the problem isn't usually that people don't get enough to drink—it's that they don't choose the right things to drink. When my patients ask me what they should drink, I tell them simply, "Drink when you're thirsty, and drink mostly water."

In this chapter, I'll discuss how I arrived at this conclusion and how to follow this advice. It's important for me to note again that this advice doesn't apply to patients with kidney stones or polycystic kidney disease; they may be well served by drinking extra water. It also doesn't apply to people on dialysis. Many people on dialysis or who have heart failure, swelling, or CKD Stage 5 should limit their fluid intake (including foods that are liquid at room temperature, such as Jell-O, popsicles, ice cream, and ice), even when they're thirsty.

How Much Water Do You Need?

The water in every liquid you drink—soda, coffee, tea, juice, beer, wine, Monster Energy drinks, and so on—is absorbed by your body in the digestive tract. You derive a lot of your water intake from the food you eat as well. All the foods and beverages you consume keep your body hydrated.

After water passes through the digestive tract, it flows around in the bloodstream until it reaches your kidneys. The kidneys then figure out how much fluid they need to retain to maintain a properly functioning body; whatever's left comes out in your urine.

For years, popular science, the media, and bottled-water companies have spread the myth that you need to drink eight glasses of water a day—each of which should be eight-ounce glasses—in order to keep your body healthy and to allow the kidneys to do their job. That's simply not true. While your primary drink *should* be water, your body doesn't need you to drink 64 ounces of plain water each day to stay hydrated. That's because you get much of the water that your body needs from the food you eat and the non-water beverages you drink, and because your body naturally works to keep you hydrated.

When your body needs water, it adjusts its normal processes and begins to conserve water. Your kidneys decrease the amount of urine you make; the urine also becomes extra concentrated to preserve the body's water levels. At the same time, your body releases hormones that make you thirsty.

There are, of course, some notable exceptions—times when you may not be able to get enough fluid. The following situations can lead to dehydration:

* Diarrhea and vomiting

* Exercising vigorously

* Staying outside in hot weather

Certain people are also more susceptible to dehydration, such as:

* Elderly adults who may be unable to concentrate their urine as well as younger adults.

* Individuals who have had an ileostomy or colostomy and thus may lose excess fluid in their stool.

* Individuals who have neurologic injuries, such as stroke, severe debility, or dementia, as they may not realize that they are thirsty or may know they are thirsty but be unable to communicate their needs or get a drink themselves.

Under typical circumstances, your body does a fantastic job of keeping you hydrated and keeping your kidneys functioning in top shape—even if you already have kidney disease. My patients often ask whether drinking more water will help flush out their kidneys and allow their kidneys to function at a higher level. According to a recent study, it doesn't. You may put more wear on your toilet and may get more exercise walking to the bathroom, but you won't help your kidneys.[1]

The Problem: The Choices You Make, Not the Amount You Drink

For most people, the problem isn't that they don't drink enough fluids to keep their kidneys hydrated. Instead, it's that the beverages they choose aren't water—in particular, that they're choosing sugar-sweetened beverages. Add to this the fact that sugary drinks are often difficult to identify, because sugar can be hidden in the unlikeliest places.

When you decide how to quench your thirst, many factors come into play. You might consider what's readily available, how thirsty you are, what your colleagues or friends are drinking, what your taste preferences are, or whether you're just trying to quench that thirst as quickly as possible.

All these thoughts can lead you away from water, the safest and healthiest drink for your kidneys. Unfortunately, water has a problem: it's tasteless. Many people don't drink it because they don't like its lack of taste. But I have good news for the no-water folks out there: there are alternatives to plain water that are also safe for your kidneys. Let's first look at these options and then consider other common drinks people choose to quench their thirst.

Alternative Waters

Fruit or vegetable water is a great way to have a refreshing, low-calorie drink easily on hand at home or at work. To fully embrace these beverages, however, you'll need to #ChangeYourBuds to truly appreciate their subtle flavors and freshness.

A visit to any supermarket will quickly reveal that the options for alternative waters are almost unlimited. I'd advise you to save money and save your kidneys: make your own flavored water. It's easy: just fill a large pitcher with ice and water, add one of the following mixtures, and let it sit overnight in the refrigerator to create more flavor. One note: make sure you wash the fruits or vegetables before adding them to the water.

ORANGE AND LEMON WATER: Add 1 orange, sliced, and 1 lemon, sliced

STRAWBERRY-LEMON-BASIL WATER: Add 6 strawberries, stemmed and quartered; ½ lemon, sliced; and 1 to 2 large sprigs of basil

CUCUMBER-LEMON-MINT WATER: Add 1 large cucumber, sliced; 1 lemon, sliced; and 1 large sprig mint

PEACH AND RASPBERRY WATER: Add 1 large peach, sliced, and 1 cup slightly crushed raspberries

If you're on the go, consider purchasing bottled waters flavored with a hint of fruit, but be sure to choose brands without added sugar or artificial sweeteners.

If you don't like anything without some fizz in it, try one of these options:

SELTZER WATER WITH ICE

SPARKLING ORANGE WATER WITH BASIL: Place 3 to 4 fresh basil leaves in the bottom of a large glass and muddle well. Fill the glass with ice and add ¼ cup of freshly squeezed orange juice. Fill the glass the rest of the way with seltzer or sparkling water.

CANNED CARBONATED AND FLAVORED WATERS: Beverages such as LaCroix, Spindrift, and Bubly: these are probably safe, but they're so new that I can't speak to any potential health risks they might pose. If you do choose one, be sure it has no added sweeteners, whether they're sugar or artificial.

Drinks with Added Sugar

It's a processed-food world these days, and as such, drinks with added sugar—namely soda, energy drinks, hydration drinks (like Gatorade), fruit juices, and sweetened tea—have replaced water as the most common ways to quench your thirst. This has had dramatic consequences for health worldwide and likely has played a significant role in the epidemics of obesity, kidney disease, and diabetes we currently face. We now know that drinking liquids with added sugar is a risk factor for developing kidney disease. This was demonstrated in a 2019 study involving a community in Mississippi, a state with one of the highest incidences of kidney disease in the country.[2]

Since my practice is in the South, I have firsthand perspective on how a pattern of choosing sugar-sweetened beverages can quickly become the norm. The recommended maximum amount of added sugar a person should consume daily, including food and drink, is 25 grams (g) for a woman and 37 g for a man. Many of my patients drink much more sugar than that each day. As an example, a 12-ounce can of Coca-Cola contains 39 g of added sugar all by itself. A large cup at McDonald's holds 32 ounces, so a large Coke there contains 80 g of sugar.

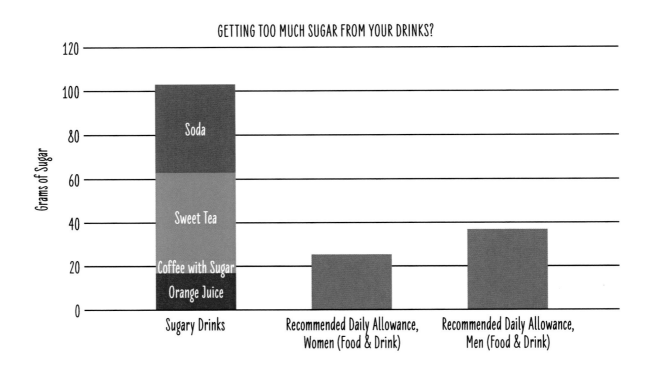

Consider how easy it is to exceed the maximum recommended amounts of sugar by double or even triple in a single day's beverages:

BREAKFAST: 1 (6-ounce) glass of orange juice (18 g sugar) + 1 (6-ounce) cup coffee with sugar (4 to 6 g)

LUNCH: 1 (8-ounce) glass sweetened tea (30 to 50 g)

DINNER/SNACK: 1 (12-ounce) can soda (30 to 50 g)

The total sugar for one day, just from those beverages alone, would amount to a whopping 82 to 124 g (versus a maximum recommended daily allowance of 25 to 37 g).

Soda is the most obvious offender of the high-sugar beverage habit, but it's not the only one. Other sugary drinks, like fruit juice, sweetened tea, and sugary coffee drinks, contribute their fair share as well. And never forget that these tallies of sugar intake don't take into consideration all the added sugar you consume every day in prepared foods. You should make a commitment today to lower your intake of all these beverages—yes, even cranberry juice.

Giving Up Sugary Drinks

If you frequently drink beverages with added sugar, stopping can be hard. I recommend slowly decreasing the amount you drink in a planned manner. It may take years for you to do it, but making some changes, rather than going "cold turkey," will make the changes more likely to stick for years down the road.

Save the sugar for your sweetie. Cut it out of your drinks!

SODA

Years ago, I drank a soda every morning and a second one every afternoon—14 a week! Each month, I cut out one soda a week. I had 14 in a week in January, but I decreased to 13 each week in February, and so on. This went on until I completely weaned myself from soda the following February. The chart on the next page gives a great visual for how I managed to quit drinking soda for good.

Over the course of the last 10 years, some of my patients' most rapid and long-lasting improvements have come from eliminating their soda consumption. I've seen diabetes put into remission, high blood pressure become easier to control, and weight loss that exceeds 50 pounds—all by making this one meaningful change.

KICK THE CAN! A simple plan for a soda-free lifestyle

	MONDAY		TUESDAY		WEDNESDAY		THURSDAY		FRIDAY		SATURDAY		SUNDAY		WEEKLY TOTAL
	AM	PM	AM	PM	AM	PM	AM	PM	AM	PM	AM	PM	AM	PM	
DECEMBER	SODA	SODA	SODA	SODA	SODA	SODA	SODA	SODA	SODA	SODA	SODA	SODA	SODA	SODA	14
JANUARY	SODA	SODA	SODA	SODA	SODA	SODA	SODA	SODA	SODA	SODA	SODA	SODA	SODA		13
FEBRUARY	SODA	SODA	SODA	SODA	SODA	SODA	SODA	SODA	SODA	SODA	SODA		SODA		12
MARCH	SODA	SODA	SODA	SODA	SODA	SODA	SODA	SODA	SODA		SODA		SODA		11
APRIL	SODA	SODA	SODA	SODA	SODA	SODA	SODA		SODA		SODA		SODA		10
MAY	SODA	SODA	SODA	SODA	SODA		SODA		SODA		SODA		SODA		9
JUNE	SODA	SODA	SODA		SODA		SODA		SODA		SODA		SODA		8
JULY	SODA		SODA		SODA		SODA		SODA		SODA		SODA		7
AUGUST	SODA		SODA		SODA		SODA		SODA		SODA				6
SEPTEMBER	SODA		SODA		SODA		SODA		SODA						5
OCTOBER	SODA		SODA		SODA		SODA								4
NOVEMBER	SODA		SODA		SODA										3
DECEMBER	SODA		SODA												2
JANUARY	SODA														1

SWEETENED OR "SWEET" TEA

Before I moved to South Carolina, I never imagined that sweetened tea could be as big a problem for my patients as soda. My patients quickly enlightened me. Down here, they make sweetened tea—better known as "sweet" tea—with 2 cups of sugar per pitcher of tea, no matter how big or small that pitcher is. If you order an iced tea at a restaurant, it's assumed you mean the sweet kind unless you specifically state otherwise. A single glass of sweet tea can exceed the recommended daily maximum intake of sugar.

For my patients who have trouble giving up sweet tea and find the taste of unsweetened tea utterly unbearable, I developed a substitute that many find satisfying.

SWEET TEA SUBSTITUTE

1/2 GALLON BOILING WATER

4 BLACK TEA BAGS

2 LARGE ORANGES, WASHED AND SLICED

2 LARGE SPRIGS FRESH MINT LEAVES, WASHED

1. Combine the boiling water and tea bags. Set aside to brew to desired strength, 3 to 5 minutes.

2. Refrigerate for 2 to 3 hours.

3. Add the orange slices and mint and return to the refrigerator for a few hours or overnight.

4. Serve over ice.

HEALTHY, NO-SUGAR BEVERAGE OPTIONS. MINT & ORANGE ICED TEA, FRUIT & VEGETABLE FLAVORED WATER, LOW-SUGAR SMOOTHIE, AND BLACK COFFEE.

CRANBERRY JUICE

I know this statement will disappointment many of you, but it must be said:

Cranberry juice provides zero benefit for the kidneys.

It's true that research has been done to see whether cranberry juice has some effect on the prevention of bladder infections, but the results have been mixed. Because many people mentally lump the bladder and kidneys together, my patients often drink extra cranberry juice in the hope that it will improve their kidney function.

Unfortunately, the only thing these extra glasses of cranberry juice are providing are sugar-saturated calories. If you are a die-hard cranberry juice lover, try two or three 4-ounce glasses of unsweetened cranberry juice each week. You'll still get some extra sugar, but much less than you would get in the sweetened version.

DIET DRINKS

The jury is still out on diet drinks. We are still learning whether the artificial sweeteners in diet drinks affect the kidneys and their function. What we *do* know is that people who drink more than seven diet sodas a week have an increased risk of developing kidney failure (end-stage kidney disease), the stage that requires a kidney transplant or dialysis, versus people who drink less than one diet soda drink a week.[3]

Although I don't believe diet drinks carry the same risk as sugar-sweetened drinks, I do recommend that my patients try to cut down on diet soda in the same way I advise them to stop drinking regular soda.

MILK AND DAIRY PRODUCTS

Just as with diet soda, we still don't know whether milk and dairy products affect the development of kidney disease. Because this question remains unanswered, the choice of how much and what kind of milk to drink must be addressed according to your stage of kidney disease and consideration of any other medical problems you have.

For many people, milk and dairy products are an excellent source of calcium in their diet, so giving them up completely without replacing them with high-calcium foods may lead to other problems. I recommend that you choose a milk that you enjoy drinking and that you can easily digest, whether it's a dairy or non-dairy milk. In general, people with early-stage disease (CKD Stages 1–3) should be safe with limiting milk intake to 1 (6-ounce) glass, or ¾ cup, three or four days each week.

If you have Stage 4 or 5 CKD or are on dialysis, you may have to be more careful about your milk choices. Cow's milk, for example, contains a high amount of both phosphorus and potassium—minerals you'll learn more about later in this book. If your kidney disease is in this range and you wish to consume more than ½ cup of dairy milk per day, speak with your doctor or dietitian first.

COFFEE

One of my favorite parts of patient visits is that I can end the visit on a high note after listing all the different foods and beverages I recommend that they give up: "Keep the coffee." Multiple studies have shown that coffee is safe for your kidneys and may also provide protection against other diseases, such as type 2 diabetes, Parkinson's disease, and cardiovascular disease. At best, coffee consumption may decrease the risk of kidney disease development and slow its progression, and at worst, it will not affect kidney disease.[4, 5, 6]

Coffee is even safe for individuals who already have chronic kidney disease. There are a few rules, however:

* If you're drinking more than four cups of coffee each day, you are unlikely to benefit from the positive health effects of drinking coffee. Stick to less than three (6-ounce) cups of coffee each day, just to be on the safe side.

* Make it black. Once you start adding sweeteners and creams or turn your coffee into a frozen milkshake, you lose a lot of the benefits and end up with lots of empty calories.

* If you have high blood pressure or an irregular heart rate, the caffeine in coffee may make these conditions more difficult to control.

* If you're on dialysis, you may need to limit your overall fluid intake, and coffee counts.

If you don't like your coffee black but still want to keep it healthy, these 10 tips can help you make the switch to black:

* Slowly wean yourself from your cream and sugar additions over time. Try one sugar instead of two, or three creamers instead of four. And over the course of months, wean down until your taste buds change enough so that you enjoy coffee in a much healthier form.

* Buy flavored coffee beans, such as hazelnut or peppermint. Most flavored beans don't add any extra calories or sugar to brewed coffee. You just might find that you like it black or at least will need less sweetener.

* Try different types of coffee beans. Ethiopian coffee is strong, so you might not be able to tolerate it without cream, but a Costa Rican coffee might be different.

* Grind your beans freshly each morning. The improved flavor of the freshly ground beans may keep you from adding as much cream or sugar to your morning cup of joe.

* If you're brewing a pot, use less coffee grounds than usual. It won't be as strong.

* Add a dash or two of cinnamon, nutmeg, or cocoa powder instead of sugar.

* Try an Americano, which is an espresso diluted with water.

* If you add a slice of lemon peel to a double shot of espresso, it takes the edge off the bitterness.

* Add a pinch of salt to your cup.

* If you must use a little something, try a small amount of real cream, half-and-half, or milk.

ALCOHOL

I find that patients commonly confuse the liver and kidneys. They'll tell me, "I don't know why I have kidney disease—I've never had a drink in my life," or "I stopped drinking alcohol as soon as I found out I have kidney disease." Alcohol affects the liver, for sure, but it doesn't seem to have much of an effect on the kidneys.

According to the most recent research, drinking one alcoholic drink (6 ounces of wine, 12 ounces of beer, 1 ounce of hard liquor) each day doesn't appear to damage the kidneys. If you're consuming much more than that, you're drinking too much, and that's not good for your health overall. Excessive drinking can contribute to weight gain;[7] can make blood pressure more difficult to control (10 g of alcohol may raise blood pressure by 1 mmHg systolic and 1 mmHg diastolic, and a typical alcoholic beverage contains 14 g of alcohol), and can elevate blood sugar as well.[8] All these health problems can contribute to kidney disease.

SMOOTHIES

A good smoothie can quench your hunger *and* your thirst, but if you don't make it yourself, you're likely to get too much sugar and too many calories. The syrupy fruit sweeteners and concentrated flavors used by smoothie shops are often loaded with sugar. By learning to make smoothies yourself with the right amounts of frozen fruit or ice; low-sugar milk or plain Greek yogurt; and chia or other seeds, you'll be able to quickly put together excellent meal replacements. Just be sure not to add too much sugar to your home smoothies; avoid this pitfall by not using presweetened yogurt, honey, agave, fruit juice, or more than two servings of fruit. The calories can add up quickly.

In short, skip the smoothie shop and invest the money you save in a good blender.

BERRY-BANANA HEMP SMOOTHIE

This recipe is perfect after a workout and as an introduction to hemp hearts, one of my favorite plant-based sources of magnesium, protein, and fiber. It's also a great way to #ChangeYourBuds as you learn to enjoy lower-sugar smoothies. If you don't have frozen bananas, use frozen fruit and a fresh banana, and lower your ice to 1/3 cup.

1 CUP ALMOND MILK, OR 2% GREEK YOGURT, PLUS MORE IF NEEDED

1 CUP FRESH BERRIES

HALF AN ORANGE, PEELED, OR SUBSTITUTE A WHOLE CLEMENTINE OR TANGERINE

2–3 TABLESPOONS HEMP HEARTS OR CHIA SEEDS

1 FROZEN BANANA, QUARTERED

2/3 CUP ICE

Pour the milk in the blender and layer with the berries, orange, hemp hearts, banana, and ice, and process until smooth. Add more milk to adjust the consistency, if needed.

NUTRITION PROFILE

YIELD: 2 servings

ANALYSIS PER SERVING

CALORIES (KCAL): 171

PROTEIN (G): 4

CARBOHYDRATES (G): 29

TOTAL DIETARY FIBER (G): 9

TOTAL SUGARS (G): 13

ADDED SUGAR (G): 0

FAT (G): 6

SATURATED FAT (G): 1

CHOLESTEROL (MG): 0

CALCIUM (MG): 91

MAGNESIUM (MG): 18

PHOSPHORUS (MG): 20

POTASSIUM (MG): 248

SODIUM (MG): 120

PUMPKIN PIE SMOOTHIE

This low-calorie, low-sodium smoothie is also a great source of fiber, potassium, and plant-based protein. Come Fall, try this seasonal alternative to break up the typical fruit and vegetable smoothie routine. It's helpful to layer smoothie ingredients in a certain order for the best texture. Always start with liquids first to create a vortex in the blender that pulls in other ingredients to be blended. Follow liquids with softer, high-moisture foods such as fresh fruits, softer vegetables, nut butters, or yogurt. Next, add hearty vegetables, such as carrots or kale, nuts, and seeds. Finish with frozen fruit or ice so the weight pushes the other ingredients down toward the vortex.

1 ½ CUPS UNSWEETENED ALMOND MILK

1 TEASPOON GROUND TURMERIC

½ TEASPOON GROUND CINNAMON, PLUS MORE FOR GARNISH

½ TEASPOON GROUND GINGER OR 1 TABLESPOON FRESHLY GRATED

2 LARGE PITTED DATES OR 2 TABLESPOONS RAISINS

1 15-OUNCE CAN UNSWEETENED PUMPKIN PURÉE

3 MEDIUM NAVEL ORANGES, PEELED AND QUARTERED

2 TABLESPOONS FLAX OR CHAI SEEDS

1 CUP ICE

NOTE: This is a high-potassium smoothie. Read Step 5 of my plan, "Get Potassium Right," to make sure this is a safe drink for your kidney health.

Layer the ingredients, in the order listed, and blend until smooth. Pour into four glasses, sprinkle with cinnamon, and serve.

NUTRITION PROFILE

YIELD: 4 servings

ANALYSIS PER SERVING

CALORIES (KCAL): 111

PROTEIN (G): 3

CARBOHYDRATES (G): 21

TOTAL DIETARY FIBER (G): 6

TOTAL SUGARS (G): 14

ADDED SUGAR (G): 0

FAT (G): 3

SATURATED FAT (G): 0

CHOLESTEROL (MG): 0

CALCIUM (MG): 249

MAGNESIUM (MG): 46

PHOSPHORUS (MG): 70

POTASSIUM (MG): 421

SODIUM (MG): 69

Kidney Cleanses

Your kidneys clean your blood. No matter what hucksters say, your kidneys don't need to be cleaned with herbal preparations or supplements. Neither foods nor herbs can cleanse or detox them.

Don't fall for kidney cleanses. They don't clean out anything other than your wallet.

RECOMMENDED BEVERAGE SCHEDULE FOR PATIENTS WITH STAGES 1 TO 3 CKD

BREAKFAST	1 (8-ounce) glass water and 1 (6-ounce) cup black coffee
LUNCH	1 (8-ounce) glass water or 1 (8-ounce) glass unsweetened iced tea
DINNER	1 (8-ounce) glass fruit-enhanced water 1 (6-ounce) cup decaffeinated tea
SNACK AND BETWEEN MEALS	2 (8-ounce) glasses water or homemade seltzer
WILDCARD (THREE TO FOUR TIMES/WEEK)	1 (6-ounce) glass of milk of your choosing or 1 alcoholic beverage
WILDCARD (ONE TO TWO TIMES/WEEK)	Diet sodas, diet fruit juices, fruit juices diluted with water, specialty alcohol cocktails, sugar-free sweetened beverages (e.g., Crystal Light)
NEVER OR RARELY	Specialty coffee drinks, sweet tea, sodas, fruit juices and juice drinks, milkshakes, flavored milks, Kool-Aid and other sugar-sweetened powdered drinks, fruit punches

People with CKD Stage 4–5 often must limit fluid intake to below these levels.

People with kidney stones or polycystic kidney disease may benefit from higher amounts of fluid intake.

STEP 3

UNCOVER HIDDEN SALT & #CHANGEYOURBUDS

Many people don't know how much salt (sodium) they consume every day in the foods they eat, and that's a big problem if you're transitioning to a low-sodium diet. Most of the salt in your diet is hidden away in processed foods, fast food, and other restaurant meals. It's relatively easy to eliminate all the salt from your cooking, but that's the wrong place to do it. You'll end up with bland home-cooked food that you don't want to eat, which will drive you to consume even more processed food and restaurant meals—resulting in a diet that's even higher in sodium than before. In this chapter, I'll teach you to be an expert at finding the hidden sources of salt in your diet, and I'll also show you how the best chefs can make a little bit of salt go a long way in terms of flavor.

Salt Is Fantastic

*"Salt has a greater impact on flavor than any other ingredient.
Learn to use it well, and your food will taste good."*

—SAMIN NOSRAT, SALT. FAT. ACID. HEAT.

Over the course of many years, I've learned how to use salt to elevate the flavor of the dishes I prepare—not by adding more, but by adding it in more intelligent ways, such as:

* Sprinkle a few crystals of kosher salt on top of a freshly sliced tomato just before your first bite to make the flavors pop and your heart sing.

* Add a small pinch of salt to a fresh salad after tossing it with a sodium-free salad dressing. Doing so improves the flavor of the salad much more than using a dressing containing sodium or by adding the salt prior to the dressing.

* Scatter one or two anchovies (a total of 300 mg of sodium) to transform the flavor of a dish much more than adding the equivalent of table salt.

* Seasoning sliced zucchini with a tiny bit of kosher salt 10 minutes before grilling it will make it cook much faster, thus preserving more of its fresh flavors and textures.

* Improve your scrambled eggs by adding a pinch of salt before they cook. They'll cook more quickly and will have a more decadent and richer flavor.

I love a little salt, and I won't make you give it up to protect your kidneys. Most of the advice doctors give patients about observing a low-sodium diet is generic. You were likely told to keep your daily intake below 2300 mg, and then it was probably left to you to figure out how. My advice is different:

* Give up as many prepackaged foods as possible.

* Dine out at restaurants less frequently.

* If you give up most of your high-sodium processed and restaurant foods, you can keep the saltshaker handy, and safely add a little salt to your food.

* Learn to cook and eat in a way that naturally lowers your sodium intake.

* Train your taste buds to enjoy less salty food.

In this book, I use the terms "sodium" and "salt" interchangeably. Sodium (Na) is the part of the specific salt, sodium chloride (NaCl), that has significant effects on your body. That's what we put on our food.

Helpful Sodium

Sodium is essential to the body. It helps the muscles contract, allows the nerves to send signals correctly, and keeps the body's fluids balanced in the right compartments. Without sodium in your diet and in your blood, you cannot exist. Sodium is essential to daily life and to good health.

The other great part about sodium is that it makes foods taste better. When used correctly, a little bit of salt can transform the blandest dish into a flavorful masterpiece. This magical seasoning brings out the sweet and sour flavors that are the hallmark of delicious dishes. At the same time, it manages to conceal some of the bitterness that can overpower more delicate flavors.

Harmful Sodium

On the other hand, sodium can cause problems—especially if you have kidney disease, high blood pressure, liver disease, or heart failure. If you have any of these conditions, too much sodium in your diet can cause you to retain excess fluid, because water follows sodium wherever it goes. This fluid is most likely to build up in your legs, abdomen, or lungs, and none of those are good. Years of research have also proven that a diet very high in sodium can make it more difficult to control blood pressure, raising the likelihood of stroke.

The Confusion

Based on my experience in medical practice, most people are confused about two things: 1) how much sodium they should eat and 2) where most of the sodium in their diet comes from. When I ask my patients whether their diet is low in sodium, most reply with either "I try to" (which usually means "no") or "Yes, doc. I never add salt to my food."

When I probe further, it usually becomes clear to me that they're on the wrong track. For example, a patient might tell me that he didn't add any salt to his lunch, but then I find out that his lunch was a hot dog on a bun with a side of potato chips. That's a whopper of a high-sodium meal. Another patient might tell me that she doesn't even own a saltshaker, but then she mentions that she eats at restaurants almost every day—a sure way to consume too much sodium.

That's the biggest source of confusion, so let's lay it to rest right now: most of the sodium in your diet doesn't come from the saltshaker. If you learn this one concept, you can quickly lower your daily sodium intake. The salt that's already in food when it's manufactured or prepared is most of what you consume every day; that includes all processed foods and the foods you order in restaurants. Only 5 to 15 percent of your daily intake comes from your saltshaker.[9]

4% found naturally in food

13% added while eating or cooking

15% found in restaurant meals

68% comes in processed foods from grocery store

Adapted from https://www.uptodate.com/contents/salt-intake-salt-restriction-and-primary-essential-hypertension

Any change you make to lower your sodium intake should focus on reducing the amounts of processed and restaurant foods you consume.

To understand why processed foods are loaded with salt, you need to think like you run a food-processing company. Imagine that you were designing factory-prepared meals that needed to be stored for months in a freezer or in a can. Now, take it a step further: imagine that in order for you to make money, you're counting on those foods to be tasty enough that people will buy and enjoy them, even though you know the natural flavors will fade over time. How would you maintain the flavor in these foods during all that processing and time? You'd do the easiest and cheapest thing you could: add a lot of salt. For example, soups that are high in sodium appeal to a lot more people than low-sodium soups.

Restaurant food works the same way. Chefs and restaurant owners often try to create food that appeals to as many people as possible. If the first bite you take is bland or under-seasoned, your entire meal experience can be negatively affected. If you've ever seen an episode of *Top Chef* where the judges take a bite and immediately complain that the food is under-seasoned, you know what I'm talking about. So, to please their diners, chefs add lots of salt and high-sodium sauces to the foods they serve, with no regard to whether it's good for your health.

I often use a turkey sandwich and fries as an example. Without even picking up a saltshaker, the amount of sodium in a turkey sandwich can be very high. Just consider the salt content of each ingredient:

BREAD: 250 mg (11 percent of recommended daily intake)

MAYONNAISE: 100 mg (4 percent)

CHEESE: 250 mg (11 percent)

TURKEY: 500 to 600 mg (22 to 26 percent)

BACON: 200 mg (9 percent)

PICKLE: 300 mg (13 percent)

FRIES: 500 to 600 mg (22 to 26 percent)

That adds up to a total sodium content in that one meal of 2100 to 2300 mg, or 91 to 100 percent of your recommended daily intake.

If you do add quite a bit of salt with the saltshaker, cutting back there can certainly be a good place to start. But if you don't reduce the amount of processed foods you consume, simply cutting out use of the saltshaker won't get you very far.

Finding the Balance

The kidneys maintain the sodium balance in your body, which means that they determine how much sodium your body needs to hold on to and how much it needs to remove via your urine. The key to using sodium in a healthy way is to learn to cook with enough of it to bring out the flavors in your food and keep the body functioning properly, without adding so much that your blood pressure goes up and your body retains fluid. This is not so easy. While it is very difficult to get too little sodium in your diet, it is extremely easy to consume too much. On the following pages, you'll find my 10 steps to help you find your perfect salty sweet spot. They are:

1. #ChangeYourBuds

2. Find Your Weakness

3. Plan Your Attack

4. Cut Down on Restaurants and Processed Foods

5. Control Your Food: Cook at Home and Pack Your Own Lunches

6. Inventory Your Pantry, Refrigerator, and Freezer

7. Stock Your Kitchen Well

8. Use Quick Hacks to Lower Your Sodium Intake

9. Forget the Numbers

10. Learn How to Maximize Flavor without Excess Salt

1. #CHANGEYOURBUDS

Believe me when I tell you that changing your taste buds will help you lower the sodium in your diet. Sometimes, I ask patients who are accustomed to a high-sodium diet to switch to a very strict low-sodium diet for a couple of weeks. At first, they complain (loudly) that the food is too bland and often say it's "inedible." Many lose weight during those two weeks, simply because they don't eat as much as they are used to. However, by the end of those few weeks, if they stick to the diet, they find that their taste buds are much more sensitive to salt, and that they can enjoy foods that are much less salty than the ones they preferred before.

As a physician, I love hearing my patients happily describe the experiences they have after adapting to a lower-sodium diet. I saw one patient, Roger, for 10 years as I helped him manage his Stage 3 CKD and uncontrolled high blood pressure. Over the course of our relationship, Roger learned to enjoy a diet that was much lower in sodium and became an expert at creating flavorful reduced-sodium dishes. He even told me once that he'd developed a healthy reduced-sodium gumbo recipe and wanted to share it with me—but I have yet to see it myself. (I still have some doubts about his "magical" roux.)

During one of my appointments with Roger, he relayed a story about a family barbecue he'd attended the previous weekend. He suddenly found himself faced with foods that had a very different flavor profile than he had become used to, and he was shocked at the result. He described the hamburger, potato salad, and baked beans he'd eaten as "tasting like the ocean," like they'd been dipped in saltwater. I hear stories like this all the time. If you invest the time and effort to #ChangeYourBuds, over time you'll find that higher-sodium foods become downright inedible.

CREATING FLAVOR WITHOUT SALT. LEEKS, ONIONS, GARLIC, SHALLOT, FRESH AND DRIED PEPPERS, FRESH AND DRIED HERBS, VINEGAR, THE JUICE AND ZEST FROM CITRUS FRUITS, PARMESAN CHEESE, AND NUTRITIONAL YEAST.

2. FIND YOUR WEAKNESS

Normally, I don't recommend that patients record every bite and sip they consume, as it's a tedious practice that's hard to follow. But I do recommend that you do it for a single week as you begin a transition to a lower-sodium diet.

First, write down everything you eat and drink for a week, including the amounts consumed, in a diet diary. For every packaged food you eat, take a look at the Nutrition Facts label and also keep track of the amount of sodium in a serving of each of those foods, and then multiply that by the number of servings you consume. If you eat out at restaurants, search online to get and record the sodium content in the meal you consume. If you can't find the exact meal, try to find a comparable one online and use that number as an estimate.

Pay close attention as you review your diet diary for what are likely the greatest sources of sodium in your diet: breads and rolls (*yes, really!*); processed meats like salami, bologna, pepperoni, or ham; fast food; canned vegetables; frozen meals; cheeses; chips, pretzels, and similar snack foods; canned soups; pizza; and sauces.

Nutrition Facts	
About 13 servings per container	
Serving size	**About 17 chips (28g)**
Amount per serving	
Calories	**160**
	% Daily Value*
Total Fat 10g	**12%**
Saturated Fat 1.5g	**7%**
Trans Fat 0g	
Cholesterol 0mg	**0%**
Sodium 170mg	**7%**
Total Carbohydrate 15g	**6%**
Dietary Fiber 1g	**5%**
Total Sugars 1g	
Protein 2g	
Vitamin D 0mcg	0%
Calcium 20mg	0%
Iron 0.5mg	2%
Potassium 330mg	6%
Vitamin C	6%
Not a significant source of added sugars.	
* The % Daily Value (DV) tells you how much a nutrient in a serving of food contributes to a daily diet. 2,000 calories a day is used for general nutrition advice	

STEP #1: Look at the Serving Size. Many products have more than 1 serving in the package. The amount of sodium (salt) listed on the label is the amount for only 1 serving.

STEP #2: Look at how much sodium is in the food. Remember, if you eat more than 1 serving you must multiply the sodium amount by the number of servings you eat. For esample, if you eat 34 chips (2 servings) from this package, you would be eating 340mg of sodium.

At the end of the week, highlight which foods had the greatest amounts of sodium, and make sure to take your serving size into account. For example, if a slice of deli meat has 200 mg of sodium and you had three of them, that's a total of 600 mg of sodium.

What you'll quickly see on your diet diary pages are your weaknesses. What are yours? For me, they're fries and potato chips. Do you have a sandwich every day? Do you eat out every evening? Do you stop by a fast-food place on your way to work every morning? Do you consume extra rolls when you eat out at restaurants? Once you know where your sodium's coming from, you can figure out how to attack it.

3. PLAN YOUR ATTACK

It's possible that you won't be able to easily cut out all the high-sodium foods all at once. Start small: review your diary, pick the high-sodium habit that shows up the most, and cut down on it a little at a time.

When it comes to dropping high-sodium foods altogether, start with the one you don't care much about, as you won't miss it much. Once you have that habit under control, move on to another. As your taste buds change, it will become easier and easier to incorporate reduced-sodium foods into your daily routine. You'll find that it won't be a struggle after all, and you'll derive a lot of pride from how far you've come.

4. CUT DOWN ON RESTAURANTS AND PROCESSED FOODS

Prepared foods are often loaded with sodium, so it's very important to limit how many of these you eat. Consider these examples:

MCDONALD'S: Big Mac with small fries: 1500 mg; Southwest Grilled Chicken Salad: 1380 mg

OLIVE GARDEN: Chicken Parmigiana: 1700 mg; Olive Garden Salad with Italian Dressing: 700 mg

CRACKER BARREL: Sunrise Sampler: 1870 mg; Grilled Chicken Salad: 1300 mg and Dressing: 350 to 700 mg

5. CONTROL YOUR FOOD: COOK AT HOME AND PACK YOUR OWN LUNCHES

This one is tied closely to step 4: the best way to manage the sodium in your diet is to make as many of your meals as you can at home. If you start with low-sodium sauces and fresh ingredients, such as fruits, vegetables, poultry, fish, and whole grains, it's much easier to maintain a lower-sodium diet. Plus, you can deploy the herbs and spices you enjoy most as much as you like to bring wonderful flavor to your food. Cooking at home puts you in total control over the amount of sodium in your food.

For example, instead of pouring a salty dressing over a vegetable or salad, sprinkle some fresh oregano and a few chile flakes on it and mix a little of your own oil and vinegar together to make your own dressing.

6. INVENTORY YOUR PANTRY, REFRIGERATOR, AND FREEZER

First, search through your pantry, refrigerator, and freezer to identify the high-sodium foods you already have on hand. Read the labels carefully, and mark anything with more than 200 mg of sodium per serving with a pen or a label so you know right away which ones are highest in sodium. When you do consume those foods, make sure you pair them with freshly prepared meats and vegetables, so you aren't adding even more sodium to that meal.

For example, if you find a can of high-sodium crushed tomatoes, use them to make a tomato sauce with sautéed mushrooms, garlic, and onions. The sauce can then serve as a seasoning for some freshly prepared meat and vegetables—for example, ground chicken and spinach. The only sodium in the meal will come from the canned tomatoes—which is already plenty.

As you survey the foods you have on hand, pay particular attention to the following items. After they're consumed, replace them with lower-sodium options.

* Canned vegetables

* Canned soups

* Frozen and prepackaged meals, appetizers, foods with sauces, breaded meats, etc.

* Pizza

* Prepared sauces and spice packets: think taco seasoning, spaghetti sauce, soy sauce, fish sauce, etc.

* Bread, rolls, and flour tortillas

* Chips, crackers, pretzels, and similar snacks

* Bottled salad dressings or marinades

* Sliced deli meats, including turkey, bologna, ham, roast beef, chicken, etc.

* Cured meats: sausages, bacon, hot dogs, etc. (turkey bacon and sausages have a lot of sodium, too—some have even more than the pork versions!)

* Cheese

* Commercially flavored rice or pasta, such as box macaroni and cheese, Rice-a-Roni, etc.

7. STOCK YOUR KITCHEN WELL

Keep the following foods on hand as staples for cooking at home. If you have them within easy reach, you'll be able to create meals with lots of depth of flavor without all the salt.

NON-PERISHABLE ITEMS

* Cans of sodium-free tomato sauce, tomato paste, and chopped and diced tomatoes*

* Sodium-free chicken, vegetable, and beef stock

* Dried or low-sodium canned beans*

* Dried lentils*

* Dijon and stone-ground mustard

* Worcestershire sauce, a low-sodium seasoning with powerful flavor; be sure to use only 1 teaspoon at a time, as it does contain some sodium in each serving

* Vinegars of all kinds: cider, balsamic, red wine, white wine, champagne, rice wine, malt, etc.

* Dried (or fresh) herbs, such as herbes de Provence or Italian seasoning; garlic powder; onion powder; regular or smoked paprika; low-sodium seasonings, such as Mrs. Dash; cayenne pepper; chile powder; thyme; parsley; cumin; nutritional yeast; and za'atar seasoning

* Sodium-free canned salmon and tuna

* Puréed pumpkin*

* Coconut milk*—use a little bit at a time in place of heavy cream

* Sodium- or salt-free nuts and seeds, including chia seeds, hemp hearts, almonds, pepitas, walnuts, and sunflower seeds*

* Your favorite frozen vegetables

* Coconut aminos, a great lower-sodium and soy-free substitute for soy sauce

* Dried mushrooms*

* *Note: These foods are high in potassium. See "Step 5: Get Potassium Right" to make sure they're safe for your stage of kidney disease.*

PERISHABLE ITEMS

* Fresh or frozen chicken or turkey (Choose the non-enhanced versions. "Enhanced" meat often means added sodium.)

* Parmesan cheese

* Fresh fish fillets or seafood (frozen is OK, too, but don't choose breaded or pre-seasoned options)

* Fresh lemons and limes to add flavor without sodium

* Onions, shallots, garlic, and ginger to serve as a flavor base or seasoning for countless low-sodium meals

* Already-chopped garlic and ginger, which you can buy in a small container usually in the produce section

It's important for me to note here my recommendations on consumption of beef and pork, which are often less expensive meat choices. Meals prepared from scratch with these meats only once a week or less often can be integrated into a healthy dietary pattern. But in the recipes in this book, you'll notice that I don't include any beef or pork ingredients. That's because red meat and pork are known to have added health risks. However, if you're choosing to eat fast-food chicken or fish or fried chicken instead of lean cuts of red meat or pork, you will benefit from making a switch to occasional dishes including freshly prepared lean red meat and pork.

Remember that all salts are the same. Sodium is sodium, and no one type of salt is better than any other. Though its rosy pink hue and online hype suggest that Himalayan salt has mystical healing powers, there's no evidence that it can improve your health.

8. USE QUICK HACKS TO LOWER YOUR SODIUM INTAKE

DELI MEATS

THE PROBLEM: A typical slice of lunch meat contains 200 to 300 mg of sodium.

THE SOLUTION: Substitute home-baked chicken and turkey breasts. It's easy to make 10 chicken breasts and then freeze them. Use them in sandwiches or on salads over the course of a month. See "Baked Chicken Breasts" in the "Chicken" chapter.

CANNED SOUPS

THE PROBLEM: Canned soups are often inexpensive, and they're also comfort foods that are filling and soothing. Many of my patients have mentioned fond childhood memories of canned soup (often paired with a grilled cheese sandwich). Unfortunately, the most inexpensive canned soups generally contain a day's worth of sodium in a single serving—along with poor-quality meats and vegetables. They also often lack fiber, which is very important for your diet.

THE SOLUTION: Start by either buying or making your own low-sodium or sodium-free chicken, beef, and vegetable stock (if you're buying them, choose ones with less than 200 mg of sodium per serving). Anytime you need to make soup, simply sauté some fresh or frozen vegetables with a little olive oil and garlic or other spices. Add the stock to the pan and simmer until fully cooked. If you like, you can add some chicken breast meat you've precooked or some low-sodium canned beans (be sure to rinse them very well) or canned tomatoes. When it's time to eat, just add a little pinch of salt and stir well. You'll have a tasty soup with far less sodium than any canned or prepackaged kind. Your homemade soup will give you the same soothing feeling, without all the salt and processed meat in the canned varieties. See "No-Sodium Chicken Stock" and "No-Sodium Vegetable Stock."

PIZZA

THE PROBLEM: Like most processed foods, pizza is high in sodium. Unless you make each element of the pizza (dough, sauce, toppings) from scratch, you simply can't avoid the salt.

THE SOLUTION: Think of pizza as a high-sodium treat, but following some rules can make it better. For one, eat no more than two slices in a meal. If you're dining out, ask the restaurant for half the cheese and twice as many fresh vegetables as they usually put on their pizzas. Be sure to leave off any processed meats, such as pepperoni, salami, and ham.

FAST FOOD

THE PROBLEM: Even if you have the very best intentions, it's nearly impossible to have a low-sodium meal at a fast-food restaurant. Even the salads—which are loaded with processed meats, cheeses, and dressings—are high in sodium.

THE SOLUTION: Cut down on the number of high-sodium fast foods you consume in a week. If you know you'll have to eat at a fast-food restaurant, plan ahead by checking the nutrition information online. You might be surprised about which menu items are the highest in sodium.

BACON, HOT DOGS, AND SAUSAGES

THE PROBLEM: No matter what kind you're talking about, these are a problem.

THE SOLUTION: These should only be eaten as a treat. If you must have one of them at a meal, make sure everything else you eat is low in sodium. Try having a little bacon with a fresh vegetable salad or roasted potatoes with lemon juice and herbs.

RESTAURANT FOODS

THE PROBLEM: The more often you eat out, the more likely you are to exceed daily limits for sodium intake.

THE SOLUTION: Restaurant foods can be tricky, but here are a few strategies that can make dining out and keeping your sodium under control a little easier:

* Ask for any sauces to be served on the side.

* When you first get your meal, decide then and there how much of it you're going to eat and push what you plan to take home to the side (or better yet, leave it on the plate). Consuming smaller portions is a great way to get things under control.

* Skip the bread. Sorry. All breads are salty.

* Ask the server to bring you oil and vinegar and make your own salad dressing.

CANNED VEGETABLES

THE PROBLEM: Generally speaking, most canned vegetables are very salty. Salt is an important part of the preservation process.

THE SOLUTION: It's best to choose fresh or frozen vegetables instead. If you absolutely must use canned vegetables, *always* drain and rinse them thoroughly, and then soak them in water for 15 minutes. Be aware, however, that doing so will remove a lot of the nutrition and flavor of the vegetables, right along with the salt.

CHIPS, PRETZELS, AND SIMILAR SNACKS

THE PROBLEM: Well, they're called salty snacks for a reason.

THE SOLUTION: Choose only low-sodium or sodium-free versions and eat only a little of them. These snacks are usually unhealthy choices in general and are processed in a way that severely diminishes their nutritional content. To satisfy any cravings you have for a tangy flavor, dip the few you do consume in hummus or a low-sodium mustard. Or, choose freshly popped popcorn with a homemade no-sodium spice blend or a sprinkle of parmesan cheese. See the "Spreads, Snacks & Sauces" section for more low-sodium dip ideas.

BOTTLED SALAD DRESSINGS

THE PROBLEM: Not a good choice.

THE SOLUTION: Avoid them altogether and make your own dressings at home. See the "Dressings & Spice Blends" section for homemade salad dressing recipes.

9. FORGET THE NUMBERS

Once you get the hang of following a low-sodium diet, forget about the numbers. In the beginning, as you're transitioning to a reduced-sodium diet, the numbers can be very helpful. But that's not how you want to live. Once you learn how to cook and how to instinctively select foods that are lower in sodium, you won't have to walk around with a calculator figuring out your dietary balance all the time.

You have a busy life, and your days are full of responsibilities. Tracking your sodium intake and keeping it below a certain level is simply too difficult to pull off in the long term. If you're one of the lucky ones with the spare time to count milligrams of sodium, aim to keep it below 2300 mg if you have heart failure, high blood pressure, or liver disease. If, like me, you don't have the time or energy to calculate the sodium in your diet, follow my other rules.

10. LEARN HOW TO MAXIMIZE FLAVOR WITHOUT EXCESS SALT

Life requires just enough salt to make food taste good. Take control. Put away the saltshaker and season your food as you prepare it. Here are some of my tips for maximizing the flavor in your meals:

* As you prepare your meals, gradually scatter a few crystals of kosher salt crystals throughout the cooking process. By adding a little bit of salt at different times, the salt will be better integrated into the dish, and a little bit will go a long way.

* Choose your sodium based on flavor and texture rather than its potential benefits or because you think one is better than another. I use kosher salt in most of my cooking because a small pinch of the bigger sodium crystals is easier to add to a dish in a controlled manner.

* Instead of salt, use vinegar or lemon juice. Sometimes a pinch of salt and the juice of half a lemon and lemon zest will add much more flavor than multiple pinches of salt. If you like vinegar instead or just find that it's easier to keep on hand than fresh lemons, experiment with different types. See "Sheet Pan Lemon-Lime Chicken & Potatoes" or "Lemon Herb Couscous Salad."

* Buy or grow your own fresh herbs. They add tremendous flavor and no sodium at all.

* Use spicy flavors such as fresh jalapeño or dried red chilies. See "Southwest Quinoa Salad."

* Experiment with dried herbs and spices of all kinds.

* Double the amount of spices or herbs suggested in a recipe.

* Learn to create flavor with aromatics such as fresh garlic, ginger, leeks, onions, and shallots. See "Leek & Yellow Squash Soup" and "Vegan Bolognese Sauce."

* Try a sprinkling of parmesan cheese or nutritional yeast (as a non-dairy substitute) to boost the flavor of food. Although both toppings contain sodium, each packs tons of flavor into a small serving. See "Roasted Brussels Sprouts."

* Avoid salt substitutes. They're loaded with potassium and can cause elevated blood potassium levels—not a good thing. And they taste bad, too. See "Step 5: Get Potassium Right."

STEP 4

EMBRACE PLANT-BASED EATING

As increasingly more research on plant-based diets accumulates, we're realizing that deep down we knew the truth all along: a diet that places emphasis on fruits and vegetables is good for your body and helps protect your kidneys. Many of the recipes on my website and YouTube channel emphasize vegetables, whole grains, beans, and fruits—the staples of a plant-based diet. I love cooking with vegetables, and I love sharing vegetable cooking tips with my followers.

In this chapter, I share how certain plant-based foods can benefit your kidneys and how you can incorporate these dietary recommendations according to your own stage of kidney disease. A diet that follows these principles can benefit your health in several ways, including:

* Improved blood pressure control
* Reduced risk of stroke
* Reduced risk of kidney stones
* Slowed progression of kidney disease

If you're unfamiliar with the idea of a whole-food, plant-based diet, here's the scoop: it's any diet that places emphasis on consumption of plants (obviously)—meaning fruits, vegetables, whole grains and whole-grain flours, legumes, seeds, and nuts. This diet should also limit refined sugars, animal products, white flours, and some oils. Plant-based diets tend to feature:

* Foods that are high in potassium
* Foods that contain more magnesium
* More alkaline (and less acid-producing) foods
* Less animal protein, thus reducing stress on the kidneys
* Fewer highly processed foods
* Fewer foods that contain artificial, highly absorbable phosphorus
* Foods that can improve blood pressure control

I will discuss all these attributes in detail in the upcoming chapters. As you read on, you'll see more clearly how a plant-based diet benefits kidney health.

Every time I talk with someone about adopting a plant-based diet, I think of a 50-year-old patient who was referred to me for uncontrolled blood pressure and Stage 4 CKD. I'll call him "Mr. H." We spent a lot of time talking about diet and exercise over the course of an hour-long appointment, and then I told him to schedule a follow-up appointment in three months.

I didn't see Mr. H again for three years. When he appeared for his appointment, I was shocked by his appearance. Mr. H had lost weight. He told me that he felt fantastic. His blood work demonstrated stable kidney function. I asked him, "Mr. H, *where have you been?*"

He chuckled, gave me a hearty smile, and replied, "Doc, I got off the hog. And I figured that if I got off the hog, I didn't have to come back to see you for a while."

It was my turn to smile. I'm not from the South originally, so my patients often share new terms and sayings with me that take some getting used to. (Ever heard of a "jockey lot"? If not, look it up. That's my favorite of all the words and sayings that I've learned since coming down here.)

Mr. H. explained: He'd decided to cut out all pork from his diet, and doing so had benefited his health tremendously. He hadn't gone vegetarian completely, much less vegan, but cutting out pork forced him to drop some of the fattiest and saltiest foods he liked to eat: pork rinds, ham, barbecued pork, bacon, etc. He replaced those foods with beans, greens, fish, and some occasional chicken. I've relayed this story to several patients over the last few years. It strikes a chord with many, and it always generates laughter.

PASS THE VEGGIES: CONVERTING TO A WHOLE-FOOD, PLANT-BASED DIET

Take a minute to think of the last dinner or lunch you had that didn't include any meat, chicken, or fish. Now try to remember the last full day in which you didn't eat any meat. Has it been a week? A month? Maybe you've *never* gone a full day without eating meat. Meat is so elemental in the typical American diet that it can be very tough to give it up all at once.

Meat is the focus of meals for most people all over the world; it is at the center of the plate. It's often the primary source of protein and the base for sauces, and it's easy to see why. The fats in animal proteins provide flavor. If you've ever braised lamb or brisket or used bacon or sausage to create the flavor base for a soup or vegetable dish, you'll understand this perfectly. But it's important to know that you *can* create the same depth of flavor using only vegan ingredients (meaning, no animal products), but it takes extra time and effort. It takes some getting used to, but it can be done!

Keep this in mind, too: if you aren't careful when transitioning away from animal products, it's easy to fall into an unhealthy rut. I often find that my patients cut out healthier animal-based dishes, such as skinless chicken or fish, and substitute them with decidedly unhealthy meatless dishes like macaroni and cheese, canned soups, or French fries.

One of the easiest ways to incorporate plant-based diet principles is to slowly add more plant-based foods to your diet and slowly reduce all the animal-based foods. As you learn to develop flavor in your food without meat, you'll bring your family along with you.

A PLANT-BASED BOUNTY.

If your current diet is heavy on meat, start with one meal a week. As you gradually develop more skills for and knowledge about plant-based diets, you'll be able to expand your efforts easily.

Here are a few more quick tips:

* On Sunday afternoons, set aside an hour for meal prep. Chop up a whole bunch of vegetables and store them in containers in your refrigerator. Then, you'll have chopped veggies at the ready for when you want a quick snack or for preparing meals.

* Substitute a low-sodium can of beans or tofu for the recommended meat ingredient in a dish. My "Spicy Chickpea Stuffed Peppers" (see www.thecookingdoc.co) and "Vegan Bolognese Sauce" with mushrooms and lentils (see Plant-Based recipes) are delicious examples of this type of substitution.

* Learn to roast vegetables. It's easy! Almost any vegetable can be roasted, and doing so helps vegetables maintain their nutritional value—especially compared to boiling them. In addition, roasting vegetables deepens their flavor and makes them even more delicious! If you roast vegetables during the weekend, you can use them throughout the week in pastas and salads and as side dishes. That said, when you're doing your Sunday vegetable prep, why not pop six sweet potatoes in the oven and roast them according to the recipe below? Or see the recipe for "Balsamic Roasted Vegetables."

ROASTED SWEET POTATOES

These sweet potatoes can serve as side dishes throughout the week. Slice them open and mash them or cut them in half and top them with veggies, beans, or a stir fry. If you are on a restricted potassium diet (more on that in the next chapter), be aware that you may have to limit sweet potatoes, as they are high in potassium.

1. Line the bottom of your oven with aluminum foil to catch any drips. Poke holes in the sweet potatoes with a fork and place them on the middle rack.
2. Set the oven at 425° F and roast the sweet potatoes for 45 to 75 minutes, depending on their size.
3. Turn off the oven and leave the sweet potatoes in for 30 minutes without opening the oven door.
4. Remove from the oven and serve or store in the refrigerator for meals later in the week.

STEP 5

GET POTASSIUM RIGHT

It's probably a coincidence, but many of my favorite foods also happen to be among the highest potassium foods you can eat: ripe bananas (more yellow than green—but no judgment here); sweet potatoes that are perfectly slow baked until the insides melt like butter and taste like honey; butternut squash soups of any variety—savory, sweet, curried, or whatever; and just-ripened avocados, whether they're sliced up in a sandwich, chopped into a salad, or crushed into guacamole.

As a matter of fact, I'm not alone in my love of high-potassium foods. During the week I wrote this chapter, three of my patients told me of their hopes that I'd loosen the restrictions they'd been given on how much potassium they could eat. One had wasted her entire tomato harvest when her previous doctor advised her to give them up. Another young man was desperate to eat guacamole once again. Last, a grandmother lamented how much she missed one of her favorite new indulgences, pomegranate juice. Similar situations occur at my office every day. Many people with kidney disease think they need to limit potassium in their diet—even though some don't need to.

Helpful Potassium

For most people, a high-potassium diet provides real health benefits. That's especially true for people with high blood pressure or those who are at high risk for strokes. One scientific review found that eating high amounts of potassium can lower blood pressure significantly.[10] Doctors and scientists still aren't exactly certain *why* a high-potassium diet improves blood pressure, but it's likely that it has something to do with my favorite organs: the kidneys. The kidneys process most of the potassium you get in your diet; if they're working correctly, the kidneys may use that extra potassium to get rid of extra sodium in the body. This helps the body retain less water, thus lowering blood pressure.

The benefits of a high-potassium diet extend even farther. High-potassium foods add to the alkalinity of your diet (see "Step 7: Discover Alkaline-Rich Foods"), reduce your risk of kidney stones (as long as you choose low-oxalate foods), and provide you with added fiber and micronutrients. And there's this: people who don't get enough potassium in their diet have a higher risk of cardiovascular disease and stroke.

Harmful Potassium

If the kidneys are working at full strength, they can handle about as much potassium as you can eat, but problems occur when the kidneys have difficulty filtering blood and can't process extra potassium in the diet. Once kidney function dips to a filtration rate below 30 ml/min (approximately 30 percent function)—and this is what occurs in Stages 4 and 5 CKD—things change. At that point, the kidneys may have trouble filtering potassium, and potassium can build up in the blood. When potassium levels become dangerously high, the heart's rhythm can become erratic. In the most extreme situations, it can stop beating completely.

The Bottom Line

A high-potassium diet is beneficial for you until your kidney disease reaches a certain point, and then you may need to switch to a diet that is lower in potassium. In some people, the need for a low-potassium diet may happen when their kidneys are functioning at 25 percent, while others—for reasons we don't completely understand—may never reach a point where they need to limit their dietary potassium. These nuances have led to some confusion, because recommendations often get lumped into a one-size-fits-all recommendation: "Everyone with kidney disease needs to limit their potassium."

How do you know which potassium camp you fall into: the eat-more camp or the eat-less camp? How do you know when your kidney function has hit the tipping point where you have to change from a high-potassium to a medium- or low-potassium diet? Below, I've included generic guidelines to get you started. But, because two people in the same category may have different potassium limits (e.g., one person with Stage 4 CKD may need a low-potassium diet while another person with Stage 4 CKD may be able to eat bananas and spinach all day), **discuss your specific case with your doctor or dietitian**.

HIGH BLOOD PRESSURE WITH NORMAL KIDNEYS: High-potassium diet, meaning a diet loaded with foods that contain high amounts of potassium.

STAGES 1 OR 2 CKD (eGFR >59 ML/MIN): High-potassium diet.

STAGE 3 CKD (eGFR 30–59 ML/MIN): Medium-high potassium diet unless your doctor tells you that you have high blood potassium levels. This means that you likely do not need to limit your potassium intake but that you should continue to monitor your levels with your physician.

STAGE 4 CKD (eGFR 15–29 ML/MIN): Varies from person to person. Discuss with your doctor or dietitian. If you have low or normal blood potassium levels, you may be able to stay on a medium potassium diet.

STAGE 5 CKD (eGFR <15 ML/MIN): Most people in this group need a lower-potassium diet. There are a few exceptions; you should discuss your specific case with your doctor or dietitian.

AUTOSOMAL DOMINANT POLYCYSTIC KIDNEY DISEASE OR SINGLE KIDNEY: Use the above recommendations and choose your dietary potassium level based on your stage of chronic kidney disease.

KIDNEY TRANSPLANT: If kidney function is normal and your serum potassium is normal, stay on a high-potassium diet. If your kidney function falls to Stages 3 through 5 CKD, follow the above recommendations. Sometimes, the medications that people take to prevent rejection of a transplanted kidney, such as tacrolimus or cyclosporine, can cause high-potassium readings.

PERITONEAL DIALYSIS: Many people who are on peritoneal dialysis have low potassium levels in their blood and can tolerate a high-potassium diet. Ask your doctor or dietitian whether you have low or high potassium levels in your blood. If your levels are low, discuss whether it is safe for you to load up on high-potassium foods.

IN-HOME HEMODIALYSIS: Varies from person to person. Discuss with your doctor or dietitian.

IN-CENTER HEMODIALYSIS: Many, but not all, people who must go to a dialysis center three times per week require a lower-potassium diet.

Though each laboratory and clinical situation is different, here is a general overview of blood potassium levels. All specific dietary guidelines and changes in your medications should be discussed with your doctor and dietitian:

BLOOD POTASSIUM LEVEL	RANGE	PLAN OF ACTION—DISCUSS WITH PHYSICIAN
3.5–5.1 mmol/L	Normal	None - Safe
5.2–5.6 mmol/L	High Normal	Monitor, change medications, and/or limit high-potassium foods
Greater than 5.6 mmol/L	High	Discuss immediate changes in medications and diet with your physician

As you learn to eat for your level of kidney disease, you may need to assess the specific amounts of potassium in each food and how much potassium you are consuming each day. Here are some general guidelines to discuss with your physician:

Low-Potassium Diet	Less than 2000 milligrams each day
Medium-Potassium Diet	Between 2000–5000 milligrams each day
High-Potassium Diet	Greater than 5000 milligrams each day

HIGH-POTASSIUM FOODS. AVOCADO, KIWI, SWISS CHARD, CANTALOUPE, DRIED BEANS, DRIED APRICOT, BEETS, PAPAYA, BANANA, ARTICHOKE, DRIED FIGS, BLACK RICE, ORANGES, ACORN SQUASH, SWEET POTATO, LENTILS, AND TOMATOES.

Tips for Increasing Your Potassium Intake

If you are in the stage of CKD that allows you to eat large amounts of potassium, try to increase your consumption using these tips.

1. Keep fresh greens in your refrigerator and a bag of frozen greens in your freezer. Some of the best choices are spinach, chard, collard greens, and kale. Whenever you make pasta, add 2 to 3 cups of fresh chopped greens 3 to 5 minutes before the sauce has finished cooking. The greens will wilt, but they won't lose any of their nutritional value.

2. Add dried fruits to your salad. Raisins, prunes, and dried apricots make excellent additions to any salad.

3. Choose fresh fruit for your snacks. Oranges and bananas are the most common fruits that are high in potassium, but you can mix things up by trying kiwi or avocado instead.

4. Learn to make butternut squash soup. It's delicious and a great source of potassium.

5. Experiment with quinoa, barley, and brown rice as substitutes for white rice or regular pasta.

6. Make sure there's something green on every plate of food you serve.

See "Corn & Black Bean Quesadilla," "Spiced Chicken, Orange & Avocado Salad," and "Sheet Pan Lemon-Lime Chicken & Potatoes" for high-potassium meals.

FIVE-MINUTE SPINACH

Nutrient-dense leafy greens, such as spinach, are high in protein, potassium, iron, vitamins, and minerals. Unlike heartier varieties, like collard greens, spinach cooks very quickly. When weeknight dinners get hectic for families juggling jobs, extracurricular activities, and homework, try this easy, flavorful side dish that goes from stove to table in a hurry.

2 TABLESPOONS EXTRA VIRGIN OLIVE OIL

2 CLOVES GARLIC, MINCED

1 POUND SPINACH, WASHED AND DRIED

JUICE OF HALF A LEMON

KOSHER SALT AND FRESHLY GROUND BLACK PEPPER, TO TASTE

1. Heat the oil in a large sauté pan over medium heat.
2. Add the garlic and cook until fragrant, 30 seconds. Add the spinach, season with a few crystals of salt and pepper, toss with the garlic and oil and cover for 1 minute.
3. Remove the lid, increase the heat to medium high, cook, while stirring, one minute. Add the lemon juice and serve hot.

NUTRITION SUMMARY & MODIFICATIONS: High potassium. Low sodium. Low phosphorus.

NUTRITION PROFILE

YIELD: 4 servings

ANALYSIS PER SERVING

CALORIES (KCAL): 89

PROTEIN (G): 3

CARBOHYDRATES (G): 5

TOTAL DIETARY FIBER (G): 3

TOTAL SUGARS (G): 1

ADDED SUGAR (G): 0

FAT (G): 7

SATURATED FAT (G): 1

CHOLESTEROL (MG): 0

CALCIUM (MG): 115

MAGNESIUM (MG): 90

PHOSPHORUS (MG): 58

POTASSIUM (MG): 643

SODIUM (MG): 90

LOW-POTASSIUM FOODS. GRAPES, CABBAGES, RADISH, CUCUMBER, BERRIES, PINEAPPLE, GREEN PEAS, CAULIFLOWER, APPLE, PEPPERS, PEAR, CAULIFLOWER, FLAX SEEDS, ONION, EGGPLANT, YELLOW SQUASH, CRANBERRIES, AND GREEN BEANS.

Recommendations for High Blood Potassium Levels and Lower Potassium Diets

Your blood potassium level is determined by much more than your kidney's filtration rate and how much potassium you eat. That's why it's so important to review your potassium levels with your doctor or dietitian to see if you need to limit potassium in your diet. Other factors that can lead to high blood potassium levels include:

* High blood sugar levels

* High blood acid levels

* Certain medications, including ACE inhibitors (e.g., lisinopril), angiotensin receptor antagonists (e.g., losartan), Bactrim (trimethoprim/sulfamethoxazole), Aldactone (spironolactone), triamterene, and amiloride.

PLEASE NOTE: **Even though these medications may increase your potassium levels, they may be very important for your overall health. Never stop or change any of your medications without first speaking to your doctor.**

If you have high blood potassium levels, your doctor may place you on a low-potassium diet. Because these diets eliminate many fruits, whole grains, and vegetables, they make following a healthy diet even more difficult.

It's important to know that following a diet that is lower in potassium isn't the only way to safely lower blood potassium levels; other adjustments may help as well. Ask your doctor if any of the following changes could make sense for your individual situation:

* Controlling your blood sugar levels.

* Stopping or lowering the doses of medications that can lead to high blood potassium levels.

* Adding a fluid pill (a diuretic), which can help the kidneys get rid of more potassium.

* Addressing any acid/base (pH) imbalance in the blood.

* Adding a medication that helps the body get rid of more potassium in the stool; these include Veltassa (patiromer), kayexalate (sodium polystyrene sulfonate), and Lokelma (sodium zirconium cyclosilicate).

Unfortunately, these alternatives don't work for everyone. Sometimes a lower-potassium diet is the only way to manage this situation. If that's the case for you, the first things you should limit in your diet are foods with concentrated potassium that you eat frequently, or that you eat too much of.

Remember, any food can be a high-potassium food if you eat too much of it. For example, bananas are often thought of as a high-potassium food, while apples and pears fall into the low-potassium category. But suppose you're making a fruit salad and you leave out the banana to keep it low-potassium, leaving you with just apples and pears. If you eat two apples and one pear worth of fruit in the salad, you've consumed more potassium than you would have if you had eaten one banana.

Some foods to limit or give up include:

* Canned soups—specifically those that are tomato based or that contain lots of potatoes.

* Tomato-based sauces and tomato paste.

* Dried fruits (specifically, raisins, figs, and prunes).

* Cooked green, leafy vegetables.

* Nuts - It's easy to eat handfuls of nuts without realizing what you've done. And the more nuts you eat, the more potassium you will get.

* Salt substitutes - These often have large amounts of potassium.

* Vegetable and orange juices.

* Dairy products - milk, yogurt, ice cream, cheese, etc.

* All the high-potassium foods in the high-potassium picture earlier in the chapter.

Sometimes, adherence to a diet that restricts potassium can result in insufficient fiber intake. Fiber is healthy for everyone—regardless of their kidney disease status—as fiber can improve gastrointestinal health, heart health, and blood sugar levels. You should know that many fruits and vegetables can add fiber to your diet without delivering an excess of potassium, and that's the key to figuring out the right low-potassium diet: one that provides enough fiber and micronutrients.

The Cooking Doc's Favorite Low-Potassium Fruits and Vegetables

* Apples
* Cauliflower
* Berries
* Eggplant
* Flax seeds
  (1 to 2 tablespoons)

* Cabbage
* Green beans
* Peas
* Radishes
* Asparagus
* Cucumbers

* Grapes
* Pineapple
* Onions
* Peppers
* Pears

When you're choosing substitutes for higher-potassium foods, it's important to choose ones that have the same color, texture, and consistency as the foods you're replacing. Some suggestions include:

* Replace dairy milk with rice milk.

* Replace lentils or beans with green peas.

* Replace half of the tomato sauce that's called for in a recipe with sodium-free chicken or vegetable stock.

* Replace tomatoes with half the amount of roasted red peppers.

* Replaced mashed potatoes with mashed cauliflower.

* Replace cooked kale, spinach, or other greens with cabbage or romaine lettuce.

* Replace tomato-based pasta sauces with garlic and olive oil.

* Replace banana, mango, and orange with blueberries, pears, and apples.

* Replace oranges or orange juice with pineapples or pineapple juice.

* Replace half of the whole grains (quinoa, brown rice, farro, whole-grain pasta, etc.) in a recipe with white rice or white pasta.

Soaking or double boiling vegetables and beans can lower the amount of potassium in each serving. To achieve the greatest effect, soak the vegetables overnight in a large pot or bowl of water. Then, boil the vegetables for 10 minutes, discard the water, and boil another 10 minutes in fresh water.

BRAISED PURPLE CABBAGE

This recipe has no right to turn out so delicious. With just a few ingredients, you will create a flavorful side dish that pairs well with grilled fish, chicken, or tofu. Cabbage is also one of my favorite low-potassium substitutions for spinach and other cooked greens.

1 TABLESPOON EXTRA-VIRGIN OLIVE OIL

1 ONION, DICED

1/2 HEAD PURPLE CABBAGE, CUT INTO 1/2 INCH STRIPS AND ROUGH CHOPPED

PINCH OF KOSHER SALT

PINCH OF RED PEPPER FLAKES

2 TABLESPOONS APPLE CIDER VINEGAR

1/2 CUP LOW-SODIUM VEGETABLE STOCK

1. Heat the oil in a large sauté pan over medium heat. Add the onions and cook until soft and translucent, stirring occasionally, 5–7 minutes. Add the cabbage, salt, and red pepper flakes and cook until cabbage is bright in color, stirring occasionally, 3–5 minutes.

2. Increase the heat to medium high, add the vinegar and vegetable stock, and bring to a boil. Cover, reduce the heat to low, and simmer until the cabbage is tender but not too soft, stirring occasionally, 8–10 minutes.

NUTRIENT PROFILE

YIELD: 4 servings

SERVING SIZE: about 6 ounces

CALORIES (KCAL): 65

PROTEIN (G): 1

CARBOHYDRATES (G): 8

TOTAL DIETARY FIBER (G): 3

TOTAL SUGARS (G): 4

ADDED SUGAR (G): 0

FAT (G): 3

SATURATED FAT (G): 1

CHOLESTEROL (MG): 0

CALCIUM (MG): 44

MAGNESIUM (MG): 13

PHOSPHORUS (MG): 31

POTASSIUM (MG): 197

SODIUM (MG): 33

Depending on how much potassium you need to remove from the vegetables, you can soak, boil, or soak and boil. Remember that all these techniques change the texture of the food significantly—often creating softer and mushier consistencies. Experiment with these cooking methods at home. To crisp up the vegetables after boiling or soaking, roast the vegetables in the oven for 10–20 minutes. See "Balsamic Roasted Vegetables."

Magnesium Is Important, Too

Over the last few years, my pantry has been transformed into something akin to a squirrel's nest. It's stuffed with seeds, nuts, and other healthy, crunchy toppings I can put on everything. This change has caused me to change my taste buds more than any other dietary adjustment I have ever made. Chia seeds, sunflower seeds, and pumpkin seeds—foods I hadn't been used to eating—now taste good to me. As I've incorporated these foods into my diet, my magnesium intake has increased significantly.

Because Western diets typically lack enough fresh greens, nuts, seeds, beans, and whole grains, most people who follow them fail to reach the recommended daily intake of magnesium: 350 to 420 mg for men and 300 to 320 mg for women.[11] A lack of magnesium both directly and indirectly impacts the kidneys. The mechanism by which dietary magnesium benefits the kidneys is unclear, but eating too little of it has been associated with speedier drops in kidney function.[12] That's the direct effect, and indirectly, magnesium intake can also affect blood pressure. Studies have associated diets that are low in magnesium with increased risk of developing high blood pressure. Although the supporting evidence remains weak, a comprehensive analysis of 22 trials that showed that high-magnesium foods can lower systolic blood pressure by 3 to 4 mm Hg and diastolic blood pressure by 2 to 3 mm Hg,[13] perhaps due to magnesium's ability to relax blood vessels.[14] Foods containing a lot of magnesium also tend to have other qualities that make them healthy. By choosing to eat more of them, you may take better control of your blood sugar and reduce your triglyceride levels.

Magnesium assists with more than 300 enzyme reactions in the body and allows the main energy source in the cells, adenosine triphosphate (ATP), to work.[15]

The evidence isn't as strong for increasing your magnesium intake as it is for some of the other recommendations in this book, but foods that are high in magnesium are also high in potassium, fiber, and plant protein (for that reason, the same restrictions apply for those who must watch their potassium intake). If you're not used to incorporating these types of foods into your diet, it may take some time to get used to them. Seize this opportunity to #ChangeYourBuds by choosing high-magnesium foods that you may not typically eat or that you and your family have never tried before, such as:

* Chia seeds
* Hemp hearts
* Unsalted pumpkin seeds
* Sunflower seeds
* Sesame seeds

They're great toppings to sprinkle on salads, pasta, or stir-fries; toss into yogurt; include in whole-grain dishes like couscous or farro; or bury in homemade chocolate or brownies.

"Go nuts (and seeds)! Eat more magnesium!"

STEP 6

AVOID HIGH-PROTEIN PITFALLS

How much protein should you eat? How much protein does your body need? How much protein can your kidneys handle? I found that this was the most difficult chapter in the book to write for two reasons: first, because the answer is so complicated, and second, because the research is all over the place. In these pages, I'll first discuss the science of protein; then, I'll cut through the controversy; and last, I'll end with some simple advice: avoid high-protein diets and substitute plant-based proteins for animal proteins whenever you can.

As you read this chapter, you'll realize that the answer to your question— what's the ideal protein intake for my kidneys and my body—can only come from a consultation with a dietitian. Getting specific, real-life guidance from a book is next to impossible, because so many different factors are involved in determining how much protein you need. If you don't already have a relationship with a dietitian, ask your doctor to refer you to one.

A Real-Life Example

Mrs. P is 48 years old. Her kidneys filter at half of the normal level, which means she's in Stage 3A CKD, and her kidneys leak too much protein into her urine. Mrs. P, who weighs 250 pounds and carries much of her weight in her abdomen, has struggled with obesity and diabetes since she was a teenager. She takes multiple medications to control her diabetes and her high blood pressure.

Over the course of her life, Mrs. P has tried many different diets, including Weight Watchers, intermittent fasting, and the Optifast meal replacement program. Six months ago, on the advice of a Facebook ad and a recommendation from a friend, she went on a low-carbohydrate, high-protein diet that involved consuming almost 2 g/kg/d (grams of protein per kilogram of body weight per day) of protein. Given her weight, that amounted to more than 200 g of protein for Mrs. P each day.

While on this diet, Mrs. P lost 30 pounds and felt well. Her diabetes control improved significantly, and her blood pressure came down as well. When she saw her nephrologist, however, he scolded her. Her blood work showed that her kidney function had worsened and that she had increased protein in her urine. He told her to limit her protein intake; within a few weeks, Mrs. P regained 10 pounds. Ultimately, Mrs. P had to see a dietitian for a consultation to sort everything out.

The Science

Proteins are composed of amino acids, some of which can only be obtained through diet because the body cannot make them. These are called *essential* amino acids. After a protein is consumed and the body breaks it down, the newly absorbed amino acids combine to form new proteins that have many responsibilities inside the body. They make reactions happen inside cells, serve as the building blocks of the hormones that circulate in the body, and help build muscle mass.

In the United States, the average person's diet already exceeds the protein intake that the body needs to function properly. According to a recent study, the average intake is approximately 1.2 g/kg/d. Even though this protein intake exceeds the minimum amount the body needs to thrive, people with normal kidney function usually don't have a problem with the extra protein. But if you are at risk for or already have kidney disease, consuming more protein than your body needs can cause trouble.

Scientists are still working to determine the exact mechanisms by which extra protein affects the kidneys. Several animal studies have looked at the relationship between protein intake and kidney disease, but the results of these studies should not be generalized to humans. We need more direct human data, and what we have collected thus far is inconclusive.

When you digest proteins, amino acids enter the blood and trigger a flood of hormones. When you eat more protein than you need, this flood of hormones may cause the kidneys to go into filter overdrive. This filter overdrive may increase pressure inside the kidneys and can lead to scarring over time. Think of it as the kidneys "burning out" in the same way an engine burns out if you run it past its capacity over a long period of time.[16] Scientists have postulated that the extra pressure and hyperfiltering causes the release a substance called transforming growth factor beta (TGF-Beta), and this over-filtering response may cause scars to form in the filters (the glomeruli) of the kidneys. When these filters develop scars, the kidneys' capacity to filter the blood is reduced, and kidney function may decline. One of the primary goals of getting your diet right for your kidneys—consuming the right foods—is to keep as many of the kidneys' filters working for as long as possible.[17, 18, 19]

If your kidneys aren't perfect—or if you have only one—your protein intake should remain at a level low enough that it doesn't put your kidney filters at risk. The tough part is determining that exact level. Although an excess may put extra stress on your kidneys, protein is essential to good health. Some recent studies have demonstrated the benefits of a diet that is lower in carbohydrates and higher in protein on blood sugar control and weight loss, and that's a source of a fair amount of the controversy. The question is a very personal one:

> How much protein do I need to eat to maintain all the positive benefits of protein without putting extra strain on my kidneys?

Then there are the other factors that come into play when determining what kind and how much protein to eat: the quality and affordability of the protein, your overall activity level, your knowledge of how to cook the protein, the taste of the finished product, obesity, and many more factors. If you are recovering from an illness or injury or are over 65, your protein requirements may be much higher. If, like Mrs. P, you are obese or diabetic (or both), you may have found that a higher-protein diet can enable you to lose weight and better control your blood sugar.

Based on my review of the research, the optimal protein intake for people who have or are at risk for chronic kidney disease is 0.6 to 0.8 g/kg/d (that means 0.8 grams of protein for each kilogram of body weight each day), and most of that protein should come from plants.

That's equivalent to 0.27 to 0.36 grams of protein for each pound of body weight each day. To provide a real-life example, a man who weighs 180 pounds would consume 49 to 65 g/d of protein, and a woman who weighs 140 pounds would consume 38 to 50 g/d. As for what 65 grams of protein looks like, it could be 4 ounces of chicken breast, ¼ cup garbanzo beans, an 8-ounce cup of milk, and a 3-ounce piece of salmon. This recommendation gets more important as your kidney function worsens. For example, a strict protein limit may provide more benefit for people with Stage 5 CKD as compared to people with Stage 3 CKD.

Here are some examples of the amount of protein in common foods:

FOOD	SERVING SIZE (APPROX)	PROTEIN (APPROX)
Egg	1 large	6 grams
Steak	3 ounces (85 grams)	22 grams
Canned solid white tuna	3 ounces	20 grams
Lentils	4 ounces (1 cup) cooked	16–20 grams
Whole milk	8 ounces	8 grams
Cheddar cheese	4 ounces (1 cup) shredded	28 grams
Broccoli	3 ounces (1 cup chopped)	3 grams
Salmon	3 ounces	20 grams
Chicken breast	3 ounces	24 grams
Peanut butter	3 ounces (2 Tbsp)	21 grams
Quinoa	3 ounces (just less than ½ cup) cooked	3.6 grams

Figuring out a diet that provides a certain amount of protein a day—let's say 60 g—can get tricky. To create a diet that conforms to a tight restriction like that, you need as many of these things as possible:

* A personal chef
* Extra money
* A dietitian
* A calculator
* Extra time to calculate protein
* Access to a variety of foods, and the income and time to make them
* Discipline

While some data has shown that lower-protein diets are effective for managing kidney disease, it's clearly difficult to make a lower-protein diet happen. Many give up on the protein restrictions of a kidney-protective diet because they find it too complicated to follow. I don't want that to happen to you, so I'll share some broad generalizations that may help you stay in a safe protein range.

1. **EAT LESS ANIMAL PROTEIN.** In the past, dietitians and doctors believed that animal-based proteins provided more energy than plant proteins. This theory was based on their higher biologic value, which refers to the fact that they contain more types of amino acids (as you recall, the building blocks of protein) than plant proteins. However, recent research suggests that the biologic value of proteins is not as important as we once believed—especially for individuals with kidney disease.

   When you consider which proteins are best, you must consider more than their biologic availability. For example, the amount of phosphorus, which can cause problems for people with kidney disease, in a piece of red meat is larger and more easily absorbed than the amounts of phosphorus in plant-based proteins. In addition, if your diet has a lot of variety, you probably get all the essential amino acids without animal protein, since different foods provide different amino acids. Diets that are lower in animal protein also may improve blood pressure and the gut microbiome and may reduce the amount of toxin build-up in people with reduced kidney function.

   Recipe Suggestion: Substitute tofu or beans for meat in at least one of your meals per week—for example, substitute crispy chickpeas for the chicken in the "Chicken & Farro Bowls" recipe.

2. **IF YOU HAVE STAGE 4 OR 5 CKD, AVOID DIETS THAT ARE VERY HIGH IN PROTEIN.** These include Atkins, South Beach, and Zone. These diets may also be unsafe for people with Stage 1–3 CKD; if you are considering one, first consult a dietitian.

3. **LIMIT MEAT, POULTRY, PORK, AND FISH CONSUMPTION TO ONE MEAL EACH DAY.** Choose vegetable-based proteins, like beans, lentils, nuts, and whole grains, instead of meats, as these generally contain less protein than similar serving sizes of animal-based proteins. Add some extra vegetables, whole grains, and non-animal fats (for example, avocados) to help fill you up.

4. **IF YOU ARE EATING ANIMAL PROTEIN AT MORE THAN ONE MEAL EACH DAY, STICK TO ONE SMALL SERVING AT EACH MEAL AND TRY TO CUT BACK.** For example, 85 g (3 ounces) of chicken contains 24 g of protein, and the same amount of canned tuna (3 ounces) has 20 g of protein.

5. **IF YOU CHOOSE ANIMAL PROTEIN, PICK A WHITE-MEAT PROTEIN, SUCH AS CHICKEN, FISH, OR TURKEY, OVER RED MEATS, LIKE BEEF, PORK, VEAL, LAMB, VENISON, AND GOAT. ALSO STAY AWAY FROM PROCESSED MEATS SUCH AS HOT DOGS, BACON, SPAM, AND SAUSAGE.** A 2017 study found that red-meat intake is directly associated with the development of end-stage kidney disease and that substituting white meats for red meats may significantly lower the risk.[20]

6. **MAKE VEGETABLES THE STAR OF EACH MEAL PLATE AND KEEP THE ANIMAL PROTEIN ON THE SIDE.**

7. **CHEAT, IF YOU WANT, BUT ONLY OCCASIONALLY.** A steak or burger once a month won't undermine all your good work.

8. **ALWAYS PLAN YOUR DIET WITH THE HELP OF A DIETITIAN.**

9. **WHEN COOKING FROM A RECIPE, TRY TO REDUCE THE AMOUNT OF MEAT THAT'S CALLED FOR AND ADD TWICE AS MANY VEGETABLES.** For example, if a recipe calls for 1 pound of ground chicken, instead use only half a pound and add an equal amount of zucchini, broccoli, or carrots to fill out the recipe. For example, in my "Za'atar Chicken Salad" recipe, you could add some chopped carrots and some no-sodium white beans to lower the overall animal protein content.

10. **USE CHEESES WITH STRONG FLAVOR, SUCH AS PARMESAN, BLUE CHEESE, OR EXTRA-SHARP CHEDDAR, SO YOU DON'T HAVE TO USE AS MUCH.** Cutting back on the amount of cheese you consume will also help you limit your sodium and phosphorus intake.

11. **LEARN TO COOK WHOLE GRAINS.** Whole-grain foods are great ways to satisfy your appetite without adding animal protein. Many people think of whole grains as a narrow group—for example, whole-grain bread, brown rice, or whole-wheat pasta—but there are lots of options. Consider whole-grain couscous, wild rice, quinoa, wheat berries, bulgur, oats, farro, barley, and other options. If you haven't cooked these grains before, it may take a few times to master the technique. See my "Southwest Quinoa Salad" or "Chicken, Kale & Farro Casserole."

A Very, Very, Very, Very Low-Protein Diet

If protein can stress your kidneys, wouldn't it make sense to cut it out almost completely—say, no more than the amount in a single 3-ounce chicken breast per day? Yes and no. Researchers have studied whether severe protein restrictions can extend the health of the kidneys and slow the time before a person needs to start dialysis, but the results have been mixed.

First, extremely low-protein diets are very hard to follow. Without a dedicated program or the full-time assistance of a dietitian, it's nearly impossible. In addition, if you consume only a tiny amount of protein each day, you're depriving your body of the essential amino acids it needs to build muscle and fight off infections. To safely adhere to a very low-protein diet, you'd have to take amino acid supplements to give your body the essential building blocks it needs. Consuming such supplements requires the strict supervision of a dietitian or a doctor.

Dialysis and Protein Intake

Once you start dialysis, your protein needs change significantly. Instead of limiting protein intake, your focus will shift to eating as much protein as you can. See "Step 10: Keep an Open Mind if You Start Dialysis" for more details.

DISCOVER ALKALINE-RICH FOODS

If you follow all the dietary advice in this book, you won't have to do anything more to ensure your diet stays focused on alkaline foods. Diets that feature lower amounts of animal protein and processed foods and higher amounts of fruits and vegetables naturally follow these guidelines. All the same, it is interesting to learn exactly why alkaline foods help the kidneys, and I hope you'll find that what you learn in this chapter will give you yet another reason to make the changes I've suggested throughout the book.

The why behind alkaline foods' benefits to kidney health is one of my favorite topics because it puts a spotlight on how the kidneys keep the body running smoothly and in balance and clearly shows how the food you eat influences your kidneys' ability to maintain this balance.

To get there, though, you must bear with me as I take you through a few pages of high-school science (don't worry—you can still skip the science and go right to the delicious recipes if you wish). I'll give you the bottom line right here, up front:

Fruits, vegetables, and herbs are good for your kidneys,
and too much animal protein can be harmful.

Remember back in high school, when you used pH papers to test different liquids to see if they were acidic, basic (alkaline), or neutral? Acidic liquids (those with a pH below 7) like lemon juice would turn the strip red. Alkaline liquids with a pH above 7, such as bleach or dish soap, would turn the strip blue or purple. Neutral liquids that had a pH of 7, like distilled water, would turn the strip green.

Using these strips to measure pH readings inside the body can be fascinating. The stomach, for example, maintains a very low acidic pH of 1.5 to 3.5; the acid helps digest and dissolve the food you eat. In contrast, the blood is almost neutral, with levels ranging from 7.35 to 7.45. The kidneys, along with the lungs and skeletal system, work hard to keep the blood pH within this range. If the blood pH were more acidic, like that of the stomach, you'd die instantly. It's amazing how the body keeps these areas separate and regulated.

pH SCALE

0 1 2 3 4 5 6 7 8 9 10 11 12 13 14

Acidic   Neutral   Alkaline

When the kidneys are functioning normally, they can easily keep the blood acid level stable with a little help from the lungs. When your kidneys sense that your blood acid level rises too high (a condition called acidosis), they remove the extra acid via the urine; when they sense that it's dropped too low, they hold on to acid, keeping it in the body. Behind the scenes, they work hard to maintain this balance every minute of every day. If they ever stop working perfectly, the results are catastrophic: even the slightest increase in blood acid level for a prolonged period will cause your bones to break down and your kidneys to be damaged.

Potential Renal Acid Load (PRAL)

Every food has its own acid/alkaline number called a potential renal acid load, or PRAL (*renal* is a synonym for kidney). Put simply, PRAL represents the amount of work that the kidneys must do to neutralize the acid that is produced by the body's metabolism of that food. The higher a food's PRAL is, the more work the kidneys must do. It's important to note that PRAL is *not* related to the acidity of the food itself; rather, PRAL is based on the acid that is produced as a result of the metabolism of that food. For example, tomatoes are acidic, but the body's metabolism of them produces base, so they have a low PRAL value.

Foods are separated into acid-producing or alkaline-producing groups based on their PRAL. Many, but not all, fruits and vegetables have PRAL scores in the alkaline or basic range, so they don't put stress on your kidneys' ability to keep the blood pH tightly regulated. On the other hand, carbonated sodas that are colored with phosphoric acid; meats; fish; and processed cheeses have more acid-producing properties, so they make your kidneys work harder. Animal proteins have some of the highest PRAL scores because they are composed of amino acids, which produce a large amount of acid as they are metabolized. This acid must be processed and discarded by the kidneys.

Though there is no standardized list of which foods are alkaline-producing and which foods are acid-producing foods, this chart summarizes my analysis of the research into some common foods:

ALKALINE (BASIC) FOODS	NEUTRAL FOODS	ACIDIC FOODS
Parsley	Blueberries	Baking soda
Oregano	Quinoa	Swiss cheese
Cilantro	Sour cream	Processed cheddar cheese
Apricots	Water	Tuna fish
Raisins		Parmigiano (parmesan) cheese
Bananas		Red meats
Paprika		Lunch (deli) meats
Broccoli		Ultra-processed foods
Cauliflower		Lentils
Zucchini		Rice
Tomatoes		
Swiss chard		
Figs		
Spinach		
Avocado		

The modern Western diet produces much more acid than the diets of our ancestors. They ate more fruits and vegetables than we do, and less white bread, hot dogs, carbonated sodas, deli meats, and cheeses.[21] Because of this difference, we are putting much more stress on the neutralizing power of our kidneys than our ancestors did, so our kidneys must work much harder than theirs did. If your kidneys aren't functioning perfectly, or if you don't have enough filters inside your kidneys to do that extra work, problems will arise.

As I mentioned in "Step 1: Understand Your Kidneys," most people are born with between 700,000 and 1.8 million functioning glomeruli, or tiny filters, per kidney.[22, 23, 24] As you get older, the number of working glomeruli drops: diabetes, vascular disease, high blood pressure, kidney cysts, kidney removal, and even aging alone all play roles in this loss of function. If you're dealing with any of these conditions, or even if you're just getting older, your kidneys may be having problems processing the acid load of your diet.

To better understand the difficulties your kidneys face with processing all that acid, think about it in terms of the heart and the lungs, two organs that are much easier to understand. If you run up a hill, your lungs will work harder as you breathe more deeply and rapidly, and your heart rate will increase, all in an effort to help your body keep up with its changing situation. If your lungs are damaged, they won't be able to keep up with your body's need for more oxygen while running, and you'll need to stop. If your heart is functioning at only 30 percent of normal capacity, it won't be able to pump hard enough to compensate for running up that hill. You'll have to stop running, or you'll have a heart attack.

It's the same principle with your kidneys. It won't happen right away, like the heart and lung analogy, but the extra work your kidneys must do when you eat more acid-producing foods can worsen your kidney disease, for a variety of complex reasons.[25, 26, 27] On a more positive note, however, eating more alkaline-producing foods, such as mushrooms, broccoli, avocados, apricots, and figs, may help protect your kidneys and slow the rate of decline of your kidney disease—especially if you cut back on red meat, soft drinks, cheese, and processed foods.

This advice is absolutely essential to follow if you have any of the following: diabetes, obesity, high blood pressure, chronic kidney disease, kidney transplant, kidney donation, kidney tumor removal, or kidney removal. But it's also important for anyone who wants to preserve the health of their kidneys. The foods you eat can help ease the kidneys' pH-stabilizing burden. If your kidneys can't get rid of excess acid because they've lost some of their function, other parts of the body must take up the burden. For example, the bones can help lessen the impact of the acid load that the kidneys can't manage, but that process causes the bones to break down over time.

Even if your blood pH doesn't change, and for most everyone it won't,
a diet focused on acid-producing foods forces the body to change the way it works
to maintain a stable balance of acid and base.

Of course, it's also important to note that your body needs both alkaline-producing and acid-producing foods. Acid-producing foods often provide important nutrients, just like alkaline-producing foods, and you can successfully integrate them into an otherwise alkaline diet. In fact, the recipes in this book use some of the most acid-producing foods, including canned tuna and parmesan cheese.

Understanding the patterns of these foods and their impact on the health of your kidneys will allow you to find the overall best diet that supports your health. Your goal is simple: eat more alkaline-producing foods than acid-producing foods. By avoiding some of the biggest offenders—red meats, foods with phosphorus additives (more on that in the next chapter), carbonated sodas (particularly dark-colored ones, like colas), and processed foods—and eating more vegetables, such as kale, broccoli, and brussels sprouts, you ensure that your diet is more alkaline than acidic.

If you have Stage 1, 2, or 3 CKD without high blood potassium levels, you should incorporate as many alkaline foods as you can into your diet. But if you have Stage 4 or 5 CKD; are on hemodialysis; have a history of high potassium levels; or are on certain medications, including angiotensin-converting-enzyme inhibitors (ACE inhibitors), angiotensin-receptor blockers (ARBs), or potassium-sparing diuretics, you must be careful about jumping into a primarily alkaline diet. High-alkaline foods are often also high in potassium. Consuming a lot of them can lead to a condition called hyperkalemia, when the potassium in the body gets to a dangerously high level. See "Step 5: Get Potassium Right" for more details, and consult your doctor or dietitian to help determine the best diet for you.

Other recipes: "Roasted Sweet Potatoes," "Roasted Brussels Sprouts," "Mediterranean Chopped Salad," "Lemony Cauliflower Rice."

KALE & GOLDEN RAISIN SALAD

Curly kale is heartier, more fibrous, and more accessible in grocery stores compared to other tender varieties such as red Russian or lacinato, also known as dinosaur or Tuscan kale. Massaging kale leaves with oil and lemon juice tenderizes the greens, making them easier to chew and digest while adding flavor. The combination of contrasting tastes, textures, and colors makes this one of my go-to salads. For low-potassium diets, substitute dried cranberries for raisins and use half kale and half romaine lettuce.

1 BUNCH CURLY KALE, ABOUT 6 OUNCES

2 TABLESPOONS EXTRA VIRGIN OLIVE OIL

1 1/2 TABLESPOONS FRESH LEMON JUICE

1 CLOVE GARLIC, MINCED

1 TABLESPOON GRATED PARMESAN CHEESE

1/3 CUP GOLDEN RAISINS

KOSHER SALT AND FRESHLY GROUND BLACK PEPPER, TO TASTE

1. Holding the thick stem end of the kale leaf in one hand, run your other hand up the stem, stripping the greens. Discard the tough bottom portion of stem left behind and chop the greens. Repeat with the remaining leaves.

2. Place the chopped kale, olive oil, and lemon juice in a large bowl and season with salt. Using clean hands, massage the leaves to soften and infuse flavors, 3 minutes. The kale will look bright green and glossy.

3. Add the garlic, parmesan, and raisins, season with pepper, and toss to combine.

NUTRITION SUMMARY & MODIFICATIONS: Medium potassium. Low sodium. Low phosphorus. For lower potassium version, substitute dried cranberries for raisins. Use 3 ounces kale and 3 ounces Romaine lettuce instead of all kale.

YIELD: 4 servings

ANALYSIS PER SERVING

CALORIES (KCAL): 131

PROTEIN (G): 3

CARBOHYDRATES (G): 15

TOTAL DIETARY FIBER (G): 2

TOTAL SUGARS (G): 11

ADDED SUGAR (G): 0

FAT (G): 8

SATURATED FAT (G): 1

CHOLESTEROL (MG): 1

CALCIUM (MG): 83

MAGNESIUM (MG): 21

PHOSPHORUS (MG): 49

POTASSIUM (MG): 323

SODIUM (MG): 101

~ LOW-POTASSIUM MODIFICATION NUTRITION PROFILE ~

YIELD: 4 servings

ANALYSIS PER SERVING

CALORIES (KCAL): 110

PROTEIN (G): 2

CARBOHYDRATES (G): 11

TOTAL DIETARY FIBER (G): 2

TOTAL SUGARS (G): 8

ADDED SUGAR (G): 5

FAT (G): 7

SATURATED FAT (G): 1

CHOLESTEROL (MG): 1

CALCIUM (MG): 52

MAGNESIUM (MG): 14

PHOSPHORUS (MG): 36

POTASSIUM (MG): 173

SODIUM (MG): 91

SAUTEED RAINBOW CHARD & APPLES

Rainbow chard is a mix of different colored varieties of chard, also known as Swiss chard, and is a relative of the beet family. The earthy, slightly bitter, green, ribbed leaves with colorful stalks vary from white to yellow, orange, red, pink, and purple. This nutritional powerhouse is high in potassium and vitamins A, C, and K. As with most sturdy greens, cooking softens the leaves and bitterness. Try chard as a great substitute for spinach recipes, raw or cooked. For low-potassium or low-oxalate recipes, substitute cabbage for the chard.

1 POUND RAINBOW CHARD

1 TABLESPOON EXTRA-VIRGIN OLIVE OIL

1 SMALL ONION, DICED

PINCH OF RED PEPPER FLAKES

1 SMALL RED APPLE, CORED AND DICED

1 CLOVE GARLIC, MINCED

½ CUP NO-SODIUM VEGETABLE STOCK

JUICE OF HALF A LEMON

1 TEASPOON GRATED PARMESAN CHEESE

1. Cut the chard stems from leaves. Chop stems and leaves, keeping them separate.

2. Heat the oil in a large sauté pan over medium high heat. Sauté the stems, onion, and red pepper flakes, stirring frequently, until onions are soft and translucent, 4 minutes. Add the apple and garlic and sauté until garlic is fragrant, 45 seconds.

3. Add the chard leaves and vegetable stock. Cover and reduce the heat to medium low. Simmer until the leaves are tender, 7 minutes, stirring occasionally. To serve, squeeze the lemon over chard and sprinkle with parmesan cheese.

NUTRITION SUMMARY & MODIFICATIONS: Medium potassium. Low sodium. Low phosphorus. For a low-potassium modification, substitute cabbage for rainbow chard.

continues ➡

SAUTEED RAINBOW CHARD & APPLES continued

~~~ NUTRITION PROFILE ~~~

YIELD: 6 servings

ANALYSIS PER SERVING

CALORIES (KCAL): 46

PROTEIN (G): 2

CARBOHYDRATES (G): 6

TOTAL DIETARY FIBER (G): 2

TOTAL SUGARS (G): 2

ADDED SUGAR (G): 0

FAT (G): 3

SATURATED FAT (G): 0

CHOLESTEROL (MG): 0

CALCIUM (MG): 44

MAGNESIUM (MG): 63

PHOSPHORUS (MG): 40

POTASSIUM (MG): 312

SODIUM (MG): 177

~~~ SAUTÉED CABBAGE & APPLES MODIFICATION NUTRITION PROFILE ~~~

YIELD: 6 servings

ANALYSIS PER SERVING

CALORIES (KCAL): 51

PROTEIN (G): 1

CARBOHYDRATES (G): 7

TOTAL DIETARY FIBER (G): 2

TOTAL SUGARS (G): 4

ADDED SUGAR (G): 0

FAT (G): 2

SATURATED FAT (G): 0

CHOLESTEROL (MG): 0

CALCIUM (MG): 36

MAGNESIUM (MG): 11

PHOSPHORUS (MG): 25

POTASSIUM (MG): 154

SODIUM (MG): 30

STEP 8

IDENTIFY & ELIMINATE SNEAKY PHOSPHORUS

Phosphorus is a mineral found in the bones. In fact, it's the second most plentiful mineral in the body. After reading this chapter, you'll know the secret about phosphorus that many dietitians and doctors don't: Some of the biggest sources of phosphorus in your diet—which are also, naturally, the first foods you should remove from your diet—are the phosphorus additives contained in sodas, processed foods, and fast foods. This chapter applies mostly to people with Stage 4 or Stage 5 CKD, but it's important for you to know about phosphorus, no matter what stage of kidney disease you're facing.

What Is Phosphorus?

The topics of how phosphorus affects your body and which high-phosphorus foods should be avoided are controversial. Unfortunately, we don't really know exactly how much phosphorus is too much, nor do we know what blood levels of phosphorus are safe for people with kidney disease. Even some of the most dedicated people who are on dialysis—those who never miss a medication and who strictly follow a diet—can't manage to bring their blood phosphorus level into the ranges prescribed by their doctors. That suggests that something is wrong with our understanding.

Although your kidneys help regulate the body's phosphorus level just as they do for sodium and potassium, they do it in a slightly different way. Most of the phosphorus in your body is stored in your bones, and a complicated hormone regulation system led by the kidneys and the foods you eat keeps the phosphorus blood level within a safe range. If the kidneys don't work as well as they should, this delicate hormonal regulation system can end up in disarray, and phosphorus blood levels can increase to high levels.

In the short term, high phosphorus in your blood can cause itching. In the long term, it can weaken your bones, lead to calcium buildup and decreased blood flow in your blood vessels, and increase your risk of death if you have kidney disease. Research has also suggested that a high-phosphorus diet can affect healthy people who don't have kidney disease.

> Studies have connected eating too much phosphorus with the development of diabetes, a higher incidence of mortality (death rate), cardiovascular disease, calcified blood vessels, osteoporosis, and many other chronic conditions—even in people who maintain normal blood phosphorus levels.[28, 29, 30]

How and why this link exists is still unclear.

On the other hand, if the phosphorus level in your blood drops too low, you can have symptoms ranging from irritability and weakness to heart rhythm problems, seizures, and coma.

As with other electrolytes and minerals in the body, when the kidneys are not working well, the body's phosphorus level can rise too high. Doctors often treat this condition by limiting phosphorus in the diet and by prescribing medications called phosphorus binders. Taking these pills at the start of each meal can help lower the blood phosphorus level by preventing the absorption of the phosphorus in food by the body.

This routine can become expensive and burdensome. The average person on dialysis takes as many as seven pills each day to help manage their phosphorus levels.[31] If you combine this with the many other medications dialysis patients may take—for high blood pressure, diabetes and heart disease, for example—some end up taking 15 to 20 pills each day. At that point, the side effects and interactions of all these drugs can become significant, and hours of a person's or caregiver's day become consumed with buying and taking medications and setting reminders for them.

Fortunately, there are ways to limit the phosphorus we consume in foods in the first place, rather than taking medications to get rid of it. Unfortunately, nephrologists and the kidney-disease community at large haven't done a great job of spreading the information needed to make this happen. For many years, diets that proclaimed they were "kidney healthy" or "renal diets" have encouraged people with kidney disease to avoid foods with high phosphorus content. But this shotgun approach—essentially blasting away at all foods that are considered high in phosphorus—has had unintended consequences without clear benefits. Shockingly, we still don't know for sure that people with kidney disease who limit their phosphorus intake fare better than those who don't.

The standard "avoid all high-phosphorus foods" advice has led many people to eliminate foods that contain other healthy nutrients like fiber, potassium, and protein. Beans, whole grains, nuts, and lentils are good examples—all high-phosphorus foods that also have significant health benefits. Later in this chapter, I'll discuss the many reasons why these organic and natural phosphorus sources should stay in your diet.

I take a different approach with low-phosphorus diets. Traditional high-phosphorus food charts don't list a priority scale—essentially, they don't tell you which foods you should give up before others. As a result, people give up healthy foods that are high in phosphorus at the same time they give up unhealthy ones.

For example, suppose your doctor or dietitian believes your phosphorus level is too high. You're given a list of foods that are high in phosphorus and asked to identify the foods on it that you regularly consume. On the list, you spot pinto beans and dark sodas, two items that frequently appear in your diet, and you're told to stop consuming them. But it's possible that you could achieve safe phosphorus levels by giving up dark sodas alone, while still eating the pinto beans and benefiting from their fiber and plant-based protein.

Another fact that most kidney disease patients never discover is that not all phosphorus is the same. The phosphorus in plants, animals, and preservatives has different chemical compositions. For example, the phosphorus in plants is stored in phytates, which cannot be broken down by the human body. So even though a plant-based dish may contain a lot of phosphorus, much of that phosphorus may not be absorbed in your intestines; therefore, it may not influence tissues and chemicals inside the body. If you eat a food with a large amount of plant-based phosphorus, most of that phosphorus may never enter your blood. Food-based phosphorus additives, on the other hand, are different. Many foods are preserved with phosphorus to extend their shelf life rather than to make them healthier. These additives easily break apart in water once they enter the digestive tract and can then be absorbed into the body, where they may have a pronounced effect.[32]

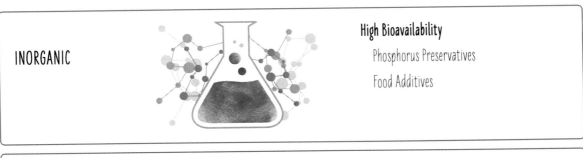

INORGANIC

High Bioavailability
Phosphorus Preservatives
Food Additives

ORGANIC

Medium Bioavailability
Dairy Products
Meat or Fish Based

Low Bioavailability
Plant Based

The difference in bioavailability (which means that it's able to enter the body and influence the tissues and chemicals inside it) of these types of phosphorus is astounding. According to one study, only 6 percent of the phosphorus in an unprocessed food, sesame seeds, is bioavailable, compared to the nearly 100 percent bioavailability of the phosphorus in food additives.[33] That means if you eat a food with 100 mg of phosphorus from a food additive, all 100 mg may be absorbed. In comparison, if you eat a food like sesame seeds with 100 mg of natural phosphorus, only 6 mg may be absorbed.

Your First Steps Toward a Healthy, Low-Phosphorus Diet

I view dietary phosphorus limitations as a small part of a safe, protective diet for people with kidney disease. Instead of eliminating all high-phosphorus foods, I recommend a different approach. Many high-phosphorus foods and beverages are bad for your health for other reasons, too, so stop consuming those first. The first ones to whack from your diet are:

DARK-COLORED SODAS. Soft drinks such as Pepsi and Coke, have very high bioavailable phosphorus levels and no redeeming health qualities. Replace them with water.

ALL FOODS WITH PHOSPHORUS ADDITIVES. This is often the hardest part of a reduced-phosphorus diet. If you don't own reading glasses or a magnifying glass, get something to enhance your vision or bring your children to the grocery store with you to decipher phosphorus content in ingredient lists. The easiest way to make this happen is to cook as many of your meals as possible from scratch at home. Phosphorus content is not usually listed on a food label like sodium or calories; instead, you need to look at the product's ingredient list and look for ingredients that contain the syllable "*phos.*" If you see it, the food contains added phosphorus, and it's best to limit that product as much as you can. Examples of these ingredients are endless, but here are some:

* Dicalcium phosphate
* Disodium phosphate
* Monosodium phosphate
* Phosphoric acid
* Sodium hexameta-phosphate
* Trisodium phosphate
* Sodium tripolyphosphate
* Tetrasodium pyrophosphate

THE FOLLOWING FOODS THAT ARE PARTICULARLY HIGH IN PHOSPHORUS ADDITIVES.

You should give these up altogether and try to create homemade versions instead:

* Canned and bottled iced teas: Make fresh, homemade iced tea instead. See the "Sweet Tea Substitute" recipe.

* Candy and caramel.

* Lunch meat: Use fresh chicken or turkey breast rather than processed deli cuts. See the "Baked Chicken Breasts" recipe.

* Ice cream: Try sorbet or frozen fruit pops instead.

* Chicken nuggets: Make these at home using Panko breadcrumbs and fresh chicken breast.

* Frozen pizzas: Make your own homemade crust.

* Evaporated milk: Use unenriched rice milk.

* American cheese: Substitute cheddar cheese.

* Hot dogs.

* Fast food.

* Frozen dinners.

* Snack foods, like cheese puffs and potato chips: Substitute fresh vegetables with homemade dips. See the recipe chapter "Spreads, Snacks & Sauces."

* Frozen waffles or pancakes: Try homemade versions.

* Boxed or canned stock or broth: Homemade versions are tastier and much healthier. See "No-Sodium Chicken Stock" and "No-Sodium Vegetable Stock."

OTHER HIGH-PHOSPHORUS FOODS WITH NO REDEEMING HEALTH VALUE.

These include beef liver and organ meats. Give these up today.

If you are still struggling with higher phosphorus levels, the next foods to give up are:

DAIRY PRODUCTS. Try to stick with cheeses that have a lower phosphorus content such as:

* Parmesan cheese

* Blue cheese

* Cottage cheese

* Neufchatel cheese

* Feta cheese

* Instead of regular milk, substitute unenriched rice milk, almond milk, or soy milk.

* Choose clear broth soups instead of creamy soups.

CHOCOLATE. Stick with small amounts eaten only occasionally.

If you still can't get your phosphorus levels under control, discuss with your doctor or dietitian the next step in limiting the phosphorus in your diet. The following foods are healthy food choices, and therefore should be the last high-phosphorus foods to consider limiting:

* Whole grains (brown rice, oat bran, wild rice, whole-grain pasta)

* Legumes

* Lentils

* Fresh or flash-frozen (without phosphorus additives) fish

* Oatmeal

STEP 9

INTEGRATE THE DASH, MEDITERRANEAN & DIABETIC DIETS INTO YOUR ROUTINE

Because many people with CKD must juggle more than just kidney disease, you can't just follow a "kidney diet" without worrying that the diet's specific recommendations could negatively affect your other medical conditions. That's particularly true if you have both diabetes and kidney disease, but confusion can also occur with heart failure, coronary artery disease, or high blood pressure. This chapter guides you through some of the difficulties that can occur when trying to find the right balance.

High Blood Pressure

The guidelines in this book adhere to two of the best-studied and most effective diets for management of high blood pressure: the Mediterranean diet and the Dietary Approaches to Stop Hypertension (DASH) diets. But before I get into the science and the specifics, I'll start with some good news: Mediterranean recipes produce some of the tastiest and freshest food on the planet. In fact, some of my all-time favorite meals were had during visits to the Mediterranean region:

* Steaming platters of paella served family-style on a sidewalk in Barcelona, just a few blocks from the beach. The soft aromas of seafood and saffron mingled perfectly with the sea breeze, jet lag, and laughter.

* Chicken shawarma, freshly sliced, consumed on the go in the streets of Jerusalem as I hurried with my family through the outdoor markets. Surrounded by the tension of armed soldiers and arguing shoppers and shopkeepers, we enjoyed the warm sun and delicious smells of the market. I've spent years trying to recreate the amazing contrast of the perfectly charred and spiced chicken; the chopped salad of cucumber, tomato, onion, and herbs; and the warm, freshly baked pita bread in my own kitchen.

* Black coffee sipped slowly in a town square in Florence as my wife and I watched the tourists stroll by.

* The amazing flavors of a sandwich my wife and I shared in San Gimignano, a small Tuscan hill town, with an afternoon glass of Brunello di Montalcino. I vividly remember the culinary masterpiece of local ingredients: tomatoes, basil, goat cheese, olive oil, balsamic vinegar, and crusty white bread.

These experiences are relevant because one of the best-studied food-based methods for treating high blood pressure is the Mediterranean diet. Imagine yourself living in an idyllic setting along the Mediterranean Sea. You're surrounded by farms growing free-range meats. There are daily farmers markets you walk a few miles to get to, providing your daily exercise; locally sourced seafood; and cheese made by your neighbors all at the same time. To me, this diet is an extension of the experiences of living in a Mediterranean town, and I try to find ways to incorporate both this style of food and the Mediterranean lifestyle into my own daily life.

Diet and High Blood Pressure

High blood pressure and kidney damage go hand in hand as a vicious cycle. Over time, uncontrolled high blood pressure can lead to kidney damage, and kidney damage can lead to worsening high blood pressure.

Of course, taking medications as they are prescribed and learning to monitor your blood pressure at home are important steps in managing your high blood pressure. At the same time, exercising, maintaining a healthy weight, and eating the right foods also play important roles. I break down the essentials of managing of high blood pressure from a food perspective into four categories:

* Follow a low-sodium diet.

* Follow a high-potassium diet, as long as you don't already have high blood potassium levels. See "Step 5: Get Potassium Right" for more details.

* Follow the DASH or Mediterranean diet.

* Be sure to include specific foods that benefit blood pressure in your diet.

In 2001, *The New England Journal of Medicine* published my favorite study on using diet to manage high blood pressure.[34] The study selected a group of people who followed a typical American diet. Before the study began, the participants regularly ate large amounts of high-sodium foods, red meats, and sweets and drank sugar-containing beverages. For the duration of the study, they switched to a lower-sodium DASH diet that placed emphasis on eating lots of fruits, vegetables, and low-fat dairy products and limited consumption of red meats, sweets, and sugar-containing beverages. It's very similar to the diet I describe throughout this book.

The results were astounding. The study found that participants who switched their typical high-sodium diet to a lower-sodium DASH diet lowered their blood pressure by 10 to 15 mm Hg—meaning that within a short period of time, their blood pressure could go from being uncontrolled to a healthy range.

A change from a typical high-sodium American diet to a low-sodium DASH diet can lower your systolic blood pressure by 10–15 mm Hg.

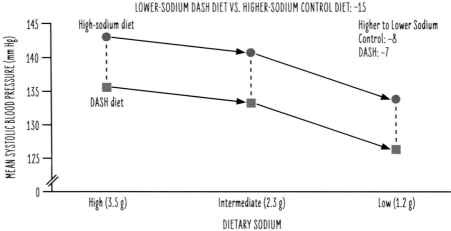

LOWER-SODIUM DASH DIET VS. HIGHER-SODIUM CONTROL DIET: –15

High-sodium diet

DASH diet

Higher to Lower Sodium
Control: –8
DASH: –7

MEAN SYSTOLIC BLOOD PRESSURE (mm Hg)

High (3.5 g)   Intermediate (2.3 g)   Low (1.2 g)

DIETARY SODIUM

* Adapted from Sacks FM, Campos H. Dietary therapy in hypertension. *N Engl J Med.* 2010;362(22):2102-2112. doi:10.1056/NEJMct0911013.

Incredibly, the best results of the intervention occurred in older individuals and people with very high blood pressure. With some lifestyle changes, doctors tell patients they're "too old" to make a change to improve their health, but with the lower-sodium DASH diet, it's just the opposite.[35] For some people, a change in diet could keep them off medication altogether, and for those with very high blood pressure that must be controlled with medication, a change in diet paired with medication could provide very significant added benefits.[36]

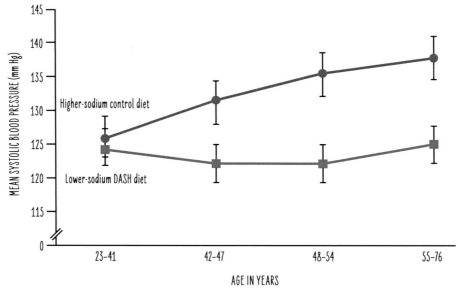

MEAN SYSTOLIC BLOOD PRESSURE (mm Hg)

Higher-sodium control diet

Lower-sodium DASH diet

23–41   42–47   48–54   55–76

AGE IN YEARS

* Adapted from Bray GA, Vollmer WM, Sacks FM, et al.[35]

The DASH diet is low in total fat, saturated fat, and cholesterol, and it focuses on fruits, vegetables, and whole grains. It's higher in fiber, potassium, calcium, and magnesium and lower in sodium than a traditional American or Western diet.

The Mediterranean diet—blessed with a name that's much more accessible and enticing than DASH—is very similar and also has excellent clinical study results. Like the DASH diet, the Mediterranean diet encourages vegetables, fruits, nuts, and whole grains. It's also been associated with improved outcomes for people who have had a kidney transplant.[37] Both diets encompass many of the recommendations in this book; in fact, most of the recommendations that I give to my patients and most of the recipes that I make at home fall within the guidelines of either a DASH or a Mediterranean diet.

Rather than advising you to choose between one of these two diets and the kidney-protective diet I describe in this book and stick exclusively to that specific set of restrictions, I recommend that you focus on the similarities that all these diets share. Keep your focus on changing your taste buds, adjusting your eating habits, and learning to cook at home. Making these changes may also help you lose weight, reduce your risk of stroke, and better control your blood sugar and cholesterol levels.

Here are some suggestions to help you get there:

* Take a cooking class at a local culinary school that's focused on healthy eating or cooking with fresh vegetables.

* Learn how to chop vegetables quickly and skillfully. Lots of great books and YouTube videos can teach you knife skills, or you can take a class.

* Give up fast food, soda, and eating on the run.

* #ChangeYourBuds so you have greater appreciation for foods that aren't as sweet or salty and cultivate a love of freshly prepared vegetables.

* Buy Mediterranean or DASH diet cookbooks to build a library of healthy recipes you love.

Specific Foods

Several studies have looked at the ability of specific foods to help lower blood pressure. Beets, one of my favorites, are a great example, because we know exactly how they work to lower blood pressure. The nitrates that naturally occur in beets are converted to nitric oxide once they are consumed. This nitric oxide dilates your blood vessels, causing your blood pressure to decrease.

But there are a few problems with studies that examine the effects of specific foods like beets on blood pressure. First, most people aren't willing to eat the same foods every day. Second, many of the foods must be consumed in large amounts if they are to lower blood pressure in a meaningful way. Third, simply adding a single specific food likely won't have much of an effect on your blood pressure or health if the rest of your diet is still loaded with processed and fast foods and lacking in fruits and vegetables. It's most important to focus on changing your diet as a whole, instead of adding individual foods.

Other foods to include in your diet that have been directly associated with blood pressure reduction are flax seeds and blueberries.

See "Seared Salmon with Tzatziki Sauce," "Lemon Caper Roasted Salmon," or "Mediterranean Chopped Salad" as examples. Most recipes in this book fit into a DASH or Mediterranean diet pattern.

Healthy Eating for Diabetes and Heart Health: Tackling the Confusion

At least one person with both chronic kidney disease and diabetes comes into my office each week boiling over with frustration—with good reason. Despite their best attempts to protect their health, they find that they're simply unable to figure out what to eat because the standard dietary advice for managing kidney disease is often in conflict with dietary recommendations for managing diabetes. This confusion, and the consequences of this confusion, provided a lot of the motivation for writing this book.

A REAL-LIFE EXAMPLE

The experience of one of my patients, Mrs. W, is a perfect illustration of how this uncertainty can lead to misguided dietary changes and how those changes lead to significant health consequences. Mrs. W had grappled with diabetes for years, and she first saw me after her primary care doctor diagnosed her with Stage 3 CKD as well. From the very beginning, she struggled with her new diagnosis. She'd had difficulty managing her diabetes in the past, but in the preceding two years, she'd improved her blood sugar levels significantly by transitioning to more whole grains, limiting white breads and pastas, and cutting out sodas.

As soon as Mrs. W received the kidney disease diagnosis from her primary care doctor, she started worrying about dialysis. This worry—when I spoke to her later about it, she characterized it as a "panic"—overwhelmed her so much that she decided to overhaul her diet on her own, basing the changes on internet research.

Before the week was out, she'd transitioned to a low-protein diet based on white bread, white pasta, and refined grains that avoided all whole-grain foods. These "white" foods and refined grains caused her blood sugar levels to rise. Unwittingly, she'd put herself at risk for the consequences of uncontrolled diabetes.

I don't want Mrs. W's situation to happen to you. In this chapter, I discuss the best ways to tackle some of these seeming contradictions and find a diet that can help you control both diabetes and chronic kidney disease. As we take a step back and look at the diet from a different perspective, you'll see that most dietary recommendations for kidney disease and most other health conditions, including diabetes and heart disease, are the same:

* Make vegetables the star of your plate.

* Control your portion sizes.

* Cook at home and eat out less often.

* Avoid high-sugar drinks and foods with added sugar.

* Closely monitor your sodium intake.

As I often tell my patients, what's good for the kidneys is good for the rest of the body. You just have to be mindful of a few adjustments and modifications.

BEET & GOAT CHEESE SALAD

ROASTED BEET, GOAT CHEESE & WALNUT SALAD WITH BLUEBERRY VINAIGRETTE

MAKES 5 SERVINGS

This recipe comes from Amy Rinkowski, the owner and head chef at Tacozzini, one of my favorite restaurants in Greenville, SC. As soon as I took my first bite of this salad, I knew I had to share it with everyone else. From both a flavor standpoint and a health standpoint, this salad tops the charts. The combination of potassium-rich spinach, nitrate-rich beets, and antioxidant-rich blueberries make this entrée salad an ideal choice for high-blood-pressure patients who can eat high-potassium foods. Contrasting flavors and textures from earthy beets to peppery arugula, creamy goat cheese, and crisp walnuts turns this salad into a light yet satisfying meal.

2 LARGE BEETS, SCRUBBED

1 TEASPOON OLIVE OIL

10 CUPS LOOSELY PACKED ARUGULA

10 CUPS LOOSELY PACKED BABY SPINACH

2 1/2 CUPS BLUEBERRIES

5 OUNCES FRESH GOAT CHEESE, CRUMBLED, ABOUT 2/3 CUP

2/3 CUP WALNUTS, TOASTED AND CHOPPED

1/2 CUP "BLUEBERRY VINAIGRETTE"

1. Heat the oven to 375°F. Rub the beets with the olive oil and wrap in foil. Place the foil on a baking sheet and cook until the beets are tender when pierced with a paring knife, about 50 minutes. Remove the beets from the foil and cool. Cut beets in half and slice them ¼-inch thick.

2. Divide arugula and spinach between five serving plates. Top each plate with the beets, blueberries, goat cheese, and walnuts. Drizzle salad with "Blueberry Vinaigrette" from Part II, "Dressings & Spice Blends."

NUTRITION SUMMARY & MODIFICATIONS: This is a low-sodium, high-potassium, and medium-phosphorus dish. Because many of the ingredients are high in potassium, it is difficult to make this an all-around low-potassium dish. However, by substituting iceberg lettuce for spinach and using only 1 beet, you can lower the potassium substantially.

NUTRITION PROFILE

YIELD: 5 servings

ANALYSIS PER SERVING

CALORIES (KCAL): 279

PROTEIN (G): 6

CARBOHYDRATES (G): 19

TOTAL DIETARY FIBER (G): 5

TOTAL SUGARS (G): 11

ADDED SUGAR (G): 0

FAT (G): 22

SATURATED FAT (G): 2

CHOLESTEROL (MG): 2

CALCIUM (MG): 145

MAGNESIUM (MG): 95

PHOSPHORUS (MG): 128

POTASSIUM (MG): 628

SODIUM (MG): 82

MODIFICATION NUTRITION PROFILE

YIELD: 5 servings

ANALYSIS PER SERVING

CALORIES (KCAL): 175

PROTEIN (G): 3

CARBOHYDRATES (G): 17

TOTAL DIETARY FIBER (G): 4

TOTAL SUGARS (G): 11

ADDED SUGAR (G): 0

FAT (G): 12

SATURATED FAT (G): 1

CHOLESTEROL (MG): 2

CALCIUM (MG): 89

MAGNESIUM (MG): 31

PHOSPHORUS (MG): 64

POTASSIUM (MG): 375

SODIUM (MG): 42

NUTRITION PROFILE FOR BLUEBERRY VINAIGRETTE

YIELD: about 1 ¾ cup

SERVING SIZE: 1 Tablespoon

CALORIES (KCAL): 55

PROTEIN (G): 0

CARBOHYDRATES (G): 1

TOTAL DIETARY FIBER (G): 0

TOTAL SUGARS (G): 0

ADDED SUGAR (G): 0

FAT (G): 6

SATURATED FAT (G): 0

CHOLESTEROL (MG): 0

CALCIUM (MG): 1

MAGNESIUM (MG): 0

PHOSPHORUS (MG): 1

POTASSIUM (MG): 3

SODIUM (MG): 2

Diabetes: The Basics

Most people know that the foods you eat can affect your blood sugar levels, but most don't know exactly how. The science behind the digestion of food and its conversion into energy has been the subject of many books, mostly because of its complexity and because of ongoing controversies. But understanding a few basics can help you understand how to select foods that are good for both diabetes control and your kidneys.

Foods are made up of carbohydrates, fats, and proteins. When you eat food, those components are broken down into glucose (sugar), lipids, and amino acids (the building blocks of protein), respectively, and the glucose, lipids, and amino acids are absorbed into your intestines. All these components are necessary for survival, but this chapter focuses only on the glucose—the sugar. Your cells need glucose for energy, but they can't use the glucose without insulin, a hormone that allows your cells to absorb and use the glucose.

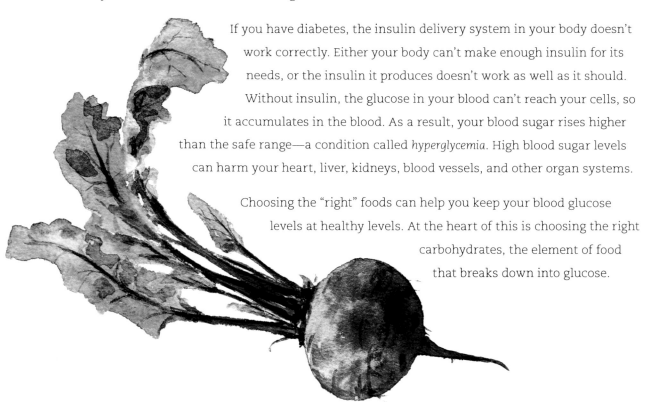

If you have diabetes, the insulin delivery system in your body doesn't work correctly. Either your body can't make enough insulin for its needs, or the insulin it produces doesn't work as well as it should. Without insulin, the glucose in your blood can't reach your cells, so it accumulates in the blood. As a result, your blood sugar rises higher than the safe range—a condition called *hyperglycemia*. High blood sugar levels can harm your heart, liver, kidneys, blood vessels, and other organ systems.

Choosing the "right" foods can help you keep your blood glucose levels at healthy levels. At the heart of this is choosing the right carbohydrates, the element of food that breaks down into glucose.

Low-Carbohydrate Foods

If you have diabetes, the most important step in controlling your blood glucose is to eliminate the high-carbohydrate foods and beverages that do not provide a lot of other health benefits. They may raise your blood sugar levels and make your diabetes more difficult to control. Here are some examples:

* White bread, white rice, white pasta

* Alcoholic drinks

* Pretzels, crackers, and chips

* Pancakes and waffles (unless they're made with whole grains)

* Fruit juice

* Milk, ice cream, and yogurt

* Cake, pie, cookies, and candy bars

* Jams, jellies, honey, and all sauces with added sugar (including ketchup and barbecue sauces)

* Soda, sweet tea, and any other sugar-sweetened drinks

The next step is to choose low-carbohydrate vegetables. The vegetables shown in the table below should be a staple of any healthy diabetic diet, but be aware that some of these foods are higher in potassium (see "Step 5: Get Potassium Right" if you need to avoid or limit these foods). It may take you some time to #ChangeYourBuds and develop a preference for these foods, but the change will be worth it.

LOW-CARBOHYDRATE VEGETABLES		
Asparagus	Chard*	Onions (all types)
Avocados*	Cucumbers	Peppers
Beets*	Eggplant	Radishes
Bok choy*	Green beans	Spinach*
Broccoli*	Greens (collard, mustard, turnip)*	Tomatillos*
Cabbage	Jicama	Tomatoes*
Carrots	Kale*	Yellow squash
Cauliflower	Lettuce (all types)	Zucchini
Celery	Okra	

* If you need to limit potassium, avoid the vegetables in italics

Whole Grains

A third step is to substitute whole grains for the white breads and pastas. Because people with Stage 4 or 5 CKD have been traditionally advised to avoid whole-grain foods, this can cause some confusion.

What Is a Whole Grain?

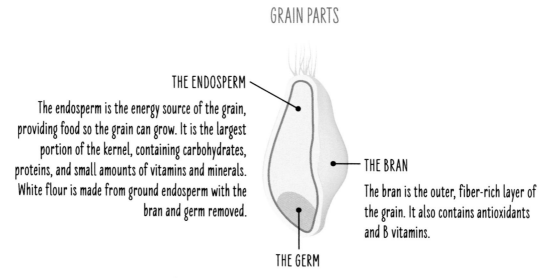

GRAIN PARTS

THE ENDOSPERM

The endosperm is the energy source of the grain, providing food so the grain can grow. It is the largest portion of the kernel, containing carbohydrates, proteins, and small amounts of vitamins and minerals. White flour is made from ground endosperm with the bran and germ removed.

THE BRAN

The bran is the outer, fiber-rich layer of the grain. It also contains antioxidants and B vitamins.

THE GERM

The germ is the embryo of the grain, which can sprout into a new plant. It contains B vitamins, protein, fats, and minerals.

Grains are made of three parts: the bran, the endosperm, and the germ. Whole-grain foods include all three of these parts and maintain all the grain's vitamins, minerals, and fiber. That's particularly beneficial for people with diabetes because the extra fiber in whole grains slows the absorption of its carbohydrate into the intestines. This, in turn, helps control spikes in blood glucose that occur after eating. Examples of whole grains include whole-wheat pasta, whole-grain bread, brown rice, whole-wheat couscous, millet, bulgur, farro, quinoa, kamut, sorghum, wheat berries, oatmeal, and even popcorn!

Whole-grain foods are much more nutritious than processed or refined grains, such as white bread, white rice, and regular pasta. In the process of refining the grains, the bran and germ, along with much of the grain's health benefits, are often removed.

If you have both kidney disease and diabetes, it's important to figure out whether you can integrate whole-grain foods into your diet. Most people can, as only those with advanced kidney disease (Stage 4 or 5, or those on dialysis) may have to limit whole grains because they contain too much potassium or phosphorus. But if you refer to the chapters on potassium and phosphorus, not everyone with CKD must limit those foods with higher levels of phosphorus and potassium. Often, the potassium can be managed by eliminating other high-potassium foods, and you can still eat some whole grains. This can help you as you attempt to manage both your diabetes and your kidney disease. And because whole grains can benefit your overall health, they should be one of the last foods you give up when limiting the phosphorus in your diet. See "Step 8: Identify and Eliminate Sneaky Phosphorus" for more details about limiting the phosphorus in your diet.

If you have been told that you have high blood potassium levels, discuss whole grains with your dietitian or doctor. Even if you need to limit whole grains, you don't have to replace them with white bread or rice or pasta. Many alternatives exist, especially non-starchy vegetables like broccoli and cauliflower.

Check out these whole-grain recipes:

* "Southwest Quinoa Salad"
* "Roasted Tomato & Zucchini Spaghetti with Vegan Basil-Cashew Pesto"

Heart-Healthy Considerations

A heart-healthy diet supports the long-term health of your heart function by reducing some of the risk factors that contribute to heart disease. These diets include many of the same highlights as kidney-healthy and diabetes-healthy diets: high-fiber and low-sodium foods, lots of fruits and vegetables, very little processed foods, and eating out infrequently. In fact, most of the recommendations in this book would be great choices for people who don't have kidney disease but want to follow a heart-healthy diet.

Putting It All Together

Trying to assemble a healthy meal with all these recommendations can be overwhelming. It may seem nearly impossible to ensure you get enough (but not too many) calories, protein, sodium, sugar, potassium, phosphorus, and carbohydrates in a single sitting. But if you follow the guidance in this book, you'll see that the recommendations for kidney disease, heart disease, diabetes, and weight loss all fall into a similar pattern: eat meals that are plant-based and not processed and that feature a lot of vegetables, whole grains, and lean protein.

STEP 10

KEEP AN OPEN MIND IF YOU START DIALYSIS

When I describe a healthy diet for someone on dialysis, I generally start by saying, "Remember everything you were told about healthy eating when you had early-stage kidney disease? Now you can forget most of it." What exactly do I mean by this? Well, here's a summary:

* The moderate- or low-protein diet you've been following will now become focused on eating as much protein as you can.

* You may now have to avoid many more fruits and vegetables.

* You aren't allowed to drink all the water or fluid you want.

* Your dietitian or doctor may tell you to avoid whole grains.

Here's what will remain the same:

* You'll still have to reduce your sodium intake.

* You must still avoid processed phosphorus additives.

* Now, you'll have to focus even harder on eating the *right* fruits and vegetables.

If you're a visual thinker, the strictest dialysis diet looks a little like this:

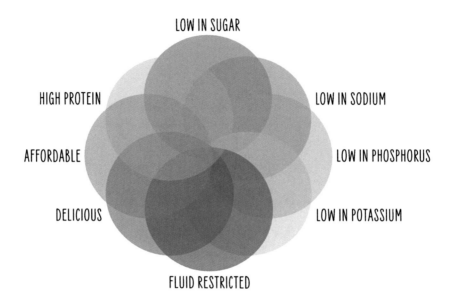

LOW IN SUGAR

HIGH PROTEIN

LOW IN SODIUM

AFFORDABLE

LOW IN PHOSPHORUS

DELICIOUS

LOW IN POTASSIUM

FLUID RESTRICTED

As your kidney function diminishes, their ability to remove the electrolytes and fluids you get from eating and drinking diminishes as well. When your kidneys can't remove them, the burden falls to dialysis. Unfortunately, the potassium and phosphorus can only be cleared when the dialysis process occurs. Most people undergo dialysis three times a week, so during the intervening 48- to 72-hour periods, too many toxins and too much fluid can build up and harm your heart and lungs. Even those who undergo dialysis every day must live without the extra benefits of a dialysis machine when they're not hooked up to it. Remember, healthy kidneys filter the blood 24 hours a day and seven days a week.

People on dialysis have different dietary requirements depending on their:

TYPE OF DIALYSIS: in-center hemodialysis, home hemodialysis, or peritoneal dialysis. People on peritoneal dialysis or home hemodialysis are often able to follow a less-restrictive diet. Because they undergo dialysis more frequently, they're able to clear their toxins and fluids more often. As a result, they may not have to be as careful about ingesting phosphorus, potassium, and fluids.

AMOUNT OF RESIDUAL (NATURAL) KIDNEY FUNCTION: Dialysis doesn't begin when kidney function is at zero; it often starts when the kidneys are still functioning in a range from 5 to 15 percent. For many, it then progresses to zero over the course of a few years. The potassium, phosphorus, sodium, and fluid restrictions for people with 15 percent kidney function and those with 0 percent kidney function are much different. If your kidneys still retain some function, your diet won't have to be as restrictive.

The *good* news about dialysis is that all dialysis centers are required to provide their patients with the services of a dietitian. If you're on dialysis, you'll have a personal dietitian assigned to help you manage your dialysis diet. If you're not getting the support and education you need, ask the dietitian you're working with about good online resources for more information. Some of my favorites include:

* American Kidney Fund's Kidney Kitchen (kitchen.kidneyfund.org/find-recipes)

* Recipes from the dialysis company DaVita (www.davita.com/diet-nutrition/recipe-collections?p=1)

* The American Association of Kidney Patients (aakp.org/center-for-patient-research-and-education/kidney-friendly-recipes)

When you meet with your dietitian, here are some best practices for making the most of your interactions:

BRING IN A FOOD LOG. For a dietitian to successfully help you, they must first understand your current diet. It's hard for a dietitian to help you if you don't provide a thorough log of exactly what, and how much of it, you're eating and drinking.

WHEN YOU MEET, REVIEW YOUR LABS AND DISCUSS SPECIFIC FOODS. If, for example, you're interested in trying a food with a higher phosphorus or potassium content, ask your dietitian if you can try it and then have them check your blood work the following week. That way, you can see whether the combination of your dialysis and residual kidney function is able to clear the extra potassium or phosphorus load.

BE WILLING TO SET GOALS. It often takes a long time and requires many small steps to adjust your diet once you're on dialysis. Your dietitian can help you set realistic goals for your lifestyle that will stay in line with a healthy dialysis diet.

REMEMBER TO KEEP EATING FRUITS AND VEGETABLES. Because of the restrictive nature of their diets, many people on dialysis don't get enough fiber. Ask your dietitian how to safely incorporate more fiber, fruits, and vegetables.

BE COMMITTED TO ENGAGE WITH YOUR DIETITIAN. Dietitians are in the best position to help you if they fully understand your lifestyle, food preferences, and barriers to making change. After all, their purpose for being there is to help you overcome these challenges!

BE WILLING TO LISTEN AND TO ADJUST YOUR BEHAVIOR. Some dietitian recommendations may seem odd to you, but you must remain open to trying new foods, flavors, and textures. You just might find that you really enjoy some of the foods that are healthiest for your kidneys!

PART II
RECIPES

These recipes embody the spirit of the food I eat every day and recommend to my patients. Carefully crafted with the help of a professionally trained chef and food critic, the head chefs and owners of my favorite local restaurants, and multiple dietitians, the final dishes are flavorful, filling, and delicious. They hit all the highlights of taste and nutrition. The dishes give you an opportunity to #ChangeYourBuds through experimentation with new vegetables, quinoa, and farro, and give you a chance to add some regular staples to your family's meal routine. Although these recipes are delicious in and of themselves, I hope you use them for even more than cooking them exactly as written. They are meant to inspire you. Find a dish or a genre you like and turn it into your own magnificent creation. Once you have a few of these techniques mastered and the recipe ideas incorporated into your knowledge of cooking, you'll have the base for a lifetime of kidney-healthy cooking and eating.

Most of these recipes can be adjusted to any level of kidney disease. When possible, I've included adjustments for lower-potassium and lower-protein options, while still trying to maintain the deliciousness of the original dish.

POTASSIUM: The biggest adjustments will be for high-potassium ingredients. If needed, be sure to make those changes when cooking these recipes at home. Also, pay attention to the serving size of the dish. Any recipe can be a high-potassium or high-protein recipe if you eat four servings at one sitting. For more information about potassium, see "Step 5: Get Potassium Right." As a reminder, here are some general recommendations for your daily potassium intake. Please discuss these numbers with your physician or dietitian before making any significant changes to your diet:

LOW-POTASSIUM DIET	Less than 2000 milligrams (mg) each day
MEDIUM-POTASSIUM DIET	Between 2000–4000 milligrams each day
HIGH-POTASSIUM DIET	Greater than 5000 milligrams each day

Recipes are categorized based on the following guidelines:

NUTRIENT PER SERVING	LOW	MEDIUM	HIGH
Sodium	Less than 200 mg	200 mg–399 mg	Greater than 399 mg
Potassium	Less than 300 mg	301 mg–499 mg	Greater than 499 mg
Phosphorus	Less than 150 mg	151 mg–299 mg	Greater than 299 mg
Protein	Less than 8 gm	9 gm–20 gm	Greater than 21 gm

SODIUM: Because these recipes start with fresh ingredients, most are low in sodium. Feel free to add a tiny pinch (a few grains' worth) of kosher salt to the recipes as you cook them to make the other flavors stand out. In "Step 3: Uncover Hidden Salt and #ChangeYourBuds," I discussed that most salt and sodium is hidden in processed and restaurant food, so I give you the option of adding a few crystals of salt to your freshly cooked dish. However, if you are incorporating these meals into a diet that includes restaurant dining, then you probably need to give up those few salt crystals in order to meet your daily low-sodium restrictions.

PHOSPHORUS: Many of these recipes fall into a high phosphorus category because they use whole grains, beans, and some dairy products. If you read "Step 8: Identify & Eliminate Sneaky Phosphorus," you'll remember that the most readily absorbed phosphorus comes from the phosphorus used for preserving foods. These recipes do not use any foods that contain phosphorus additives, so the high phosphorus amounts listed in the nutrition profiles are likely not 100% absorbed into your body. Nevertheless, I have provided some ideas about how to lower the phosphorus content in some of the recipes if you are struggling with higher phosphorus levels.

Beverages

ALTERNATIVE WATERS

See the section "Alternative Waters" in Part I, "Step 2: Choose Your Beverages Wisely" for several flavored, sparkling, and seltzer waters. You'll find very simple recipes for "Orange and Lemon Water," "Strawberry-Lemon-Basil Water," "Cucumber-Lemon-Mint Water," "Peach and Raspberry Water," and more.

SWEET TEA SUBSTITUTE

See Part I, "Step 2: Choose Your Beverages Wisely."

BERRY-BANANA HEMP SMOOTHIE

See Part I, "Step 2: Choose Your Beverages Wisely."

PUMPKIN PIE SMOOTHIE

See Part I, "Step 2: Choose Your Beverages Wisely."

HEARTY LENTIL VEGETABLE SOUP

SOUPS

NO-SODIUM CHICKEN STOCK ⁓⁓⁓⁓⁓⁓⁓⁓⁓⁓⁓⁓⁓⁓⁓⁓⁓⁓⁓ 134

NO-SODIUM VEGETABLE STOCK ⁓⁓⁓⁓⁓⁓⁓⁓⁓⁓⁓⁓⁓⁓⁓⁓⁓ 136

GRANDMA JULIE'S CHICKEN SOUP ⁓⁓⁓⁓⁓⁓⁓⁓⁓⁓⁓⁓⁓⁓⁓ 137

HEARTY LENTIL VEGETABLE SOUP ⁓⁓⁓⁓⁓⁓⁓⁓⁓⁓⁓⁓⁓⁓⁓ 139

LEEK & YELLOW SQUASH SOUP ⁓⁓⁓⁓⁓⁓⁓⁓⁓⁓⁓⁓⁓⁓⁓⁓ 141

NO-SODIUM CHICKEN STOCK

Homemade chicken stock is wholesome and cost effective. The rich results are the foundation for delicious soups, stews, and sauces. I like to make this recipe over the weekend and take advantage of its double-duty kitchen prep. My freezer gets replenished with a batch of nutritious stock, and I start the week with plenty of no-sodium, unprocessed chicken. Having the cooked chicken on hand for "Chicken, Kale & Farro Casserole," "Za'atar Chicken Salad," "Spiced Chicken, Orange & Avocado Salad," or "Grandma Julie's Chicken Soup" means carefree weeknight dinners and encourages smart, healthy eating choices. The recipe will yield about 2 pounds of cooked chicken.

2 3-4 POUND WHOLE CHICKENS

2 ONIONS, SKIN ON, ROUGH CHOPPED

3 STALKS CELERY, ROUGH CHOPPED

8 CARROTS, SCRUBBED, ROUGH CHOPPED

1/4 TEASPOON BLACK PEPPERCORNS

6 WHOLE CLOVES

4 CLOVES GARLIC, SKIN ON, CRUSHED

2 BAY LEAVES

2 TEASPOONS DRIED THYME

10 SPRIGS PARSLEY

1. Combine all the ingredients in a large stock pot and cover with 2 inches of cold water, about 5 quarts. Bring to a boil, reduce the heat, and simmer until a thermometer inserted into the thickest part of the thigh, without touching the bone, reaches an internal temperature of 165°F, about 45 minutes depending on the size of the bird.

2. Using a pair of tongs, carefully transfer the chicken to a rimmed baking sheet. Break the chicken apart with the tongs to help cool more quickly. Return the wings to the pot.

3. Once the chicken is cool enough to handle, remove the meat from the bones and set aside. Return the bones to the pot and simmer on low, partially covered, for 2 hours. While the stock is simmering, divide the cooled chicken meat into resealable bags or airtight containers and refrigerate or freeze as needed.

4. Using a fine mesh sieve or a colander lined with a double layer of cheesecloth, strain the stock in a few batches. Use a wooden spoon or ladle to coax any liquids out of the vegetables. Discard the bones and vegetables. Allow stock to cool, cover and refrigerate overnight.

5. Skim off any fat on the surface and discard. Divide the stock into jars and refrigerate up to a week, or pour into resealable bags, lay flat on a baking sheet, and freeze for up to 3 months.

NUTRITION SUMMARY & MODIFICATIONS: Low sodium. Low potassium. Low phosphorus.

FREEZER SCRAP SAVER BAGS Homemade stocks enhance the flavor of a recipe, are healthier than store-bought, lower food costs, and minimize kitchen waste. Designate a resealable gallon-sized freezer bag to store vegetable scraps until you accumulate enough for your next batch of stock. You will be surprised how quickly the trimmings, peelings, stems, and stalks of onions, leeks, celery, carrots, garlic, broccoli, leafy greens, mushrooms, corn cobs, herbs, and more add up. Use separate bags for poultry, fish, or beef bones.

~~~~~~~~~~~ NUTRITION PROFILE ~~~~~~~~~~~

YIELD: 1 gallon

SERVING SIZE: 1 cup

CALORIES (KCAL): 27

PROTEIN (G): 3

CARBOHYDRATES (G): 1

TOTAL DIETARY FIBER (G): 0

TOTAL SUGARS (G): 1

ADDED SUGAR (G): 0

FAT (G): 1

SATURATED FAT (G): 0

CHOLESTEROL (MG): 0

CALCIUM (MG): 0

MAGNESIUM (MG): 2

PHOSPHORUS (MG): 69

POTASSIUM (MG): 197

SODIUM (MG): 69

NO-SODIUM VEGETABLE STOCK

MAKES 4 QUARTS

There are many advantages to preparing homemade stocks that make it worth your time and effort. Topping the list, it is simply better for you. Store-bought stock can be loaded with sodium and preservatives. Homemade stock is made from vegetable scraps that typically end up in the trash, so economically it's a big savings. Essentially, it's free! The aroma and flavor can't be beat. Great soups, sauces, and gravies all begin with great stock. Stocks also elevate ho-hum dishes to the next level. Try stocks in place of water when cooking rice and grains, in stir-fries and casseroles, or for steaming vegetables. Use this recipe as a baseline. Adjust it with whatever vegetables scraps your kitchen accumulates and find a flavor profile that your family enjoys.

8 OUNCES MUSHROOMS, QUARTERED

2 MEDIUM ONIONS, QUARTERED, SKIN ON

1 HEAD GARLIC, SKIN ON, CLOVES SEPARATED AND CRUSHED

3 STALKS CELERY, COARSELY CHOPPED

3 MEDIUM CARROTS, COARSELY CHOPPED

1 TEASPOON DRIED THYME

10 SPRIGS PARSLEY

1 TEASPOON BLACK PEPPERCORN

1 BAY LEAF

1 TABLESPOON NO SODIUM TOMATO PASTE

1. Place all ingredients in a large stock pot. Fill the pot with enough cold water to cover the vegetables by 2 inches, about 5 quarts. Bring to a boil, reduce the heat to medium low, and simmer for 2 hours.

2. Place a fine mesh strainer over a large bowl or use a colander lined with a double layer of cheesecloth, strain the stock, and set aside to cool.

3. Divide cooled stock into airtight containers and refrigerate up to 5 days, or pour into resealable bags, lay flat on a baking sheet, and freeze up to 3 months.

NUTRITION SUMMARY & MODIFICATIONS: Low sodium. Low potassium. Low phosphorus.

NUTRITION PROFILE

YIELD: 4 quarts

SERVING SIZE: 1 cup

CALORIES (KCAL): 17

PROTEIN (G): 0

CARBOHYDRATES (G): 4

TOTAL DIETARY FIBER (G): 0

TOTAL SUGARS (G): 1

ADDED SUGAR (G): 0

FAT (G): 0

SATURATED FAT (G): 0

CHOLESTEROL (MG): 0

CALCIUM (MG): 17

MAGNESIUM (MG): 8

PHOSPHORUS (MG): 26

POTASSIUM (MG): 122

SODIUM (MG): 18

GRANDMA JULIE'S CHICKEN SOUP

Homemade chicken soup is the perfect elixir for colds. The ginger-infused chicken broth eases congestion and upset stomachs. Surprise family or friends who are under the weather with a mason jar of this soothing remedy. The aroma of this soup simmering on the stove transports me back to my childhood and my grandma Julie's kitchen. She was a wonderful grandmother and a fantastic cook. Consider this adaptation of her recipe as a general guide and experiment with variations using whatever vegetables and herbs you have in the fridge or the garden. For a heartier meal, add a few cups of cooked couscous or farro.

2 TABLESPOONS OLIVE OIL

2 STALKS CELERY, FINELY CHOPPED

2 MEDIUM CARROTS, SLICED

1 MEDIUM ONION, DICED

2 QUARTS "NO-SODIUM CHICKEN STOCK"

1 TEASPOON GROUND GINGER

1 BAY LEAF

1 POUND COOKED CHICKEN MEAT FROM "NO-SODIUM CHICKEN STOCK" OR "BAKED CHICKEN BREASTS" (SEE "CHICKEN")

1/4 CUP CHOPPED PARSLEY

FRESHLY GROUND BLACK PEPPER, TO TASTE

1. Heat the oil in a large saucepan over medium-high heat. Sauté the celery, carrot, and onion until the onion is translucent, 5 minutes.

2. Add the chicken stock, ginger, and bay leaf and bring to a boil. Reduce to medium low and simmer, partially covered, until the vegetables are tender, 25 minutes.

3. Remove the bay leaf, add the cooked chicken and parsley, season with pepper. Turn off the heat and cover until the chicken is heated through, 5 minutes.

NUTRITION SUMMARY & MODIFICATIONS: Low sodium. Medium potassium. Low phosphorus. If you are on a low-potassium diet, serve with white rice.

NUTRITION PROFILE

YIELD: 10 servings

SERVING SIZE: 1 cup

CALORIES (KCAL): 149

PROTEIN (G): 15

CARBOHYDRATES (G): 3

TOTAL DIETARY FIBER (G): 1

TOTAL SUGARS (G): 2

ADDED SUGAR (G): 0

FAT (G): 8

SATURATED FAT (G): 2

CHOLESTEROL (MG): 42

CALCIUM (MG): 18

MAGNESIUM (MG): 16

PHOSPHORUS (MG): 148

POTASSIUM (MG): 350

SODIUM (MG): 115

HEARTY LENTIL VEGETABLE SOUP

Packed with fiber, potassium, and plenty of nutrients, this vegetarian soup also scores high points for adaptability. Add whatever dribs and drabs of vegetables you have in the fridge or freezer to the pot, substitute low-sodium canned beans for lentils, or put last night's leftover farro or couscous to good use. If you happen to have any "Crispy Chickpeas" (see "Spreads, Snacks & Sauces") in the pantry, they make great "croutons" sprinkled on top.

2 TABLESPOONS OLIVE OIL

1 ONION, DICED

2 STALKS CELERY, CHOPPED

2 CARROTS, CHOPPED

2 CLOVES GARLIC, MINCED

8 OUNCES MUSHROOMS, SLICED

2 CUPS CHOPPED CABBAGE, PACKED

2 TABLESPOONS TOMATO PASTE

1 QUART WATER

1 QUART LOW-SODIUM VEGETABLE STOCK, PLUS MORE IF NEEDED

2 15-OUNCE CANS NO-SODIUM DICED TOMATOES

1 1/2 CUPS BROWN LENTILS

2 TEASPOONS ITALIAN HERB SEASONING

PINCH OF CRUSHED RED PEPPER FLAKES, OR TO TASTE

2 CUPS CHOPPED COLLARD GREENS, PACKED OR OTHER LEAFY GREENS, STEMS REMOVED

GRATED PARMESAN CHEESE, FOR SERVING, OPTIONAL

FRESH BASIL, CHOPPED, FOR SERVING, OPTIONAL

FRESHLY GROUND BLACK PEPPER, TO TASTE

continues ➡

A SHARP KNIFE IS A SAFE KNIFE Great kitchen knives are essential tools of the trade. Investing in a reputable brand of knives and a honing steel will provide years of enjoyment. A sharp knife requires little effort and cuts precisely, efficiently, and safely. A dull knife blade requires more force and tends to slip off the food, putting your fingers in harm's way. Keeping your knives properly sharpened is only half of the equation. Over time, the blade's edge becomes rounded and loses its point. Using a honing steel maintains the edge and should be done routinely between sharpenings, preferably before each use. To hone a knife, hold the steel with the tip pointing down on a stable, flat surface, such as a cutting board. Position the knife blade at a 15-degree angle to the steel. Draw the knife downward and across, from the heel of the blade to the tip, along the length of the steel. Repeat the motion on both sides of the blade several times. Wipe the blade clean with a cloth.

1. Heat the oil in a large pot or Dutch oven over medium-high heat. Sauté the onions until translucent, 5 minutes. Add the celery and carrots and sauté 3 minutes. Add the garlic and sauté until fragrant, 30 seconds. Add the mushrooms and sauté until their juices are released. Add the cabbage and tomato paste, stirring to coat the vegetables, and cook for 2 minutes.

2. Add the water, vegetable stock, diced tomatoes, lentils, Italian herbs, and crushed red pepper and bring to a boil. Reduce the heat to a simmer and cook 20 minutes.

3. Add the collard greens and simmer until the lentils are soft but not mushy, 20–25 minutes, season with pepper. If the liquid reduces below the surface of the lentils while cooking, add more stock or water as needed.

4. Ladle soup into warm serving bowls and top with grated parmesan and basil, if desired.

NUTRITION SUMMARY & MODIFICATIONS: Low sodium. Medium potassium. Low phosphorus.

To lower the potassium, omit the tomato paste, substitute cabbage for the collard greens, use only ¾ cup of lentils and, for the liquid, substitute 1 15-ounce can of tomatoes and 1 cup of water for the original version of 2 15-ounce cans of tomatoes. This modification is also medium potassium but has about ¼ less.

~~~~~~~~ NUTRITION PROFILE ~~~~~~~~

YIELD: 12 servings	**TOTAL SUGARS (G):** 4	**MAGNESIUM (MG):** 22
SERVING SIZE: 1 cup	**ADDED SUGAR (G):** 0	**PHOSPHORUS (MG):** 105
CALORIES (KCAL): 138	**FAT (G):** 3	**POTASSIUM (MG):** 466
PROTEIN (G): 7	**SATURATED FAT (G):** 0	**SODIUM (MG):** 34
CARBOHYDRATES (G): 23	**CHOLESTEROL (MG):** 0	
TOTAL DIETARY FIBER (G): 5	**CALCIUM (MG):** 54	

~~~~~~~~ LOW-POTASSIUM MODIFICATION NUTRITION PROFILE ~~~~~~~~

YIELD: 12 servings	**TOTAL SUGARS (G):** 3	**MAGNESIUM (MG):** 17
SERVING SIZE: 1 cup	**ADDED SUGAR (G):** 0	**PHOSPHORUS (MG):** 74
CALORIES (KCAL): 92	**FAT (G):** 3	**POTASSIUM (MG):** 331
PROTEIN (G): 4	**SATURATED FAT (G):** 0	**SODIUM (MG):** 25
CARBOHYDRATES (G): 14	**CHOLESTEROL (MG):** 0	
TOTAL DIETARY FIBER (G): 3	**CALCIUM (MG):** 37	

LEEK & YELLOW SQUASH SOUP

MAKES 10 1-CUP SERVINGS OR 2½ QUARTS

Leeks are milder and sweeter than regular onions. They add another layer of flavor and complexity without the use of salt or fat, making them perfect for this light summer soup. When washing leeks, split them in half lengthwise and place under cold running water to rinse away any dirt trapped inside the layers. Save the top, dark green part of the leek for homemade stock. If leeks are unavailable, substitute Vidalia onion.

2 TABLESPOONS OLIVE OIL

2 LARGE LEEKS, SLICED, WHITE AND LIGHT GREEN PARTS

½ CUP WHITE WINE

1 ½ POUNDS YELLOW SQUASH, ABOUT 5 CUPS, CUT INTO ½-INCH CUBES

1 ½ QUARTS LOW-SODIUM VEGETABLE BROTH

1 TABLESPOON FRESH THYME, LEAVES PICKED AND CHOPPED, PLUS MORE FOR GARNISH

GRATED PARMESAN, FOR SERVING

FRESHLY GROUND BLACK PEPPER, TO TASTE

1. Heat the olive oil in a large pot or Dutch oven over medium heat. Sweat the leeks until soft, 10–15 minutes. Increase the heat to medium-high, add the wine, and reduce by three-fourths.

2. Add the squash, vegetable broth, and thyme and bring to a boil. Reduce the heat to a simmer and cook until the squash is soft when pierced with a paring knife, 15–20 minutes.

3. Using a blender, working in batches, purée the soup until smooth. Alternatively, you can use an immersible stick blender. Return the soup to the pot, reheat, and season with pepper.

4. Ladle the soup into serving bowls and garnish with thyme and parmesan.

NUTRITION SUMMARY & MODIFICATIONS: Low potassium. Low phosphorus. Low sodium.

NUTRITION PROFILE

YIELD: 10 servings	TOTAL SUGARS (G): 3	MAGNESIUM (MG): 15
SERVING SIZE: 1 cup	ADDED SUGAR (G): 0	PHOSPHORUS (MG): 28
CALORIES (KCAL: 54	FAT (G): 3	POTASSIUM (MG): 183
PROTEIN (G): 1	SATURATED FAT (G): 0	SODIUM (MG): 83
CARBOHYDRATES (G): 6	CHOLESTEROL (MG): 0	
TOTAL DIETARY FIBER (G): 2	CALCIUM (MG): 32	

SMOKY EGGPLANT SPREAD, SALSA FRESCA WITH JALAPEÑO GARNISH,
CRISPY CHICKPEAS, AND DEVILED EGGS WITH PICKLED RED ONIONS.

SPREADS, SNACKS & SAUCES

DEVILED EGGS WITH PICKLED RED ONION...........144

QUICK PICKLED RED ONIONS...........145

CRISPY CHICKPEAS...........146

SMOKY EGGPLANT SPREAD...........148

ROASTED RED PEPPER & WHITE BEAN HUMMUS...........149

SALSA FRESCA...........150

EDAMAME DIP...........152

BUTTER BEAN DIP...........153

TZATZIKI SAUCE...........154

AVOCADO LIME CREMA...........155

DEVILED EGGS WITH PICKLED RED ONION

~ MAKES 1 DOZEN ~

Deviled eggs are an easy and economical finger food, perfect for picnics or backyard barbeques. Boil and peel the eggs in advance to help reduce day-of-party prep time. This healthy version cuts the fat with Greek yogurt while pickled onions add color and an unexpected tangy topping. Feel free to substitute other fresh herbs for dill such as thyme, tarragon, parsley, or chives.

6 LARGE EGGS

2 TABLESPOONS 2% PLAIN GREEK YOGURT

2 TABLESPOONS AVOCADO MAYONNAISE

1 TEASPOON DIJON MUSTARD

FRESHLY GROUND BLACK PEPPER, TO TASTE

2 TABLESPOONS CHOPPED "QUICK PICKLED RED ONIONS"

DILL SPRIGS, FOR GARNISH

1. Place the eggs in a saucepan large enough to hold them in a single layer. Add cold water to cover the eggs by 1 inch. Bring to a boil over high heat. Remove from the heat, cover, and let the eggs stand in hot water for 12 minutes. Drain and cool completely in ice water.

2. Peel and slice the eggs in half lengthwise. Place the yolks in a medium bowl and mash with a fork. Add the yogurt, mayonnaise, and mustard, season with pepper, and stir until smooth.

3. Place the filling in a resealable plastic bag and snip a corner with a pair of scissors. Pipe the filling into the whites. Top with "Quick Pickled Red Onions" and dill sprigs. Refrigerate until ready to serve.

NUTRITION SUMMARY & MODIFICATIONS: Low sodium. Low potassium. Low phosphorus.

~ NUTRITION PROFILE ~

YIELD: 1 dozen

SERVING SIZE: 1 deviled egg with pickled red onions

CALORIES (KCAL): 58

PROTEIN (G): 3

CARBOHYDRATES (G): 1

TOTAL DIETARY FIBER (G): 0

TOTAL SUGARS (G): 0

ADDED SUGAR (G): 0

FAT (G): 5

SATURATED FAT (G): 1

CHOLESTEROL (MG): 96

CALCIUM (MG): 16

MAGNESIUM (MG): 3

PHOSPHORUS (MG): 47

POTASSIUM (MG): 38

SODIUM (MG): 63

QUICK PICKLED RED ONIONS

Keep a jar of these onions in the refrigerator for sandwiches, burgers, and salads. Experiment with different flavors by adding whole spices such as peppercorn, star anise, allspice, or a pinch of cumin or caraway seeds. Store the onions refrigerated up to two weeks, if they last that long!

1 SMALL, THINLY SLICED RED ONION

½ CUP WATER

½ CUP APPLE CIDER VINEGAR

1 TEASPOON SUGAR

Combine ingredients in a small saucepan and bring to a boil. Reduce heat to medium low and simmer 3 minutes. Remove from heat and cool completely. Store refrigerated in a glass jar.

NUTRITION SUMMARY & MODIFICATIONS: Low sodium. Low potassium. Low phosphorus.

NUTRITION PROFILE

YIELD: 1 cup

SERVING SIZE: 2 Tablespoons

CALORIES (KCAL): 8

PROTEIN (G): 0

CARBOHYDRATES (G): 2

TOTAL DIETARY FIBER (G): trace

TOTAL SUGARS (G): 1

ADDED SUGAR (G): 1

FAT (G): 0

SATURATED FAT (G): 0

CHOLESTEROL (MG): 0

CALCIUM (MG): 3

MAGNESIUM (MG): 2

PHOSPHORUS (MG): 4

POTASSIUM (MG): 33

SODIUM (MG): 1

CRISPY CHICKPEAS

Chickpeas, also known as garbanzo beans, are part of the legume family and a great source of plant-based protein. Available dried or canned, chickpeas are inexpensive and versatile. Incorporate them into your diet by making a batch of homemade hummus or add to salads, soups, burritos, or veggie burgers. These healthy, crispy chickpeas fit the bill when you're craving a crunchy snack. Experiment with different flavors by sprinkling with "No-Sodium All-Purpose Seasoning" or "No-Sodium Cajun Seasoning" (see "Dressings & Spice Blends") blends after roasting.

1 15-OUNCE CAN LOW-SODIUM CHICKPEAS

1 TEASPOON OLIVE OIL

FRESHLY GROUND BLACK PEPPER, TO TASTE

1. Heat the oven to 350°F. Line a baking sheet with parchment paper, set aside. Drain the chickpeas in a colander and rinse in cold water. Place the chickpeas on one half of a clean kitchen towel. Fold the towel over the chickpeas and gently rub to remove as much moisture as possible. Discard any skins that come off during the process and place the chickpeas on the prepared baking sheet.

2. Drizzle the chickpeas with the oil, toss to coat, and bake for 50 minutes, stirring halfway through the baking time. Season with pepper. Cool and store in an airtight container.

NUTRITION SUMMARY & MODIFICATIONS: Low sodium. Low potassium. Low phosphorus. Note that the serving size is only ¼ cup. Because they taste so good, you may not be able to limit your munching to such a tiny amount. Be mindful.

NUTRITION PROFILE

YIELD: ¾ cup

SERVING SIZE: ¼ cup

CALORIES (KCAL): 84

PROTEIN (G): 4

CARBOHYDRATES (G): 11

TOTAL DIETARY FIBER (G): 4

TOTAL SUGARS (G): 2

ADDED SUGAR (G): 0

FAT (G): 3

SATURATED FAT (G): 0

CHOLESTEROL (MG): 0

CALCIUM (MG): 28

MAGNESIUM (MG): 22

PHOSPHORUS (MG): 64

POTASSIUM (MG): 115

SODIUM (MG): 106

SMOKY EGGPLANT SPREAD

This recipe was inspired by my favorite Greek restaurant in downtown Greenville, Jī-rōz, and the owner and chef, John Makkas. His delicious, authentic Greek menu reflects the traditional flavors and cooking methods of a healthy Mediterranean diet, plant-based foods with limited amounts of dairy, eggs, poultry, and seafood, and little red meat. Serve this spread with raw vegetables, crackers, or toasted pita triangles.

1 EGGPLANT

2 CLOVES GARLIC

JUICE OF ONE LEMON

¼ CUP FRESH PARSLEY LEAVES, PACKED

2 TABLESPOONS EXTRA-VIRGIN OLIVE OIL

FRESHLY GROUND BLACK PEPPER, TO TASTE

PINCH OF SALT (OPTIONAL—NOT INCLUDED IN NUTRITION PROFILE)

1. Heat the broiler and position the oven rack 8 inches from the heat source. Pierce the eggplant in several places with a paring knife and place on a foil-lined rimmed baking sheet. Broil until the eggplant is soft and the skins are charred, about 20–25 minutes, using a pair of tongs to give the eggplant a quarter turn every 5 minutes. Alternatively, roast the eggplant on an outdoor grill over high heat.

2. Keep the eggplant on the baking sheet to catch any liquid that is released. Once the eggplant is cool enough to handle, cut off the stem and peel away the skin.

3. Place the flesh of the eggplant, garlic, lemon juice, and parsley in a food processor or blender. While the machine is running, slowly add the olive oil and process until smooth, season with salt and pepper.

4. Transfer to an airtight container and refrigerate several hours or overnight.

NUTRITION SUMMARY & MODIFICATIONS: Low sodium. Low potassium. Low phosphorus.

~~~ NUTRITION PROFILE ~~~

YIELD: 1 ½ cups

SERVING SIZE: 1 Tablespoon

CALORIES (KCAL): 16

PROTEIN (G): 0

CARBOHYDRATES (G): 2

TOTAL DIETARY FIBER (G): 1

TOTAL SUGARS (G): 1

ADDED SUGAR (G): 0

FAT (G): 1

SATURATED FAT (G): 0

CHOLESTEROL (MG): 0

CALCIUM (MG): 2

MAGNESIUM (MG): 2

PHOSPHORUS (MG): 3

POTASSIUM (MG): 25

SODIUM (MG): 1

ROASTED RED PEPPER & WHITE BEAN HUMMUS

~~~ MAKES 2½ CUPS ~~~

Unlike traditional hummus made with garbanzo beans, cannellini beans add a creamy texture without added fat from olive oil. Great northern or navy beans make good substitutions. Allow the hummus to sit a few hours refrigerated, or overnight, so flavors meld and consistency thickens. Serve the hummus with raw vegetables or toasted pita triangles or use as a spread on veggie wraps.

2 RED BELL PEPPERS

1 15-OUNCE CAN LOW-SODIUM CANNELLINI BEANS, RINSED AND DRAINED

1 CUP 2% GREEK YOGURT

1 CLOVE GARLIC

2 TABLESPOONS LEMON JUICE

¼ TEASPOON CAYENNE PEPPER

1. Heat the broiler and position the oven rack 8 inches from the heat source. Place the peppers on a foil-lined baking sheet. Broil the peppers until the skins are charred, about 20–25 minutes, using a pair of tongs to give the peppers a quarter turn every 5 minutes.

2. Place the roasted peppers in a heat-proof bowl and cover with plastic wrap. Allow peppers to steam 10 minutes.

3. Transfer the peppers to a cutting board. Pull on the stem to remove. Peppers will collapse and break open. Remove the core cluster of seeds. Use the back of a paring knife to scrape away any remaining seeds. Peel the skin from the flesh.

4. Combine the peppers and remaining ingredients in a food processor or blender and process until smooth. Transfer to an airtight container and refrigerate several hours or overnight.

NUTRITION SUMMARY & MODIFICATIONS: Low sodium. Low potassium. Low phosphorus. Pair it with low-potassium vegetables to help minimize the potassium content of the overall snack.

~~~ NUTRITION PROFILE ~~~

YIELD: 10 servings

SERVING SIZE: ¼ cup

CALORIES (KCAL): 55

PROTEIN (G): 4

CARBOHYDRATES (G): 8

TOTAL DIETARY FIBER (G): 2

TOTAL SUGARS (G): 2

ADDED SUGAR (G): 0

FAT (G): 1

SATURATED FAT (G): 0

CHOLESTEROL (MG): 2

CALCIUM (MG): 42

MAGNESIUM (MG): 22

PHOSPHORUS (MG): 68

POTASSIUM (MG): 168

SODIUM (MG): 20

SALSA FRESCA

This quick homemade salsa will add a spark of freshness and flavor to your dinner plate. Make a large batch and serve it over grilled fish or chicken, or a plate of beans. While most jarred and canned salsas are high sodium, this version uses jalapeño, lime, and fresh cilantro to create flavor without added salt.

1 JALAPEÑO, SEEDED AND MINCED

JUICE OF HALF A LIME

2 TABLESPOONS CHOPPED CILANTRO

1 LARGE RIPE TOMATO, DICED

1 SCALLION, CHOPPED

FRESHLY GROUND BLACK PEPPER, TO TASTE

PINCH OF SALT (OPTIONAL—NOT INCLUDED IN NUTRITION PROFILE)

Combine ingredients in a small bowl, season with pepper. Store refrigerated in an airtight container.

NUTRITION SUMMARY & MODIFICATIONS: This is a low-sodium, low-potassium, and low-phosphorus dip when you use only 1 tablespoon. If you are using a larger amount of this salsa and you are on a lower-potassium diet, substitute 2 large cucumbers for the tomatoes.

— NUTRITION PROFILE —

YIELD: 1 cup

SERVING SIZE: 1 Tablespoon

CALORIES (KCAL): 3

PROTEIN (G): 0

CARBOHYDRATES (G): 1

TOTAL DIETARY FIBER (G): 0

TOTAL SUGARS (G): 0

ADDED SUGAR (G): 0

FAT (G): 0

SATURATED FAT (G): 0

CHOLESTEROL (MG): 0

CALCIUM (MG): 2

MAGNESIUM (MG): 2

PHOSPHORUS (MG): 3

POTASSIUM (MG): 33

SODIUM (MG): 1

EDAMAME DIP

I like to keep a bag of edamame in the freezer for this quick, last-minute appetizer. Substitute fresh fava beans or green peas when they are in season. Serve with raw vegetables or toasted pita triangles.

2 CUPS SHELLED EDAMAME, ABOUT 2 POUNDS FRESH OR FROZEN

JUICE OF 1 SMALL LEMON

2 CLOVES "ROASTED GARLIC" (SEE "VEGETABLE SIDES") OR 1 FRESH CLOVE, CRUSHED

1 SCALLION, ROUGH CHOPPED

2 TABLESPOON GRATED PARMESAN CHEESE

1/4 CUP PARSLEY, LEAVES PICKED

1/4 CUP EXTRA-VIRGIN OLIVE OIL

FRESHLY GROUND BLACK PEPPER, TO TASTE

1. Bring a large pot of water to boil and cook the edamame until tender, 5 minutes. Drain, reserve a ½ cup of liquid, and set aside to cool.

2. Place the edamame, lemon juice, garlic, scallion, parmesan, and parsley in a food processor or blender and process until combined. While the machine is running, slowly add the olive oil and process until smooth. Season with pepper. If necessary, add a few tablespoons of cooking liquid at a time to achieve desired consistency.

3. Store refrigerated in an airtight container.

NUTRITION SUMMARY & MODIFICATIONS: Low sodium. Low potassium. Low phosphorus. Please note that the serving size is only 1 tablespoon. Pair it with low-potassium vegetables such as cucumber or celery to help minimize the potassium content of the overall snack.

~ NUTRITION PROFILE ~

YIELD: 2 cups

SERVING SIZE: 1 Tablespoon

CALORIES (KCAL): 30

PROTEIN (G): 1

CARBOHYDRATES (G): 1

TOTAL DIETARY FIBER (G): 1

TOTAL SUGARS (G): 0

ADDED SUGAR (G): 0

FAT (G): 2

SATURATED FAT (G): 0

CHOLESTEROL (MG): 0

CALCIUM (MG): 11

MAGNESIUM (MG): 7

PHOSPHORUS (MG): 20

POTASSIUM (MG): 49

SODIUM (MG): 7

BUTTER BEAN DIP

～ MAKES 4 CUPS ～

Butter beans range in size from small to large and in color from pale green to white, based on when they are harvested. Depending on what part of the country you live in, butter beans and lima beans are used interchangeably. Their natural buttery flavor and creamy texture make them ideal for a tasty dip. Serve with raw vegetables or pita bread or use as a spread for sandwiches and filling for veggie wraps. Although I prefer fresh beans, you can use frozen, dried, or canned beans, cooked according to package directions. Just like the "Smoky Eggplant Spread," this recipe was inspired by chef John Makkas.

4 CUPS FRESH BUTTER BEANS, SHELLED, ABOUT 3 POUNDS UNSHELLED

ZEST AND JUICE OF 1 MEDIUM LEMON

4 CLOVES "ROASTED GARLIC" (SEE "VEGETABLE SIDES") OR 4 CLOVES, CRUSHED

1/4 CUP PARSLEY LEAVES, PACKED

1/2 CUP EXTRA-VIRGIN OLIVE OIL

FRESHLY GROUND BLACK PEPPER, TO TASTE

PINCH OF SALT (OPTIONAL—NOT INCLUDED IN NUTRITION PROFILE)

1. Cover the butter beans with water in a medium pot and bring to a boil. Reduce the heat to a simmer and cook until tender, about 30 minutes. Drain the beans and reserve 1/2 cup of the cooking liquid.

2. Place the beans, lemon zest, juice, garlic, and parsley in a food processor or blender and process until combined. While the machine is running, slowly add the olive oil and process until smooth. Season with salt and pepper. If necessary, add a few tablespoons of cooking liquid at a time to achieve desired consistency.

3. Store refrigerated in an airtight container.

NUTRITION SUMMARY & MODIFICATIONS: Low sodium. Low potassium. Low phosphorus. Because each tablespoon has 120 mg of potassium, the potassium content can add up quickly if you eat much more than that. Pair it with low-potassium vegetables to help minimize the potassium content.

～ NUTRITION PROFILE ～

YIELD: 4 cups

SERVING SIZE: 1 Tablespoon

CALORIES (KCAL): 47

PROTEIN (G): 2

CARBOHYDRATES (G): 5

TOTAL DIETARY FIBER (G): 2

TOTAL SUGARS (G): 1

ADDED SUGAR (G): 0

FAT (G): 2

SATURATED FAT (G): 0

CHOLESTEROL (MG): 0

CALCIUM (MG): 5

MAGNESIUM (MG): 10

PHOSPHORUS (MG): 26

POTASSIUM (MG): 120

SODIUM (MG): 48

TZATZIKI SAUCE

This sauce gets better as it sits in the refrigerator, allowing the flavors to develop and meld. If possible, make a few hours ahead of time or overnight. Try this versatile sauce with grilled chicken, as a sandwich spread, or as a healthy dip alternative with raw vegetables or toasted pita triangles.

1 LARGE CUCUMBER

1 ½ CUPS 2% PLAIN GREEK YOGURT

1 LARGE CLOVE GARLIC, MINCED

2 TABLESPOONS EXTRA-VIRGIN OLIVE OIL

1 TABLESPOON LEMON JUICE

2 TABLESPOONS MINCED FRESH DILL

KOSHER SALT AND FRESHLY GROUND BLACK PEPPER, TO TASTE

1. Cut off the stem end of the cucumber. Using the large holes of a box grater, grate the cucumber, you should have about 2 cups. Place the grated cucumber in a fine mesh strainer set over a bowl and sprinkle with a little salt to draw out the excess moisture. After 10 minutes, use the bottom of a coffee mug or a potato masher and press the cucumber to release the liquid. Repeat two more times for a total of 30 minutes.

2. While the cucumber is draining, combine the remaining ingredients in a medium bowl and season with pepper. Add the drained cucumbers and store refrigerated in an airtight container until needed.

NUTRITION SUMMARY & MODIFICATIONS: This is a low-sodium, low-potassium, and low-phosphorus dip. Please note the serving size is 1 tablespoon.

~ NUTRITION PROFILE ~

YIELD: 2 cups

SERVING SIZE: 1 Tablespoon

CALORIES (KCAL): 17

PROTEIN (G): 1

CARBOHYDRATES (G): 1

TOTAL DIETARY FIBER (G): 0

TOTAL SUGARS (G): 0

ADDED SUGAR (G): 0

FAT (G): 1

SATURATED FAT (G): 0

CHOLESTEROL (MG): 1

CALCIUM (MG): 12

MAGNESIUM (MG): 2

PHOSPHORUS (MG): 14

POTASSIUM (MG): 23

SODIUM (MG): 3

AVOCADO LIME CREMA

Using only four ingredients, this sauce will quickly become a household favorite. Because it has so much flavor, you can spice up your favorite Mexican dishes with a tablespoon of this sauce rather than adding multiple tablespoons of plain whole-fat sour cream or cheese.

1 RIPE AVOCADO, CUBED

1/2 CUP LIGHT SOUR CREAM

JUICE OF HALF A LIME

FRESHLY GROUND BLACK PEPPER, TO TASTE

Mash the avocado with a fork in a small bowl. Add the sour cream and lime juice and season with pepper. Store refrigerated in an airtight container until needed.

NUTRITION SUMMARY & MODIFICATIONS: This is a low-sodium, low-potassium, and low-phosphorus condiment. Note that the serving size is only 1 tablespoon.

~ NUTRITION PROFILE ~

YIELD: 1 cup

SERVING SIZE: 1 Tablespoon

CALORIES (KCAL): 26

PROTEIN (G): 0

CARBOHYDRATES (G): 1

TOTAL DIETARY FIBER (G): 1

TOTAL SUGARS (G): 0

ADDED SUGAR (G): 0

FAT (G): 2

SATURATED FAT (G): 1

CHOLESTEROL (MG): 3

CALCIUM (MG): 12

MAGNESIUM (MG): 4

PHOSPHORUS (MG): 11

POTASSIUM (MG): 63

SODIUM (MG): 7

EGG MUFFINS

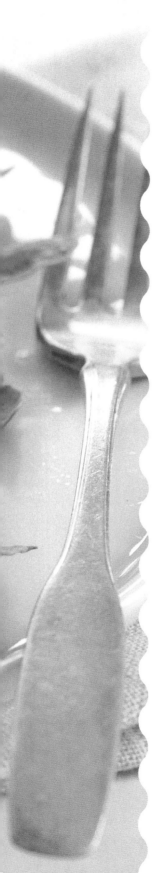

BREAKFAST

MAPLE CINNAMON CHIA PUDDING 158

SLOW-COOKED STEEL-CUT OATS 160

SPICED APRICOT WALNUT MUFFINS 161

EGG MUFFINS WITH SPINACH & ARTICHOKE HEARTS 162

SUNFLOWER BUTTER & BLUEBERRY TOAST 164

AVOCADO TOAST WITH CHILE FLAKES 165

NOTE

Breakfast is often one of the hardest meals for people with advanced kidney disease because typical "American" breakfast dishes are often high in sodium, protein, and fat—think bacon and eggs on toast with butter or a sausage biscuit. My patients often find success by picking two or three breakfast dishes and sticking with them for the long haul.

MAPLE CINNAMON CHIA PUDDING

Despite their size, chia seeds pack a dense nutritional punch, making them a perfect start to energize your day and your workouts. These tiny, protein-rich, high-fiber seeds are prized for their ability to absorb 10 times their weight in liquid while forming a gel-like consistency, similar to tapioca pudding or agar-based bubble or boba teas. Used as a thickening agent, chia seeds are a popular egg alternative in vegan baking or as a binder for veggie burgers. If you're new to chia seeds, allow yourself time to adjust to their unique texture; it grows on you. Experiment with incorporating chia into your diet by adding the seeds to yogurt, smoothies, oatmeal, or granola, and #ChangeYourBuds.

1/2 CUP ALMOND MILK, PLUS MORE IF NEEDED, OR OTHER NON-DAIRY MILK

1/4 TEASPOON VANILLA EXTRACT

1 TEASPOON MAPLE SYRUP

1/4 TEASPOON CINNAMON

2 TABLESPOON CHIA SEEDS

1 TABLESPOON NO SUGAR ADDED SUNFLOWER OR PEANUT BUTTER

1/2 BANANA, SLICED, OR BERRIES

1 TABLESPOON CHOPPED WALNUTS

1. Combine the almond milk, vanilla, maple syrup, cinnamon, and chia seeds in a small bowl. Whisk with a fork and set aside for 5 minutes. Whisk and repeat after another 5 minutes, to prevent clumping. Cover the bowl with plastic wrap, refrigerate and chill at least 2 hours or overnight.

2. Add the nut butter, stirring until combined. Adjust the consistency with a few tablespoons of almond milk, if needed. Top with the sliced banana and walnuts. Or, top with blueberries if you are on a lower-potassium diet.

NUTRITION SUMMARY & MODIFICATIONS: Low sodium. Medium potassium. High phosphorus. Substitute blueberries for banana to lower the potassium content a bit but note that it is still a medium-potassium dish even with blueberries. The phosphorus content is also elevated due to the chia seeds. Refer to the phosphorus chapter to see whether this breakfast can fit safely into your diet.

BANANA MODIFICATION NUTRITION PROFILE

YIELD: 1 serving

SERVING SIZE: 6 ounces

CALORIES (KCAL): 376

PROTEIN (G): 9

CARBOHYDRATES (G): 39

TOTAL DIETARY FIBER (G): 12

TOTAL SUGARS (G): 20

ADDED SUGAR (G): 11

FAT (G): 22

SATURATED FAT (G): 2

CHOLESTEROL (MG): 0

CALCIUM (MG): 398

MAGNESIUM (MG): 171

PHOSPHORUS (MG): 354

POTASSIUM (MG): 502

SODIUM (MG): 147

BLUEBERRIES MODIFICATION NUTRITION PROFILE

YIELD: 1 serving

SERVING SIZE: 6 ounces

CALORIES (KCAL): 365

PROTEIN (G): 9

CARBOHYDRATES (G): 36

TOTAL DIETARY FIBER (G): 12

TOTAL SUGARS (G): 20

ADDED SUGAR (G): 11

FAT (G): 22

SATURATED FAT (G): 2

CHOLESTEROL (MG): 0

CALCIUM (MG): 400

MAGNESIUM (MG): 160

PHOSPHORUS (MG): 350

POTASSIUM (MG): 348

SODIUM (MG): 147

SLOW-COOKED STEEL-CUT OATS

This recipe takes time to develop its creamy flavor. Try not to rush the cooking process. Oats are a nutritious source of fiber, and the peanut butter adds some plant-based protein to the finished dish.

1 TABLESPOON COCONUT OIL, OR NON-DAIRY BUTTER SUBSTITUTE

1 CUP STEEL-CUT OATS

2 CUPS UNSWEETENED OAT MILK, OR OTHER NON-DAIRY MILK

1 CUP WATER

2 TEASPOONS VANILLA EXTRACT

1 TABLESPOON PURE MAPLE SYRUP

1/4 CUP AND 2 TABLESPOONS UNSWEETENED PEANUT BUTTER

1 1/2 CUPS FRESH BLUEBERRIES

1. Heat the oil in a medium saucepan over medium heat. Add the oats and toast for 3 minutes, stirring frequently to prevent burning.

2. Increase the heat to medium high, add the milk, water, and vanilla to boil, and stir to combine. Reduce the heat to a low simmer. Cover and cook 20–30 minutes, stirring occasionally. Cooking time will vary depending on desired texture and consistency.

3. Add the maple syrup and peanut butter, stirring to combine. Place the oatmeal in serving bowls and top with blueberries.

NUTRITION SUMMARY & MODIFICATIONS: Low sodium. Low potassium. Low phosphorus.

NUTRITION PROFILE

YIELD: 6 servings

ANALYSIS PER SERVING

CALORIES (KCAL): 241

PROTEIN (G): 7

CARBOHYDRATES (G): 28

TOTAL DIETARY FIBER (G): 4

TOTAL SUGARS (G): 9

ADDED SUGAR (G): 3

FAT (G): 12

SATURATED FAT (G): 4

CHOLESTEROL (MG): 0

CALCIUM (MG): 25

MAGNESIUM (MG): 30

PHOSPHORUS (MG): 58

POTASSIUM (MG): 205

SODIUM (MG): 110

SPICED APRICOT WALNUT MUFFINS

~ MAKES 12 MUFFINS ~

These hearty muffins use spelt flour to add fiber and an earthy flavor that pairs perfectly with the oats, apricots, and walnuts. They are great to make ahead for a quick breakfast option or to take with you on the run. Simply make ahead and store in an airtight container and reheat when ready to serve. They can be served cold too, if you don't have the time to reheat.

1/4 CUP OLIVE OIL, PLUS MORE FOR PAN

1 CUP UNBLEACHED ALL-PURPOSE FLOUR, SIFTED

1 CUP UNBLEACHED SPELT FLOUR, SIFTED

1/3 CUP SUGAR

1/8 TEASPOON SALT

1 TABLESPOON BAKING POWDER

2 TEASPOONS PUMPKIN PIE SPICE

1/2 CUP ROLLED OATS

1 CUP DRIED APRICOTS, CHOPPED

1/2 CUP WALNUTS, CHOPPED

2 LARGE EGGS

1 1/3 CUPS ALMOND MILK, OR OTHER NON-DAIRY MILK

1. Lightly grease a muffin pan, set aside. Preheat the oven to 350°F. In a large bowl, sift flours, sugar, salt, baking powder, and pumpkin pie spice. Add oats, apricots, and walnuts and stir to combine.

2. In a medium bowl, lightly whisk the eggs. Add the milk and olive oil and whisk until well blended. Add the egg mixture to the dry ingredients and stir until just moistened, being careful not to overmix the batter. Divide the batter evenly among muffin cups, filling each about three-quarters full.

3. Bake until golden brown and tops spring back when touched, about 18–20 minutes. Transfer to a wire rack to cool.

NUTRITION SUMMARY & MODIFICATIONS: Low sodium. Low potassium. Low phosphorus.

~ NUTRITION PROFILE ~

YIELD: 12 muffins

SERVING SIZE: 1 muffin

CALORIES (KCAL): 232

PROTEIN (G): 6

CARBOHYDRATES (G): 33

TOTAL DIETARY FIBER (G): 3

TOTAL SUGARS (G): 14

ADDED SUGAR (G): 7

FAT (G): 9

SATURATED FAT (G): 1

CHOLESTEROL (MG): 31

CALCIUM (MG): 238

MAGNESIUM (MG): 59

PHOSPHORUS (MG): 41

POTASSIUM (MG): 197

SODIUM (MG): 53

EGG MUFFINS WITH SPINACH & ARTICHOKE HEARTS

Eggs are a versatile, healthy, and delicious breakfast food, and this recipe is perfect for mixing up your egg routine when you get tired of scrambling them. It can be prepared ahead of time and reheated for a quick morning meal. To minimize the phosphorus and cholesterol, I use half whole eggs and half egg whites. This maintains the flavor of the egg yolks in the final dish—a trick I also use when making scrambled eggs. Try diced bell pepper (as shown in the accompanying picture) instead of onion, kale instead of spinach, or add lightly sautéed mushrooms.

NONSTICK COOKING SPRAY

1 TEASPOON BUTTER OR BUTTER SUBSTITUTE

½ ONION, DICED

1 CUP (LIGHTLY PACKED) RAW SPINACH, CUT INTO RIBBONS

½ CUP MARINATED ARTICHOKE HEARTS, CHOPPED

½ CUP NON-DAIRY MILK SUBSTITUTE (RICE, ALMOND, OR OAT)

5 LARGE EGGS AND 5 LARGE EGG WHITES

1 TABLESPOON HOT SAUCE

½ CUP NON-DAIRY SHREDDED CHEESE SUBSTITUTE

1. Preheat oven to 350°F. Grease muffin tins generously with nonstick spray or add muffin liners to muffin tins and coat with nonstick spray.

2. Add the butter and onion to a small sauté pan and turn heat to medium high. Cook 3–5 minutes until the onions just start to turn translucent. Remove from heat and let cool. Mix onion, spinach, and artichoke heart in a bowl and divide evenly into 12 muffin tins.

3. Whisk the eggs, egg whites, hot sauce, and non-dairy milk together and pour evenly into the lined muffin tins, over the vegetable mix. Top each muffin with a pinch of cheese.

4. Bake 15–20 minutes until the eggs are cooked through. Run the blade of a knife around the outside of the muffins to help remove them cleanly from the tins. Serve immediately or refrigerate for 2–3 days.

NUTRITION SUMMARY & MODIFICATIONS: Low sodium. Low potassium. Low phosphorus.

~~~~~ NUTRITION PROFILE ~~~~~

YIELD: 12 cups

SERVING SIZE: 1 cup

CALORIES (KCAL): 72

PROTEIN (G): 6

CARBOHYDRATES (G): 3

TOTAL DIETARY FIBER (G): 1

TOTAL SUGARS (G): 1

ADDED SUGAR (G): 0

FAT (G): 4

SATURATED FAT (G): 1

CHOLESTEROL (MG): 78

CALCIUM (MG): 62

MAGNESIUM (MG): 11

PHOSPHORUS (MG): 77

POTASSIUM (MG): 96

SODIUM (MG): 123

SUNFLOWER BUTTER & BLUEBERRY TOAST

This alternative to the traditional peanut butter and jelly sandwich substitutes fresh berries for a sugar-sweetened jelly. Add some hemp hearts, chia seeds, or pumpkin seeds to give the toast a little crunch.

2 TABLESPOONS UNSWEETENED SUNFLOWER BUTTER, OR UNSWEETENED PEANUT BUTTER

2 SLICES THIN, WHOLE-GRAIN BREAD, TOASTED

1/4 CUP FRESH BLUEBERRIES, OR FROZEN AND THAWED

Spread sunflower butter on toast and top with blueberries.

NUTRITION SUMMARY & MODIFICATIONS: High sodium. Medium potassium. High phosphorus. The sodium level is high due to the bread. If you can find a low-sodium bread, that will lower the sodium significantly. The potassium and phosphorus are elevated due to the sunflower butter and the whole grains. If you are on a very strict low-potassium and low-phosphorus diet, stick to 1 slice of whole-grain bread or substitute white bread for the whole-grain bread.

NUTRITION PROFILE

YIELD: 1 serving

SERVING SIZE: 2 slices

CALORIES (KCAL): 404

PROTEIN (G): 15

CARBOHYDRATES (G): 42

TOTAL DIETARY FIBER (G): 11

TOTAL SUGARS (G): 8

ADDED SUGAR (G): 3

FAT (G): 20

SATURATED FAT (G): 2

CHOLESTEROL (MG): 0

CALCIUM (MG): 525

MAGNESIUM (MG): 147

PHOSPHORUS (MG): 329

POTASSIUM (MG): 309

SODIUM (MG): 477

AVOCADO TOAST WITH CHILE FLAKES

Korean chile flakes should become one of your pantry staples. It allows you to add a smoky and fruity spice to your dish, elevating the flavor without added salt. This spice is delicious on tofu, chicken, or eggs, or when used to jazz up a yogurt dip. Because avocados are a high-potassium fruit, limit your serving to 1 slice if you are on a low-potassium diet. Top with a fried egg to turn this toast into a satisfying lunch or dinner.

½ RIPE AVOCADO, PITTED AND PEELED

2 SLICES THIN, WHOLE-GRAIN BREAD, TOASTED

¼ LIME

¼ TEASPOON KOREAN CHILE FLAKES, OR CRUSHED RED PEPPER FLAKES

Slice the avocado and place on the toast. Use a fork to smash the avocado. Squeeze the lime juice over the avocado and sprinkle with Korean chile flakes.

NUTRITION SUMMARY & MODIFICATIONS: High sodium. High potassium. Medium phosphorus. The sodium level is high due to the bread. If you can find a low-sodium bread, that will lower the sodium significantly. The potassium is elevated due to the avocado and it is difficult to replace the flavor of the avocado with another fruit or vegetable.

NUTRITION PROFILE

YIELD: 2 slices

SERVING SIZE: 2 slices

CALORIES (KCAL): 299

PROTEIN (G): 10

CARBOHYDRATES (G): 38

TOTAL DIETARY FIBER (G): 9

TOTAL SUGARS (G): 4

ADDED SUGAR (G): 3

FAT (G): 13

SATURATED FAT (G): 28

CHOLESTEROL (MG): 0

CALCIUM (MG): 127

MAGNESIUM (MG): 75

PHOSPHORUS (MG): 192

POTASSIUM (MG): 549

SODIUM (MG): 333

STUFFED ZUCCHINI BOATS

PLANT BASED

STUFFED ZUCCHINI BOATS 168

CORN & BLACK BEAN QUESADILLA 170

CURRIED SWEET POTATOES & CHICKPEAS 173

CRANBERRY, PEPITA & BROCCOLI SALAD 175

VEGAN BOLOGNESE SAUCE 176

MEDITERRANEAN CHOPPED SALAD 178

ROASTED SWEET POTATOES
See Part I, "Step 4: Embrace Plant-Based Eating."

KALE & GOLDEN RAISIN SALAD
See Part I, "Step 7: Discover Alkaline-Rich Foods."

ROASTED BEET, GOAT CHEESE & WALNUT SALAD WITH BLUEBERRY VINAIGRETTE See Part I, "Step 9: Integrate the DASH, Mediterranean & Diabetic Diets into Your Routine."

STUFFED ZUCCHINI BOATS

This recipe puts summer zucchini bumper crops to great use. Serve as a side dish or as a vegetarian main course over a bed of quinoa or stewed lentils. Change the filling depending on whatever you have on hand—sautéed ground chicken, low-sodium cannellini beans, bell peppers, or corn are just a few of the endless possibilities!

4 MEDIUM ZUCCHINIS

1 TABLESPOON EXTRA-VIRGIN OLIVE OIL

2 MEDIUM TOMATOES, DICED

1/2 CUP CHOPPED ONION

2 CLOVES GARLIC, MINCED

2 TABLESPOONS GRATED PARMESAN

2 TABLESPOONS PANKO BREADCRUMBS

1 TABLESPOON BALSAMIC VINEGAR

8 LARGE BASIL LEAVES, THINLY SLICED

FRESHLY GROUND BLACK PEPPER, TO TASTE

PINCH OF SALT (OPTIONAL—NOT INCLUDED IN NUTRITION PROFILE)

1. Heat the oven to 400°F. Line a baking sheet with foil or parchment paper, set aside. Slice the zucchini in half lengthwise. Using a melon baller or a teaspoon, remove the seeds and flesh, leaving about ¼-inch of the flesh intact to form a hollowed shell or "boat." Place the zucchini boats on prepared baking sheet. Chop the zucchini flesh.

2. Heat the olive oil in a large sauté pan over medium-high heat. Sauté the zucchini flesh, tomato, and onions until onions soften, 5 minutes. Add the garlic and sauté until fragrant, 1 minute, season with salt and pepper. Remove from the heat and set aside to cool slightly.

3. Divide the tomato mixture between the zucchini boats. Combine the parmesan and breadcrumbs in a small bowl and sprinkle on top of the tomato filling.

4. Bake until the zucchini is tender and the tops are golden brown, 30 minutes, rotating pan halfway through baking. Remove from the oven, drizzle the zucchini boats with balsamic vinegar, and sprinkle with basil.

NUTRITION SUMMARY & MODIFICATIONS: Low sodium. Medium potassium. Low phosphorus. To lower the potassium, leave off the tomatoes, though it will still be a medium-potassium dish.

SLICING LEAFY GREENS *Chiffonade* translates to "made of rags" in French. The culinary technique references a specific knife cut commonly used on leafy greens or tender large leaf herbs such as basil or sage. The cut creates uniform, thin strips that can be used during cooking for soups, stews, and salads or as a delicate garnish before serving. To chiffonade collard greens or kale, remove the thick center stems and stack the leaves on top of each other. Roll the leaves tightly, end-to-end, to form a cylinder. Using a sharp chef's knife, slice the leaves into thin strips. Toss the leaves gently with your fingers to separate the tangle of ribbons. When using fresh herbs as a garnish, slice the leaves just before using to minimize browning from oxidation.

~~~~~~ NUTRITION PROFILE ~~~~~~

YIELD: 8 servings

ANALYSIS PER SERVING

CALORIES (KCAL): 54

PROTEIN (G): 2

CARBOHYDRATES (G): 7

TOTAL DIETARY FIBER (G): 2

TOTAL SUGARS (G): 4

ADDED SUGAR (G): 0

FAT (G): 2

SATURATED FAT (G): 1

CHOLESTEROL (MG): 1

CALCIUM (MG): 38

MAGNESIUM (MG): 25

PHOSPHORUS (MG): 58

POTASSIUM (MG): 359

SODIUM (MG): 35

CORN & BLACK BEAN QUESADILLA

Quesadillas are popular for their ease of preparation and versatility. Serve them topped with a poached egg for breakfast, over greens for lunch, or with a side of brown rice for dinner. This Mexican favorite offers a healthy version by reducing the size of the tortillas and the amount of cheese and using low-sodium beans.

1 15-OUNCE CAN LOW-SODIUM BLACK BEANS

1/4 CUP WATER

1/2 TEASPOON CHILE POWDER

1/2 TEASPOON CUMIN

8 6-INCH CORN TORTILLAS

1/2 CUP CORN, FRESH, CANNED, OR FROZEN, COOKED

1/2 CUP SHREDDED CHEDDAR CHEESE

1 TEASPOON EXTRA-VIRGIN OLIVE OIL

"AVOCADO LIME CREMA" (SEE "SPREADS, SNACKS & SAUCES")

"SALSA FRESCA" (SEE "SPREADS, SNACKS & SAUCES")

LIME WEDGES AND CILANTRO SPRIGS, FOR SERVING, OPTIONAL

1. Place a colander over a bowl and drain the beans, reserving the juice. Rinse the beans in cold water. Combine the beans, ¼ cup reserved bean juice, ¼ cup water, chile powder, and cumin in a small saucepan over medium-low heat. Simmer until heated through, stirring occasionally, 10 minutes. Using a potato masher or fork, mash the beans.

2. Spread 4 tortillas with ¼ cup mashed black beans. Sprinkle 2 tablespoons of corn and 2 tablespoons of cheese over the beans and top with a tortilla.

3. Heat the olive oil in a large nonstick sauté pan over medium heat. Place the tortillas in the pan and cook until golden brown, about 3 minutes per side, working in batches if necessary.

4. Transfer the quesadillas to a cutting board and slice into quarters. Top each quarter with a tablespoon of avocado lime crema and salsa fresca. Serve with lime wedges and cilantro sprigs, if desired.

NUTRITION SUMMARY & MODIFICATIONS: Low sodium. Medium potassium. Medium phosphorus. For a low-potassium version, omit the avocado lime crema and salsa fresca, and use only 1 cup of black beans in the dish. You will use about 1 tablespoon of black beans per tortilla. If you need more flavor with these changes, experiment with toppings such as salsa fresca made with cucumbers instead of tomatoes, extra cilantro, or thin slices of jalapeño.

YIELD: 8 servings

ANALYSIS PER SERVING

CALORIES (KCAL): 203

PROTEIN (G): 8

CARBOHYDRATES (G): 27

TOTAL DIETARY FIBER (G): 7

TOTAL SUGARS (G): 1

ADDED SUGAR (G): 0

FAT (G): 8

SATURATED FAT (G): 3

CHOLESTEROL (MG): 12

CALCIUM (MG): 143

MAGNESIUM (MG): 50

PHOSPHORUS (MG): 203

POTASSIUM (MG): 418

SODIUM (MG): 136

~~~~ LOWER-POTASSIUM MODIFICATION NUTRITION PROFILE ~~~~

YIELD: 8 servings

ANALYSIS PER SERVING

CALORIES (KCAL): 130

PROTEIN (G): 5

CARBOHYDRATES (G): 20

TOTAL DIETARY FIBER (G): 4

TOTAL SUGARS (G): 1

ADDED SUGAR (G): 0

FAT (G): 4

SATURATED FAT (G): 2

CHOLESTEROL (MG): 7

CALCIUM (MG): 108

MAGNESIUM (MG): 33

PHOSPHORUS (MG): 156

POTASSIUM (MG): 171

SODIUM (MG): 96

CURRIED SWEET POTATOES & CHICKPEAS

— SERVES 4 —

This hearty side dish also makes an excellent vegetarian meal when served over the "Kale & Golden Raisin Salad" (see "Step 7: Discover Alkaline-Rich Foods"). Cut the vegetables the same size to ensure uniform roasting times. Leftovers can be used as an excellent filling for tacos, grain bowls, and sandwich wraps.

1 15-OUNCE CAN LOW-SODIUM CHICKPEAS

1 TABLESPOON OLIVE OIL, DIVIDED

1 LARGE SWEET POTATO, PEELED AND CUT INTO 1-INCH PIECES

1 SMALL ONION, CUT INTO 1-INCH PIECES

1 CLOVE GARLIC, CHOPPED

1 TEASPOON CURRY POWDER

FRESH CHOPPED PARSLEY, FOR GARNISH

FRESHLY GROUND BLACK PEPPER, TO TASTE

PINCH OF SALT (OPTIONAL—NOT INCLUDED IN NUTRITION PROFILE)

1. Heat the oven to 350°F. Line a baking sheet with parchment paper, set aside.

2. Drain the chickpeas and rinse in cold water. Place the chickpeas on a clean kitchen towel and gently rub to remove as much moisture as possible. Discard any skins that come off during the process and place the chickpeas on the prepared baking sheet. Drizzle with one teaspoon of oil, toss to coat, and bake for 15 minutes.

3. While the chickpeas are baking, combine the sweet potato, onion, and garlic in a medium bowl. Sprinkle with curry powder and remaining 2 teaspoons of oil and toss to coat.

4. Remove the chickpeas from the oven after 15 minutes and push to one half of the baking sheet. Place the sweet potato mixture on the opposite half of the sheet. Bake until the chickpeas are crispy and the sweet potatoes are tender, stirring halfway through the cooking time without combining the two, about 35 minutes.

5. Season the sweet potato and chickpeas with salt and pepper. Transfer to a serving dish and sprinkle with chopped parsley.

NUTRITION SUMMARY & MODIFICATIONS: Low sodium. Medium potassium. Low phosphorus. For a low-potassium version, substitute thick slices of shredded cabbage for the sweet potatoes.

continues ➡

CURRIED SWEET POTATOES & CHICKPEAS continued

∼ NUTRITION PROFILE ∼

YIELD: 4 servings

SERVING SIZE: 1 serving

CALORIES (KCAL): 159

PROTEIN (G): 6

CARBOHYDRATES (G): 24

TOTAL DIETARY FIBER (G): 6

TOTAL SUGARS (G): 6

ADDED SUGAR (G): 0

FAT (G): 5

SATURATED FAT (G): 1

CHOLESTEROL (MG): 0

CALCIUM (MG): 57

MAGNESIUM (MG): 39

PHOSPHORUS (MG): 104

POTASSIUM (MG): 378

SODIUM (MG): 134

∼ LOW-POTASSIUM MODIFICATION NUTRITION PROFILE ∼

YIELD: 4 servings

SERVING SIZE: 1 serving

CALORIES (KCAL): 122

PROTEIN (G): 5

CARBOHYDRATES (G): 15

TOTAL DIETARY FIBER (G): 5

TOTAL SUGARS (G): 4

ADDED SUGAR (G): 0

FAT (G): 5

SATURATED FAT (G): 1

CHOLESTEROL (MG): 0

CALCIUM (MG): 47

MAGNESIUM (MG): 30

PHOSPHORUS (MG): 84

POTASSIUM (MG): 196

SODIUM (MG): 122

CRANBERRY, PEPITA & BROCCOLI SALAD

This salad is a perfect example of how a few small changes to a classic recipe create a healthier dish without sacrificing taste. Smoked paprika replaces the flavor of bacon while reducing fat, a sprinkle of parmesan stands in for cheddar cheese, and vinegar eliminates salt and makes the dish come alive. This hearty salad can be made in advance and improves in flavor as it sits in the fridge. Add the pepitas just before serving so they stay crisp.

1/4 TEASPOON SMOKED PAPRIKA

1/3 CUP MAYONNAISE

4 TEASPOONS APPLE CIDER VINEGAR

2 TABLESPOONS GRATED PARMESAN

1/3 CUP DRIED CRANBERRIES

2 SCALLIONS, CHOPPED

1 HEAD BROCCOLI, CUT INTO SMALL FLORETS, ABOUT 4 CUPS

1/4 CUP UNSALTED, ROASTED PEPITAS

FRESHLY GROUND BLACK PEPPER, TO TASTE

Whisk together the paprika, mayonnaise, vinegar, and parmesan in a large bowl. Add the cranberries, scallions, and broccoli, season with pepper and toss to combine. Refrigerate until ready to serve. Sprinkle with pepitas just before serving.

NUTRITION SUMMARY & MODIFICATIONS: Low sodium. Low potassium. Low phosphorus.

NUTRITION PROFILE

YIELD: 6 servings

ANALYSIS PER SERVING

CALORIES (KCAL): 147

PROTEIN (G): 3

CARBOHYDRATES (G): 8

TOTAL DIETARY FIBER (G): 2

TOTAL SUGARS (G): 5

ADDED SUGAR (G): 3

FAT (G): 12

SATURATED FAT (G): 2

CHOLESTEROL (MG): 5

CALCIUM (MG): 26

MAGNESIUM (MG): 12

PHOSPHORUS (MG): 34

POTASSIUM (MG): 202

SODIUM (MG): 91

VEGAN BOLOGNESE SAUCE

— MAKES 9 CUPS —

Bolognese is a traditional Italian meat sauce prized for its concentrated rich taste. After several attempts to develop a lean, meatless version, I am pleased to share my results. The earthiness and texture of the mushrooms lend themselves to a classic meaty ragù yet eliminate saturated fats. The key to this sauce is patience. A low, slow simmer is necessary to reduce the liquid and achieve the intense flavor. Serve this sauce over pasta topped with vegan grated parmesan, or as a filling for baked stuffed peppers, or toss with spaghetti squash.

1/2 OUNCE DRIED PORCINI MUSHROOMS

1 TABLESPOON EXTRA-VIRGIN OLIVE OIL

3 TABLESPOONS VEGAN BUTTER

1 ONION, FINELY CHOPPED

2 CARROTS, FINELY CHOPPED

2 STALKS CELERY, FINELY CHOPPED

1 POUND SHIITAKE MUSHROOMS, FINELY CHOPPED

1 CUP UNSWEETENED OAT MILK, OR OTHER NON-DAIRY MILK

1/4 TEASPOON FRESHLY GRATED NUTMEG

1 CUP DRY WHITE WINE

1 28-OUNCE CAN ITALIAN PLUM TOMATOES, CUT UP WITH THEIR JUICES

3/4 CUP BLACK OR GREEN FRENCH LENTILS, COOKED ACCORDING TO PACKAGE DIRECTIONS

FRESHLY GROUND BLACK PEPPER, TO TASTE

1. Reconstitute the porcini mushrooms by placing them in a bowl and cover with warm water for 30 minutes. Carefully lift the mushrooms from the water without disturbing any dirt or debris that may have fallen to the bottom of the bowl and finely chop. Pour the mushroom water through a fine mesh sieve and reserve. Alternatively, strain through a coffee filter.

2. Add the olive oil, butter, and onions to a large saucepan and turn the heat to medium. Sauté the onion, until translucent, 5 minutes, add the carrot and celery and cook, stirring occasionally, 3 minutes. Add the porcini and shiitake mushrooms and cook until the mushrooms release their juices and are tender, stirring occasionally, 6 minutes.

3. Increase the heat to medium high, add the reserved mushroom water, oat milk, and nutmeg and bring to boil. Reduce the heat to medium and simmer until most of the liquid is evaporated, stirring occasionally, 12 minutes. Add the wine and simmer until evaporated.

4. Increase the heat to medium high, add the tomatoes and their juices, and bring to a boil. Reduce the heat to a low simmer so the sauce is barely bubbling. Cook until the flavors are concentrated, 2½–3 hours, stirring occasionally. If necessary, add a little water while simmering to prevent scorching.

5. Add the cooked lentils, season with pepper, and simmer 10 minutes.

NUTRITION SUMMARY & MODIFICATIONS: Low sodium. Low potassium. Low phosphorus. Note serving size is ¼ cup. Because it has so much flavor, you might not need much more than that.

~~~~~~~~~~~~~ NUTRITION PROFILE ~~~~~~~~~~~~~

YIELD: 9 cups	TOTAL SUGARS (G): 2	MAGNESIUM (MG): 10
SERVING SIZE: ¼ cup	ADDED SUGAR (G): 0	PHOSPHORUS (MG): 44
CALORIES (KCAL): 45	FAT (G): 2	POTASSIUM (MG): 165
PROTEIN (G): 2	SATURATED FAT (G): 0	SODIUM (MG): 49
CARBOHYDRATES (G): 6	CHOLESTEROL (MG): 0	
TOTAL DIETARY FIBER (G): 1	CALCIUM (MG): 22	

MEDITERRANEAN CHOPPED SALAD

Sumac is a tangy spice made from berries that are picked, dried, and ground into a coarse, red powder. Commonly used in Middle Eastern cooking, the sumac bush is a subtropical flowering plant and a member of the cashew family. It has similar yet muted sour and acidic characteristics of lemon. Sumac is used to enhance flavor in the Mediterranean vinaigrette and acts as a salt replacement, balancing the overall taste of the salad. This versatile spice can be used as a rub for grilled meats, in citrusy marinades, sprinkled over fresh vegetables, or dusted on desserts for a pop of color. If you do not have sumac for the dressing, substitute 1 teaspoon of lemon zest.

15 OZ CAN LOW-SODIUM CHICKPEAS

1 TEASPOON EXTRA-VIRGIN OLIVE OIL

1/2 TEASPOON CUMIN

1 PINT GRAPE TOMATOES, QUARTERED

1 CUCUMBER, CHOPPED

1/2 CUP CHOPPED PARSLEY

1/4 CUP DICED RED ONION

1/4 CUP "MEDITERRANEAN VINAIGRETTE" (SEE "DRESSINGS & SPICE BLENDS")

FRESHLY GROUND BLACK PEPPER, TO TASTE

PINCH OF SALT (OPTIONAL—NOT INCLUDED IN NUTRITION PROFILE)

1. Heat the oven to 350°F. Line a baking sheet with parchment paper, set aside. Drain the chickpeas and rinse in cold water. Place the chickpeas on a clean kitchen towel and gently rub to remove as much moisture as possible. Discard any skins that come off during the process and place the chickpeas on the prepared baking sheet. Drizzle with oil and toss to coat. Bake until crispy, stirring halfway through baking time, about 50 minutes. Cool slightly and toss with cumin.

2. Combine chickpeas, tomatoes, cucumbers, parsley, onion, and Mediterranean vinaigrette in a large bowl, season with salt and pepper, and toss to combine. If not serving salad immediately, add chickpeas just before serving to maintain crispness.

NUTRITION SUMMARY & MODIFICATIONS: Low sodium. Medium potassium. Low phosphorus. For a low-potassium modification, use three chopped cucumbers instead of tomatoes and decrease the parsley to ¼ cup.

YIELD: 6 servings

SERVING SIZE: ¼ cup

CALORIES (KCAL): 130

PROTEIN (G): 4

CARBOHYDRATES (G): 14

TOTAL DIETARY FIBER (G): 3

TOTAL SUGARS (G): 3

ADDED SUGAR (G): 0

FAT (G): 7

SATURATED FAT (G): 1

CHOLESTEROL (MG): 0

CALCIUM (MG): 44

MAGNESIUM (MG): 29

PHOSPHORUS (MG): 66

POTASSIUM (MG): 303

SODIUM (MG): 20

~~~~~ LOWER-POTASSIUM MODIFICATION NUTRITION PROFILE ~~~~~

YIELD: 6 servings

SERVING SIZE: ¼ cup

CALORIES (KCAL): 126

PROTEIN (G): 4

CARBOHYDRATES (G): 13

TOTAL DIETARY FIBER (G): 3

TOTAL SUGARS (G): 2

ADDED SUGAR (G): 0

FAT (G): 7

SATURATED FAT (G): 1

CHOLESTEROL (MG): 0

CALCIUM (MG): 42

MAGNESIUM (MG): 27

PHOSPHORUS (MG): 62

POTASSIUM (MG): 208

SODIUM (MG): 17

SPICED CHICKEN, ORANGE & AVOCADO SALAD

CHICKEN

SHEET PAN LEMON-LIME CHICKEN & POTATOES........................182

ZA'ATAR CHICKEN SALAD........................185

CHICKEN FARRO BOWLS........................187

CREOLE CHICKEN BURGERS........................189

SPICED CHICKEN, ORANGE & AVOCADO SALAD........................191

SEARED CAJUN CHICKEN THIGHS........................193

BAKED CHICKEN BREASTS........................194

SHEET PAN LEMON-LIME CHICKEN & POTATOES

This is an old favorite family recipe that relies on fresh citrus to create an extremely flavorful meal. It is sure to please kids and adults alike. To complete the meal, add broccoli florets or asparagus spears to the pan for the last 15 minutes of roasting. For low-carbohydrate diets, substitute rutabaga, parsnips, or turnips for the potatoes.

8 BONE-IN, SKIN-ON CHICKEN THIGHS

1/2 CUP FRESHLY SQUEEZED LIME JUICE, ABOUT 4 LIMES

1/2 CUP FRESHLY SQUEEZED LEMON JUICE, ABOUT 2 LEMONS

ZEST OF 1 LEMON

ZEST OF 2 LIMES

2 CLOVES GARLIC, MINCED

1/2 CUP DRY WHITE WINE

2 POUNDS YUKON GOLD POTATOES, CUT INTO 1/2-INCH CUBES

1 TABLESPOON EXTRA-VIRGIN OLIVE OIL

2 TABLESPOONS CHOPPED PARSLEY

FRESHLY GROUND BLACK PEPPER, TO TASTE

1. Trim the chicken thighs of any excess skin and place in a gallon size resealable bag. Add the lemon and lime juices and zests, garlic, and white wine, season with pepper. Seal and toss the bag to combine, lay flat on a baking sheet and refrigerate. Marinate the chicken 4 to 6 hours, turning the bag over halfway through.

2. Remove the chicken from the bag, pat dry with a paper towel and place skin side up on half of a rimmed baking sheet to catch any juices. Allow chicken to air dry 20 minutes.

3. Heat the oven to 425°F. Place the potatoes on the opposite side of the baking sheet, drizzle with olive oil, season with pepper, and toss to combine. Roast until the internal temperature of the thickest part of the chicken thigh reaches 165°F, about 35 minutes, tossing the potatoes halfway through. For crispier chicken skin, lay a piece of foil over the potatoes and broil the thighs for 3–5 minutes. Remove the pan from the oven, toss the potatoes with the chicken juice, sprinkle with parsley, and serve.

NUTRITION SUMMARY & MODIFICATIONS: Low sodium. High potassium. Medium phosphorus. There are multiple ways to lower the potassium, but it is difficult to make it a low-potassium dish because of the potatoes and the chicken. Here are two options for modification. First, double boil the potatoes before you roast them. See "The Cooking Doc's Favorite Low-Potassium Fruits and Vegetables" in Step 5 for directions. A second option is to substitute 1/2 a head of cabbage cut into thick slices for the potatoes. Both modifications will create a medium-potassium dish.

YIELD: 8 servings

ANALYSIS PER SERVING

CALORIES (KCAL): 291

PROTEIN (G): 23

CARBOHYDRATES (G): 20

TOTAL DIETARY FIBER (G): 2

TOTAL SUGARS (G): 1

ADDED SUGAR (G): 0

FAT (G): 15

SATURATED FAT (G): 4

CHOLESTEROL (MG): 76

CALCIUM (MG): 23

MAGNESIUM (MG): 44

PHOSPHORUS (MG): 237

POTASSIUM (MG): 704

SODIUM (MG): 138

~~~~~~~~~~~~ BOILED POTATOES MODIFICATION NUTRITION PROFILE ~~~~~~~~~~~~

YIELD: 8 servings

ANALYSIS PER SERVING

CALORIES (KCAL): 279

PROTEIN (G): 22

CARBOHYDRATES (G): 18

TOTAL DIETARY FIBER (G): 2

TOTAL SUGARS (G): 1

ADDED SUGAR (G): 0

FAT (G): 15

SATURATED FAT (G): 4

CHOLESTEROL (MG): 76

CALCIUM (MG): 17

MAGNESIUM (MG): 36

PHOSPHORUS (MG): 207

POTASSIUM (MG): 496

SODIUM (MG): 74

~~~~~~~~~~~~ CABBAGE MODIFICATION NUTRITION PROFILE ~~~~~~~~~~~~

YIELD: 8 servings

ANALYSIS PER SERVING

CALORIES (KCAL): 227

PROTEIN (G): 22

CARBOHYDRATES (G): 5

TOTAL DIETARY FIBER (G): 2

TOTAL SUGARS (G): 3

ADDED SUGAR (G): 0

FAT (G): 15

SATURATED FAT (G): 4

CHOLESTEROL (MG): 76

CALCIUM (MG): 44

MAGNESIUM (MG): 29

PHOSPHORUS (MG): 195

POTASSIUM (MG): 362

SODIUM (MG): 85

SHEET PAN LEMON-LIME CHICKEN & POTATOES continued

CUT THE SALT, NOT THE FLAVOR Adapting to a low-sodium diet can be challenging. Luckily, there are ways to help you overcome a salt habit *without* sacrificing *flavor*. Gradually, you will #ChangeYourBuds and won't even miss the saltshaker.

* Aromatics like garlic, onions, shallots, and leeks are foundations for imparting depth of flavor during cooking.

* Spices and fresh herbs add complexity while cooking or freshness when tossed in before serving. Be sure to try my "No-Sodium All-Purpose Seasoning" (see "Dressings & Spice Blends").

* Experiment with fresh, dried, or roasted peppers that offer a wide range of taste and heat such as cayenne, *espelette*, jalapeños, poblano, habanero, serrano, or chipotle peppers.

* A splash of vinegar goes a long way to balance flavor and provide a subtle acidic note. Stock your pantry with a variety: apple cider, sherry, rice wine, balsamic, or champagne.

* Citrus juice or zest brings life to a dish by brightening the overall flavor composition or when used as a finishing touch.

* Use grated parmesan sparingly, or nutritional yeast, common in vegan diets, as a salt substitute to sprinkle over pastas, soups, vegetables, or popcorn or add to dressings, dips, and sauces.

ZA'ATAR CHICKEN SALAD

Za'atar is a Middle Eastern aromatic spice blend commonly made from marjoram, thyme, sumac, and sesame seeds. This unique mixture creates a tangy, herbaceous flavor profile with a wide range of culinary uses. Try Za'atar as a rub for grilled meats or seafood, sprinkle on vegetables or hummus, or mix with olive oil and brush on pita or flatbread before toasting. This recipe also makes a delicious filling for sandwich wraps.

3 TABLESPOONS AVOCADO MAYONNAISE

2 TABLESPOONS CHOPPED DILL

1 TABLESPOON ZA'ATAR SEASONING

1 TABLESPOON LEMON JUICE

1 POUND "BAKED CHICKEN BREASTS," DICED OR SHREDDED

1 CUP RED GRAPES, CUT IN HALF

1/2 CUP THINLY SLICED CELERY

4 CUPS MIXED GREENS, FOR SERVING

FRESHLY GROUND BLACK PEPPER, TO TASTE

1. Whisk together the mayonnaise, dill, Za'atar, and lemon juice in a medium bowl. Fold in the chicken, grapes, and celery and season with pepper.

2. Divide the greens among serving plates and top with the chicken salad.

NUTRITION SUMMARY & MODIFICATIONS: High potassium. High phosphorus. High protein. Most of the potassium comes from the chicken breast, but the greens and grapes also add to the potassium content. To lower the potassium, phosphorus, and protein, decrease the serving size to 1/2 cup and serve with iceberg lettuce instead of mixed greens and grapes.

NUTRITION PROFILE

YIELD: 4 servings

SERVING SIZE: 1 cup

CALORIES (KCAL): 299

PROTEIN (G): 38

CARBOHYDRATES (G): 10

TOTAL DIETARY FIBER (G): 2

TOTAL SUGARS (G): 7

ADDED SUGAR (G): 0

FAT (G): 13

SATURATED FAT (G): 2

CHOLESTEROL (MG): 143

CALCIUM (MG): 64

MAGNESIUM (MG): 58

PHOSPHORUS (MG): 306

POTASSIUM (MG): 629

SODIUM (MG): 169

CHICKEN FARRO BOWLS

Unlike other food trends that come and go, the popularity of nutritious, colorful grain bowls continues to rise. Adaptability, versatility, and healthy options fuel the momentum. Grain bowls accommodate vegans, vegetarians, and meat eaters at one table. Build your own bowl creations by starting with a base of nutritious grains such as quinoa or farro. **Keep a container of precooked grains on hand to reduce prep time.** *Toppings are limitless and should include a variety of tastes and textures. Choose vegetables, fruits, legumes, nuts, seeds, and plant- or animal-based proteins that complement each other or a specific ethnic cuisine. Finish your bowl with a dip, sauce, or dressing that ties the ingredients all together. A few of my favorite toppings include "Sautéed Broccolini & Garlic" (see "Vegetable Sides"), "Crispy Chickpeas," "Roasted Red Pepper & White Bean Hummus," and "Tzatziki Sauce" (see "Spreads, Snacks & Sauces").*

1 POUND BONELESS, SKINLESS CHICKEN BREAST, CUT INTO CUBES

1 1/2 TEASPOONS "NO-SODIUM ALL-PURPOSE SEASONING" (SEE "DRESSINGS & SPICE BLENDS")

1 TABLESPOON OLIVE OIL

4 OUNCES BABY KALE OR SPINACH

1 1/2 CUPS COOKED FARRO

12 CHERRY TOMATOES, HALVED

1 MEDIUM CARROT, PEELED INTO THIN STRIPS

1/2 CUCUMBER, SLICED

2 SCALLIONS, SLICED

1/4 CUP CRUMBLED FETA CHEESE

1/4 CUP "RED WINE VINAIGRETTE" (SEE "DRESSINGS & SPICE BLENDS")

1. Place the chicken in a medium bowl and toss with the "No-Sodium All-Purpose Seasoning" to coat. Heat the oil in a medium sauté pan over medium-high heat. Sauté the chicken until cooked through, about 5 minutes. Add the kale and sauté until just wilted, 1 minute.

2. Divide the farro between 4 serving bowls. Top each bowl with ¼ of the chicken-kale mixture, tomatoes, carrots, cucumbers, scallions, and feta. Drizzle each bowl with a tablespoon of "Red Wine Vinaigrette."

NUTRITION SUMMARY & MODIFICATIONS: Low sodium. High potassium. Medium phosphorus. High protein. To make it into a low-potassium, medium-protein dish, use only 8 ounces of chicken breast, substitute shredded cabbage for the kale or spinach, use white rice instead of farro, and leave off the tomatoes.

continues ➡

CHICKEN FARRO BOWLS continued

∼∼∼∼∼∼∼∼∼∼ NUTRITION PROFILE ∼∼∼∼∼∼∼∼∼∼

YIELD: 4 servings

ANALYSIS PER SERVING

CALORIES (KCAL): 447

PROTEIN (G): 36

CARBOHYDRATES (G): 38

TOTAL DIETARY FIBER (G): 5

TOTAL SUGARS (G): 3

ADDED SUGAR (G): 0

FAT (G): 18

SATURATED FAT (G): 4

CHOLESTEROL (MG): 81

CALCIUM (MG): 157

MAGNESIUM (MG): 50

PHOSPHORUS (MG): 274

POTASSIUM (MG): 763

SODIUM (MG): 197

∼∼∼∼∼∼ LOWER POTASSIUM AND PROTEIN MODIFICATION NUTRITION PROFILE ∼∼∼∼∼∼

YIELD: 4 servings

ANALYSIS PER SERVING

CALORIES (KCAL): 272

PROTEIN (G): 16

CARBOHYDRATES (G): 17

TOTAL DIETARY FIBER (G): 1

TOTAL SUGARS (G): 2

ADDED SUGAR (G): 0

FAT (G): 16

SATURATED FAT (G): 4

CHOLESTEROL (MG): 44

CALCIUM (MG): 79

MAGNESIUM (MG): 27

PHOSPHORUS (MG): 163

POTASSIUM (MG): 266

SODIUM (MG): 133

CREOLE CHICKEN BURGERS

Ground chicken burgers are a wholesome alternative to ground beef and equally tasty prepared on the stove top or grill. For grilling, be sure to clean and oil the grill generously so the burgers don't stick. A touch of mayonnaise keeps these burgers juicy and moist while the onions and homemade "No-Sodium Cajun Seasoning" (see "Dressings & Spice Blends") ramp up the flavor. Serve the burgers in whole-wheat pita pockets or on romaine or bibb lettuce "buns" with your favorite toppings. Leave off the avocado for a lower-potassium version.

1-POUND GROUND CHICKEN

1 TEASPOON "NO-SODIUM CAJUN SEASONING"

1/2 CUP FINELY DICED ONION

1 TABLESPOON MAYONNAISE

1 TABLESPOON OLIVE OIL

1 AVOCADO, PITTED, PEELED, AND SLICED

SPICY BROWN MUSTARD, FOR SERVING

1. Line a plate with waxed or parchment paper. Combine the ground chicken, Cajun seasoning, onion, and mayonnaise in a large bowl. Dampen hands with water and form ground chicken mixture into 5 patties and place on prepared plate.

2. Heat the oil in a large nonstick sauté pan over medium heat. Cook the burgers until browned and an internal temperature reaches 165°F, 5 minutes per side. If necessary, reduce heat to medium-low, cover, and continue cooking burgers to required temperature.

3. Top burgers with sliced avocado and a dollop of mustard.

NUTRITION SUMMARY & MODIFICATIONS: Low sodium. Medium potassium. Medium phosphorus. For a lower-potassium and lower-protein modification, leave off the avocado and create 6 smaller burgers instead of 5 larger ones.

NUTRITION PROFILE

YIELD: 5 servings

ANALYSIS PER SERVING

CALORIES (KCAL): 283

PROTEIN (G): 23

CARBOHYDRATES (G): 5

TOTAL DIETARY FIBER (G): 2

TOTAL SUGARS (G): 1

ADDED SUGAR (G): 0

FAT (G): 19

SATURATED FAT (G): 4

CHOLESTEROL (MG): 77

CALCIUM (MG): 17

MAGNESIUM (MG): 27

PHOSPHORUS (MG): 168

POTASSIUM (MG): 332

SODIUM (MG): 96

SPICED CHICKEN, ORANGE & AVOCADO SALAD

MAKES 4 SERVINGS

This salad is a favorite among patients with early-stage kidney disease or no potassium restrictions. Depending on what's in season, peach, pear, and mango also work well in place of the oranges.

2 8-OUNCE BONELESS, SKINLESS CHICKEN BREASTS

1 TEASPOON CUMIN

1 TEASPOON GARLIC POWDER

1 TABLESPOON AVOCADO OIL (OR OTHER NEUTRAL OIL)

1 HEAD BUTTER LETTUCE, CHOPPED

3 OUNCES BABY SPINACH, ABOUT 2 CUPS PACKED

1/4 CUP "DIJON VINAIGRETTE" (SEE "DRESSINGS & SPICE BLENDS")

1 CUP GRAPE TOMATOES, HALVED

1 LARGE RADISH, THINLY SLICED

1 LARGE ORANGE, PEELED AND CUT INTO SLICES

1 LARGE AVOCADO, SLICED

1 TABLESPOON FRESH CILANTRO LEAVES

FRESHLY GROUND BLACK PEPPER, TO TASTE

PINCH OF SALT (OPTIONAL—NOT INCLUDED IN NUTRITION PROFILE)

1. Place the chicken breasts in a single layer between two pieces of plastic wrap. Using the smooth side of a meat mallet or a rolling pin, pound the breasts evenly until ¾-inch thick. Season the chicken with cumin, garlic, salt, and black pepper. Heat the avocado oil in a large, heavy-bottomed sauté pan or cast-iron skillet over medium-high heat. Cook the chicken breast until nicely browned on both sides with an internal temperature of 165°F, about 4–5 minutes per side. Remove from heat and transfer the breasts to a cutting board for 5 minutes. The resting time allows the breasts to continue cooking slightly and the natural juices to redistribute. Slice the breasts into strips across the grain.

2. Combine the butter lettuce and spinach in a large bowl and toss with the Dijon vinaigrette. Place the lettuce on a large serving platter. Top with chicken, tomatoes, radish, oranges, and avocado. Sprinkle with cilantro. Serve additional dressing on the side, if desired.

NUTRITION SUMMARY & MODIFICATIONS: Low sodium. High potassium. High phosphorus. High protein. To lower the potassium, use butter lettuce instead of spinach, replace the orange with a pear, replace the tomato with ¼ cup of roasted red pepper, and omit the avocado (shown in modification). Because of the chicken and so many vegetables, even the low-potassium version is high in potassium and should be paired only with low-potassium foods if you are on a low-potassium diet. To further lower the potassium and the protein, use only 1 boneless, skinless chicken breast instead of 2 (nutrition profile not included).

continues ➡

SPICED CHICKEN, ORANGE & AVOCADO SALAD continued

RIPENING AND STORING AVOCADOS   A ripe avocado is ready to eat when firm but yields to pressure when gently squeezed. To speed up the ripening time, place the avocado in a brown paper bag at room temperature with an apple or banana. Store ripe avocados in the refrigerator and use within a few days.

Once an avocado is cut in half and exposed to air, oxidation occurs, causing the cut surface to brown. To prevent this, squeeze fresh lemon or lime juice over the cut surface. The citric acid acts as a natural preservative and prevents oxidation. If you don't want to impart the citrus flavor, store the cut avocado in a bowl of clean, cool water in an airtight container or place the cut side face down on a plate and cover with plastic wrap. For guacamole, take a piece of plastic wrap and press it down to cover the entire surface or cover with a ¼-inch of water, store refrigerated in an airtight container. Drain the water before using.

NUTRITION PROFILE

YIELD: 4 servings

ANALYSIS PER SERVING

CALORIES (KCAL): 380

PROTEIN (G): 39

CARBOHYDRATES (G): 12

TOTAL DIETARY FIBER (G): 5

TOTAL SUGARS (G): 6

ADDED SUGAR (G): 0

FAT (G): 21

SATURATED FAT (G): 3

CHOLESTEROL (MG): 132

CALCIUM (MG): 57

MAGNESIUM (MG): 68

PHOSPHORUS (MG): 320

POTASSIUM (MG): 845

SODIUM (MG): 100

PEAR MODIFICATION NUTRITION PROFILE

YIELD: 4 servings

ANALYSIS PER SERVING

CALORIES (KCAL): 343

PROTEIN (G): 37

CARBOHYDRATES (G): 12

TOTAL DIETARY FIBER (G): 3

TOTAL SUGARS (G): 7

ADDED SUGAR (G): 0

FAT (G): 16

SATURATED FAT (G): 3

CHOLESTEROL (MG): 96

CALCIUM (MG): 48

MAGNESIUM (MG): 49

PHOSPHORUS (MG): 297

POTASSIUM (MG): 574

SODIUM (MG): 119

SEARED CAJUN CHICKEN THIGHS

Salt is usually the first ingredient listed in store-bought Cajun seasoning, making it very high in sodium. My homemade version contains all the distinct, spicy flavors without added salt. The heat level can be adjusted by adapting the amount of cayenne pepper to satisfy personal tastes. Try this recipe served with "Broccoli-Cauliflower Mash with Roasted Garlic" (see "Vegetable Sides").

4 BONE-IN, SKIN-ON CHICKEN THIGHS

4 TEASPOONS "NO-SODIUM CAJUN SEASONING" (SEE "DRESSINGS & SPICE BLENDS")

1 TABLESPOON CANOLA OIL

1. Heat the oven to 400°F. Pat the chicken thighs with a paper towel to remove moisture. Season both sides with "No-Sodium Cajun Seasoning." Heat the oil in a cast-iron or heavy-bottomed skillet over medium-high heat. Place the chicken thighs skin side down and cook until browned, 2 to 3 minutes. Turn the chicken thighs and place the skillet in the oven.

2. Cook until the thighs reach an internal temperature of 165°F, 15 minutes. Let the thighs rest a few minutes before serving to allow juices to redistribute throughout the meat.

NUTRITION SUMMARY & MODIFICATIONS: Low sodium. Low potassium. Medium phosphorus.

PREHEATING PANS   For stovetop cooking, choose stainless steel or cast-iron pans that distribute heat evenly. Heat the pan on medium high before adding the oil. This minimizes the amount of time the oil is in contact with the heat, which causes it to break down. To test if the pan is hot enough, add ¼ teaspoon of water. If one or two beads form immediately and dance around the pan, it is ready. If several small beads of water form, the pan is too hot and should be removed from the heat source to cool. When the pan is ready, add the oil, and swirl the pan to evenly coat the bottom. Allow the oil to heat until it shimmers before adding the food. This prevents foods from sticking to the pan. Avoid overcrowding the pan, which causes a sudden drop in temperature, releasing moisture that turns into steam.

NUTRITION PROFILE

YIELD: 4 servings

ANALYSIS PER SERVING

CALORIES (KCAL): 279

PROTEIN (G): 21

CARBOHYDRATES (G): 1

TOTAL DIETARY FIBER (G): 0

TOTAL SUGARS (G): 0

ADDED SUGAR (G): 0

FAT (G): 23

SATURATED FAT (G): 4

CHOLESTEROL (MG): 76

CALCIUM (MG): 12

MAGNESIUM (MG): 20

PHOSPHORUS (MG): 177

POTASSIUM (MG): 228

SODIUM (MG): 72

BAKED CHICKEN BREASTS

Use these chicken breasts as a substitute for store-bought deli meat, which is high in sodium—yes, even the "low-sodium" varieties—and often contains caramel coloring and preservatives. I like to make this recipe on Sunday to have on hand for sandwiches during the week or last-minute dinners for pastas, fajitas, or salads. For a zesty version, sprinkle the chicken with "No-Sodium Cajun Seasoning" (see "Dressings & Spice Blends").

2 POUNDS BONELESS, SKINLESS CHICKEN BREASTS

1 TABLESPOON EXTRA-VIRGIN OLIVE OIL

KOSHER SALT (¼ TSP USED FOR NUTRITION PROFILE) AND FRESH GROUND BLACK PEPPER, TO TASTE

1. Heat the oven to 400°F. Place the chicken breasts on a baking sheet and rub both sides with oil. Season with salt and pepper.

2. Bake until the internal temperature reaches 165°F when inserted into the thickest portion of the breast, about 20 minutes.

3. Cool and slice, dice, or shred, as needed.

NUTRITION SUMMARY & MODIFICATIONS: This is a low-sodium, low-potassium, and medium-phosphorus dish.

YIELD: 8 servings

SERVING SIZE: 3 ounces

CALORIES (KCAL): 154

PROTEIN (G): 26

CARBOHYDRATES (G): 0

TOTAL DIETARY FIBER (G): 0

TOTAL SUGARS (G): 0

ADDED SUGAR (G): 0

FAT (G): 5

SATURATED FAT (G): 1

CHOLESTEROL (MG): 72

CALCIUM (MG): 13

MAGNESIUM (MG): 25

PHOSPHORUS (MG): 194

POTASSIUM (MG): 218

SODIUM (MG): 63

DEMYSTIFYING CHICKEN LABELS

* Natural means there are no preservatives, colorings, or artificial ingredients and minimal processing.

* Fresh means the chicken has never been cooled below 26 degrees Fahrenheit.

* Enhanced birds are injected with a saltwater solution or broth to enhance flavor and texture and add water weight. This method results in very high sodium contents.

* Farm-raised is a bogus marketing label since all commercial chickens are raised on farms.

* No hormones added is another pointless designation since the use of hormones in poultry production was banned in the United States in the 1950s.

* Raised without antibiotics means the bird was not given antibiotics while it was raised. However, other drugs may have been used to control other health risks.

* Antibiotic-free is different than raised without antibiotics. Antibiotic-free means antibiotic treatment was stopped prior to slaughter and that no antibiotic residue remains when the bird is processed.

* Free range broadly defines chickens having access to the outdoors, according to the USDA. This deceiving, unspecified term does not require a length of time, environmental quality, or space requirements. In short, a chicken that is outside for a few minutes a day could be classified as "free range." Humane Farm Animal Care (HFAC), a non-profit certification organization, sets precise standards for responsible farm animal practices. The HFAC "free range" designation requires 2 square feet per bird and outdoor access at least 6 hours per day.

* To be labeled organic, the USDA requires certified organic feed without pesticides or fertilizers, outdoor access, and no antibiotics. Chickens can be given antibiotics while the chick is still in the egg and on its first day of life. A "raised without antibiotics" label used with a USDA organic label means no antibiotics were ever used.

* Certified humane is a designation by the HFAC, and endorsed by the Center for Food Safety, that indicates processors have met all the organization standards from raising to processing.

* All-vegetable or vegetarian diet chickens are fed diets that do not contain any fats and proteins.

SEARED SALMON WITH TZATZIKI

SEAFOOD

LEMON CAPER ROASTED SALMON 198

TUNA, CANNELLINI & DILL SALAD 200

SEARED SALMON WITH TZATZIKI SAUCE 203

SALMON BURGER 205

THAI SHRIMP SALAD 206

LEMON CAPER ROASTED SALMON

Salmon is one of my favorite fish to cook because it's readily available, easy to prepare, and a crowd-pleaser. Full of omega-3s, it's heart healthy, too. This recipe is a twist on a classic French dish called Trout Grenobloise. I eliminated the traditional butter, white wine, and croutons, but not the flavor! If there is leftover salmon, flake it and toss with a green salad for a satisfying lunch the next day.

4 5-OUNCE SALMON FILLETS

1 1/2 TABLESPOONS EXTRA-VIRGIN OLIVE OIL

1 TABLESPOON FRESH LEMON JUICE

1 TABLESPOON CAPERS, DRAINED AND CHOPPED

2 TABLESPOONS CHOPPED PARSLEY, PLUS SPRIGS FOR GARNISH

1/4 CUP PANKO BREADCRUMBS

ZEST OF 1 LEMON

FRESHLY GROUND BLACK PEPPER, TO TASTE

1. Heat the oven to 400°F. Line a baking sheet with foil or parchment paper. Pat the salmon dry with a paper towel and place the fillets, skin side down, on the baking sheet.

2. Combine the oil, lemon juice, capers, parsley, and breadcrumbs in a small bowl and season with pepper. Spread the breadcrumb mixture evenly over the top of the fillets.

3. Roast until the thickest part of the fillet reaches an internal temperature of 125°F for medium or 145°F for well done, as recommended by the USDA. Keep in mind that the temperature will continue to rise once the salmon is removed from the oven. For medium doneness, the exterior flesh should be opaque, and the center will be slightly translucent pink and begin to separate with a fork but not completely flake, about 10 minutes. Roasting times will vary slightly depending on the thickness of the fillets.

4. Sprinkle salmon with lemon zest, garnish with parsley sprigs, and serve.

NUTRITION SUMMARY & MODIFICATIONS: Low sodium. High potassium. High phosphorus. High protein. To change to a low-potassium, medium-phosphorus, and medium-protein dish, use 3 ounces of salmon per person.

YIELD: 4 servings

ANALYSIS PER SERVING

CALORIES (KCAL): 231

PROTEIN (G): 28

CARBOHYDRATES (G): 2

TOTAL DIETARY FIBER (G): 0

TOTAL SUGARS (G): 0

ADDED SUGAR (G): 0

FAT (G): 12

SATURATED FAT (G): 2

CHOLESTEROL (MG): 62

CALCIUM (MG): 13

MAGNESIUM (MG): 38

PHOSPHORUS (MG): 357

POTASSIUM (MG): 513

SODIUM (MG): 156

~~~~~~~~~~~~~~~~~~ 3 OUNCE PORTION MODIFICATION NUTRITION PROFILE ~~~~~~~~~~~~~~~~~~

YIELD: 4 servings

ANALYSIS PER SERVING

CALORIES (KCAL): 188

PROTEIN (G): 21

CARBOHYDRATES (G): 2

TOTAL DIETARY FIBER (G): 0

TOTAL SUGARS (G): 0

ADDED SUGAR (G): 0

FAT (G): 10

SATURATED FAT (G): 2

CHOLESTEROL (MG): 47

CALCIUM (MG): 11

MAGNESIUM (MG): 29

PHOSPHORUS (MG): 268

POTASSIUM (MG): 389

SODIUM (MG): 131

TUNA, CANNELLINI & DILL SALAD

This protein-rich salad makes the perfect summer meal when temperatures soar and you don't feel like turning on the oven. From the peppery bite of arugula to the sweetness of sundried tomatoes, to the crisp celery against the creamy cannellini bean, the flavor and texture combinations hit all the right notes. If cannellini beans, also known as white kidney beans, aren't available, use red kidney beans, garbanzo, or butter beans.

1/4 CUP RED WINE VINEGAR

2 TABLESPOONS EXTRA-VIRGIN OLIVE OIL

2 TABLESPOONS CHOPPED SUNDRIED TOMATOES

1/4 CUP CHOPPED FRESH DILL

1/4 TEASPOON RED PEPPER FLAKES

1 12-OUNCE CAN WATER-PACKED TUNA, LOW-SODIUM IF AVAILABLE, DRAINED

1 15-OUNCE CAN LOW-SODIUM CANNELLINI BEANS, RINSED AND DRAINED

1/2 CUP DICED RED ONION

1 CUP PACKED ARUGULA, CHOPPED

1 STALK CELERY, THINLY SLICED

FRESHLY GROUND BLACK PEPPER, TO TASTE

Whisk together the vinegar, olive oil, sundried tomatoes, dill, and red pepper flakes in a medium bowl. Add the tuna, beans, onion, arugula, and celery. Season with pepper and toss to combine.

NUTRITION SUMMARY & MODIFICATIONS: Medium sodium. Medium potassium. Low phosphorus. To lower the potassium, substitute roasted red peppers for the sundried tomatoes, use chopped green pepper and only ½ of a can of cannellini beans. The dish will still have a moderate amount of potassium even with these adjustments, so pair it with low-potassium sides.

YIELD: 4 servings

SERVING SIZE: 1 cup

CALORIES (KCAL): 205

PROTEIN (G): 18

CARBOHYDRATES (G): 15

TOTAL DIETARY FIBER (G): 4

TOTAL SUGARS (G): 2

ADDED SUGAR (G): 0

FAT (G): 8

SATURATED FAT (G): 1

CHOLESTEROL (MG): 26

CALCIUM (MG): 59

MAGNESIUM (MG): 26

PHOSPHORUS (MG): 117

POTASSIUM (MG): 454

SODIUM (MG): 346

~~~ LOWER-POTASSIUM MODIFICATION NUTRITION PROFILE ~~~

YIELD: 4 servings

SERVING SIZE: 1 cup

CALORIES (KCAL): 177

PROTEIN (G): 16

CARBOHYDRATES (G): 10

TOTAL DIETARY FIBER (G): 3

TOTAL SUGARS (G): 2

ADDED SUGAR (G): 0

FAT (G): 8

SATURATED FAT (G): 1

CHOLESTEROL (MG): 26

CALCIUM (MG): 54

MAGNESIUM (MG): 30

PHOSPHORUS (MG): 122

POTASSIUM (MG): 367

SODIUM (MG): 267

SEARED SALMON WITH TZATZIKI SAUCE

This dish combines the spicy flavor of cumin with the fresh Mediterranean flavors of tzatziki sauce. Searing salmon takes practice, but after a few attempts, you'll be able to create a perfect sear on the outside and tender flesh on the inside.

4 5-OUNCE SALMON FILLETS, ABOUT ¾-INCH THICK

1 TEASPOON GROUND CUMIN

1 TABLESPOON EXTRA-VIRGIN OLIVE OIL

½ CUP "TZATZIKI SAUCE" (SEE "SPREADS, SNACKS & SAUCES")

LEMON WEDGES, FOR SERVING

4 DILL SPRIGS FOR GARNISH

FRESHLY GROUND BLACK PEPPER, TO TASTE

1. Season the salmon with cumin and black pepper.

2. Heat the oil in a large skillet over medium-high heat. Place the salmon skin side down and cook the salmon until the skin is crispy and golden brown, 3 minutes. Turn the fillets and cook until the thickest part of the fillet reaches an internal temperature of 125°F for medium or 145°F for well done, as recommended by the USDA. Keep in mind that the temperature will continue to rise once the salmon is removed from the heat. For medium doneness, the exterior flesh should be opaque, and the center will be slightly translucent pink and begin to separate with a fork but not completely flake, about 3–4 minutes depending on thickness.

3. Place fillets on serving plates, top each fillet with 2 tablespoons "Tzatziki Sauce" from "Spreads, Snacks & Sauces" and serve with lemon wedges and dill.

NUTRITION SUMMARY & MODIFICATIONS: Low sodium. High potassium. High phosphorus. High protein. To change to a low-potassium, medium-phosphorus, and high-protein dish, use 3 ounces of salmon per person. To further reduce the protein, phosphorus, and potassium, leave off the tzatziki sauce.

continues ➡

PROPER COOKING TAKES TIME AND SCIENCE   When food is cooked at proper temperatures and times, desired browning, aromas, and flavors are created, as in a perfectly roasted chicken or seared, golden brown crusted salmon fillets. This is due to a chemical reaction that takes place between amino acids, sugars, and heat, known as the Maillard reaction. Sautéing, searing, and roasting caramelize the natural sugars present in food and intensify the flavor. Avoid over stirring or turning foods too frequently during cooking. Be patient and allow foods to cook undisturbed.

NUTRITION PROFILE

YIELD: 4 servings

ANALYSIS PER SERVING

CALORIES (KCAL): 242

PROTEIN (G): 32

CARBOHYDRATES (G): 1

TOTAL DIETARY FIBER (G): 0

TOTAL SUGARS (G): 1

ADDED SUGAR (G): 0

FAT (G): 12

SATURATED FAT (G): 2

CHOLESTEROL (MG): 71

CALCIUM (MG): 39

MAGNESIUM (MG): 45

PHOSPHORUS (MG): 374

POTASSIUM (MG): 540

SODIUM (MG): 112

3-OUNCE PORTION MODIFICATION NUTRITION PROFILE

YIELD: 4 servings

ANALYSIS PER SERVING

CALORIES (KCAL): 198

PROTEIN (G): 25

CARBOHYDRATES (G): 1

TOTAL DIETARY FIBER (G): 0

TOTAL SUGARS (G): 1

ADDED SUGAR (G): 0

FAT (G): 11

SATURATED FAT (G): 2

CHOLESTEROL (MG): 54

CALCIUM (MG): 36

MAGNESIUM (MG): 34

PHOSPHORUS (MG): 288

POTASSIUM (MG): 417

SODIUM (MG): 86

SALMON BURGER

Using fresh versus canned salmon eliminates added salt, increases flavor, and creates a more appealing texture. No-sodium canned salmon will also work in a pinch. This recipe is perfect for easy, quick weeknight dinners. Try serving the burgers in pita pockets paired with "Tzatziki Sauce" (see "Spreads, Snacks & Sauces") or on a bed of salad greens drizzled with "Lemon Shallot Vinaigrette" (see Dressings & Spice Blends).

1 POUND FRESH SKINLESS SALMON, CUT INTO LARGE CHUNKS

1 TEASPOON DIJON MUSTARD

1 TABLESPOON CAPERS, DRAINED

1 SCALLION, ROUGH CHOPPED

¼ CUP PANKO BREADCRUMBS

1 TABLESPOON OLIVE OIL

FRESH GROUND BLACK PEPPER, TO TASTE

LEMON WEDGES, FOR SERVING

1. Place ¼ of the salmon in a food processor and process to a finely ground paste. Add the remaining salmon, Dijon, capers, and scallion. Pulse just until the salmon is chopped, but not ground. Do not over pulse, the salmon pieces should be no less than ¼-inch.

2. Transfer the salmon mixture to a medium bowl. Using a rubber spatula, fold in the breadcrumbs and season with pepper.

3. Dampen your hands with water and form the salmon mixture into 4 patties.

4. Heat the oil in a large nonstick sauté pan over medium-high heat. Gently place the patties in the pan and cook until golden brown flipping once, about 2–3 minutes per side. Check the center for doneness by making a small slit with a paring knife. The salmon should be opaque on the outside and just beginning to flake, but still slightly translucent pink in the middle. The salmon will continue to cook when removed from the heat.

5. Serve as a sandwich or over greens with lemon wedges.

NUTRITION SUMMARY & MODIFICATIONS: Low sodium. Medium potassium. Medium phosphorus. For a lower potassium and phosphorus meal, divide the salmon into 5 or 6 smaller burgers.

— NUTRITION PROFILE —

YIELD: 4 servings

ANALYSIS PER SERVING

CALORIES (KCAL): 205

PROTEIN (G): 26

CARBOHYDRATES (G): 5

TOTAL DIETARY FIBER (G): 0

TOTAL SUGARS (G): 0

ADDED SUGAR (G): 0

FAT (G): 9

SATURATED FAT (G): 1

CHOLESTEROL (MG): 57

CALCIUM (MG): 14

MAGNESIUM (MG): 35

PHOSPHORUS (MG): 289

POTASSIUM (MG): 421

SODIUM (MG): 181

THAI SHRIMP SALAD

Once you become a good cook, you will enjoy the flavor of home-cooked meals more than the restaurant meals. Preparing home-cooked meals is also good for your health and your wallet. This shrimp salad combines the colors, textures, and flavors of fresh shrimp, carrots, cabbage, cucumber, mint, and cilantro. By making it at home, you take control of the fat content, sodium levels, and the amount of empty carbohydrates compared to what you would get at a restaurant, where a dish like this could easily have 1000 mg of sodium per serving.

1 POUND MEDIUM SHRIMP, PEELED AND DEVEINED

JUICE OF ONE LIME

¼ TEASPOON RED PEPPER FLAKES

1 SHALLOT, FINELY GRATED

2 TABLESPOONS SESAME OIL

¼ CUP RICE VINEGAR

1 TABLESPOON LOW-SODIUM SOY SAUCE, OR TAMARI FOR GLUTEN-FREE DIETS

¼ CUP CHOPPED CILANTRO, PLUS MORE FOR GARNISH

¼ CUP CHOPPED MINT, PLUS MORE FOR GARNISH

2 TABLESPOONS CHOPPED CHIVES

3 MEDIUM CARROTS, PEELED AND GRATED

1 SMALL CUCUMBER, SLICED INTO HALF CIRCLES

¼ SMALL HEAD RED CABBAGE, SHREDDED AND CHOPPED, ABOUT 2 CUPS

1 SMALL HEAD ROMAINE, CHOPPED

¼ CUP UNSALTED, ROASTED PEANUTS, CHOPPED

1. Prepare an ice bath in a medium bowl, set aside. Bring a medium pot of water to boil. Add the shrimp, turn off the heat, and poach until cooked through, 1 minute. Drain and place shrimp in ice bath to cool and drain.

2. Whisk together the lime juice, red pepper flakes, shallot, sesame oil, vinegar, and soy sauce in a large bowl. Add the shrimp, tossing to coat, and transfer to a separate bowl.

3. Add the cilantro, mint, chives, carrot, cucumber, cabbage, and romaine to the remaining sesame-soy dressing and toss to combine.

4. To serve, divide salads between plates, top with the shrimp and chopped peanuts, and garnish with cilantro and mint leaves.

NUTRITION SUMMARY & MODIFICATIONS: High sodium. High potassium. Low phosphorus. To turn it into a medium-potassium dish, omit the romaine lettuce and peanuts, use only 1 carrot, and serve over ½ cup of white rice. Leave off the soy sauce for a lower-sodium version.

EXTEND THE LIFE OF FRESH HERBS   To best way to extend the life of fresh herbs depends on the herb. For tender leafed herbs such as parsley, cilantro, chervil, tarragon, mint, or dill, give the stem ends a fresh cut and remove any wilted or discolored leaves. Place herb bundles in a glass jar with a few inches of water. Drape the jar with a plastic bag, produce bags work well for this, and refrigerate. Refresh the water every few days. Basil should be prepped the same way but kept uncovered at room temperature. For hardy herbs like chives, rosemary, or thyme, roll the herb bundles in damp paper towels, place in resealable plastics bags, and refrigerate.

NUTRITION PROFILE

YIELD: 4 servings

ANALYSIS PER SERVING

CALORIES (KCAL): 267

PROTEIN (G): 26

CARBOHYDRATES (G): 13

TOTAL DIETARY FIBER (G): 5

TOTAL SUGARS (G): 5

ADDED SUGAR (G): 0

FAT (G): 13

SATURATED FAT (G): 2

CHOLESTEROL (MG): 172

CALCIUM (MG): 147

MAGNESIUM (MG): 50

PHOSPHORUS (MG): 100

POTASSIUM (MG): 797

SODIUM (MG): 441

LOWER-POTASSIUM MODIFICATION NUTRITION PROFILE

YIELD: 4 servings (with rice)

ANALYSIS PER SERVING

CALORIES (KCAL): 294

PROTEIN (G): 25

CARBOHYDRATES (G): 29

TOTAL DIETARY FIBER (G): 2

TOTAL SUGARS (G): 3

ADDED SUGAR (G): 0

FAT (G): 9

SATURATED FAT (G): 1

CHOLESTEROL (MG): 172

CALCIUM (MG): 104

MAGNESIUM (MG): 28

PHOSPHORUS (MG): 70

POTASSIUM (MG): 488

SODIUM (MG): 409

ROASTED CARROTS, CRANBERRIES & COUSCOUS

BEANS, GRAINS & PASTA

SOUTHWEST QUINOA SALAD……………………………………………………210

LIGHT MACARONI & CHEESE WITH PEAS……………………………………212

CHICKEN, KALE & FARRO CASSEROLE………………………………………214

ROASTED TOMATO & ZUCCHINI SPAGHETTI WITH
VEGAN BASIL-CASHEW PESTO…………………………………………………216

ROASTED CARROTS, CRANBERRIES & COUSCOUS…………………………219

LEMON HERB COUSCOUS SALAD………………………………………………221

VEGETARIAN SUMMER PASTA SALAD…………………………………………222

SOUTHWEST QUINOA SALAD

If you are tasting quinoa for the first time you are in for a real treat. This salad is a great chance for you and your family to #ChangeYourBuds and reap the benefits of quinoa's rich plant-based protein and high fiber. Quinoa makes a hearty base for this colorful, flavor-packed Tex-Mex–inspired salad. Try adding it to soups, green salads, and baked goods or simply have it on its own as a side dish in place of rice or for breakfast instead of oatmeal.

1 CUP QUINOA, RINSED IF NOT PREWASHED

2 CUPS LOW-SODIUM VEGETABLE STOCK

1 15-OUNCE CAN LOW-SODIUM BLACK BEANS, DRAINED AND RINSED

1 JALAPEÑO, MINCED

1 GREEN, RED, OR YELLOW BELL PEPPER, CHOPPED

1 CUP THINLY SLICED RED ONION

1 PINT GRAPE TOMATOES, HALVED

2 TABLESPOONS CHOPPED CILANTRO, PLUS MORE FOR GARNISH

1/4 CUP "CUMIN LIME VINAIGRETTE" (SEE "DRESSINGS & SPICE BLENDS")

1 AVOCADO, CUT INTO CUBES

1. Cook the quinoa according to package directions, substituting stock for water. After fluffing with a fork, set aside to cool.

2. Combine the quinoa, beans, jalapeño, bell pepper, onion, tomato, and cilantro in a large bowl. Drizzle salad with the cumin lime vinaigrette and toss to combine.

3. Divide the quinoa between serving bowls and top with the avocado and a few cilantro leaves. Serve at room temperature or chilled.

NUTRITION SUMMARY & MODIFICATIONS: Low sodium. Medium potassium. Medium phosphorus. To lower the potassium, omit the tomato and avocado, and use only ½ can of black beans.

RINSING QUINOA   Quinoa, pronounced "keen-wah," is a flowering plant that originated thousands of years ago in the Andes. Although a seed, quinoa is classified as a whole grain, high in plant-based protein and fiber. It compares in nutrition to grains and is prepared similarly, yet quinoa falls into the pseudo-cereal group. Grown for its protein-rich seeds and available in white, red, purple, and black varieties, quinoa is light yet filling, gluten-free, and easy to digest and it cooks in just 15 minutes. The outside of the seed has a bitter residue of saponins, mother nature's clever way of repelling insects and birds. Nowadays, most quinoa is prewashed and doesn't require rinsing. However, it is still a good idea to check the packaging and if you are unsure, rinse before using.

NUTRITION PROFILE

YIELD: 8 servings

SERVING SIZE: 1 cup

CALORIES (KCAL): 201

PROTEIN (G): 7

CARBOHYDRATES (G): 28

TOTAL DIETARY FIBER (G): 7

TOTAL SUGARS (G): 3

ADDED SUGAR (G): 1

FAT (G): 7

SATURATED FAT (G): 1

CHOLESTEROL (MG): 0

CALCIUM (MG): 39

MAGNESIUM (MG): 66

PHOSPHORUS (MG): 162

POTASSIUM (MG): 484

SODIUM (MG): 98

LOW-POTASSIUM MODIFICATION NUTRITION PROFILE

YIELD: 8 servings

SERVING SIZE: 1 cup

CALORIES (KCAL): 146

PROTEIN (G): 5

CARBOHYDRATES (G): 21

TOTAL DIETARY FIBER (G): 4

TOTAL SUGARS (G): 3

ADDED SUGAR (G): 2

FAT (G): 5

SATURATED FAT (G): 1

CHOLESTEROL (MG): 0

CALCIUM (MG): 30

MAGNESIUM (MG): 53

PHOSPHORUS (MG): 130

POTASSIUM (MG): 248

SODIUM (MG): 65

LIGHT MACARONI & CHEESE WITH PEAS

My version of macaroni and cheese takes on a healthier profile with a few minor ingredient changes while still maintaining the creaminess of a traditional recipe. Olive oil, low-fat milk, and vegetable stock reduces fat, whole-grain pasta increases fiber, and peas add protein and vitamins. Reduced-fat and vegan cheeses can also be used with equally tasty results.

1 16-OUNCE BOX WHOLE-GRAIN ELBOW PASTA

2 TABLESPOONS ALL-PURPOSE FLOUR

1 TABLESPOON BUTTER, OR BUTTER SUBSTITUTE

1 TABLESPOON EXTRA-VIRGIN OLIVE OIL

1 1/4 CUPS 1% MILK

1 1/4 CUPS "NO-SODIUM VEGETABLE STOCK" (SEE "SOUPS")

1/2 TEASPOON LOW-SODIUM HOT SAUCE, OR TO TASTE

2 CUPS FRESHLY GRATED CHEDDAR CHEESE

1 10-OUNCE BAG FROZEN PEAS

1. Bring a large pot of water to boil and add the pasta, stirring to prevent pasta from sticking together, cook for 2 minutes. Add the peas and cook until the pasta is al dente, about another 3–4 minutes, drain and set aside.

2. Place the pot over medium-low heat and add butter and olive oil to melt. Add the flour and stir with a wooden spoon, making sure to reach the edges of the pot. Cook for 2 minutes, stirring frequently to prevent the roux from scorching.

3. Increase heat to medium and gradually whisk in a few tablespoons of milk at a time, whisking until the milk is incorporated before adding more. Add the vegetable stock and simmer until the sauce thickens slightly, whisking occasionally, 5 minutes.

4. Gradually add the cheese, whisking until melted. Add the pasta and peas to the cheese sauce, stir to combine, and serve immediately.

NUTRITION SUMMARY & MODIFICATIONS: Medium sodium. Low potassium. High phosphorus. To lower the potassium and phosphorus, use regular pasta instead of whole-grain pasta and decrease the cheese amount to 1 cup total.

NUTRITION PROFILE

YIELD: 8 servings

SERVING SIZE: 1 cup

CALORIES (KCAL): 443

PROTEIN (G): 20

CARBOHYDRATES (G): 56

TOTAL DIETARY FIBER (G): 8

TOTAL SUGARS (G): 5

ADDED SUGAR (G): 0

FAT (G): 17

SATURATED FAT (G): 7

CHOLESTEROL (MG): 35

CALCIUM (MG): 313

MAGNESIUM (MG): 104

PHOSPHORUS (MG): 408

POTASSIUM (MG): 267

SODIUM (MG): 283

CHICKEN, KALE & FARRO CASSEROLE

MAKES 8 1-CUP SERVINGS

For many families, casseroles are a staple comfort food but often made with canned cream soups, bacon, and cheese. This wholesome recipe replaces those high-sodium, carbohydrates, and fat ingredients with lean protein, vitamin-rich leafy greens, and whole grains without sacrificing flavor. For vegetarian meals, substitute the chicken and chicken stock with beans and vegetable stock.

1 TABLESPOON EXTRA-VIRGIN OLIVE OIL, PLUS MORE FOR PAN

1 TABLESPOON VEGAN BUTTER, OR BUTTER SUBSTITUTE

1 MEDIUM ONION, DICED

2 CLOVES GARLIC, MINCED

2 TABLESPOONS ALL-PURPOSE FLOUR

1 1/4 CUPS 1% MILK

1 1/4 CUPS "NO-SODIUM CHICKEN STOCK" (SEE "SOUPS")

8 OUNCES KALE, CHOPPED OR BABY KALE

1-POUND BONELESS, SKINLESS CHICKEN BREAST, CUT INTO 1-INCH CUBES

1 TEASPOON "NO-SODIUM ALL-PURPOSE SEASONING" (SEE "DRESSINGS & SPICE BLENDS")

2 MEDIUM YELLOW SQUASH, CUT IN 1-INCH CUBES, ABOUT 1 POUND

1 CUP SEMI-PEARLED FARRO, COOKED ACCORDING TO PACKAGE DIRECTIONS

1/2 CUP GRATED PARMESAN, DIVIDED

1/2 CUP NON-FAT PLAIN GREEK YOGURT

1/4 CUP LOW-SODIUM OR HOMEMADE BREADCRUMBS

FRESHLY GROUND BLACK PEPPER, TO TASTE

2 TABLESPOONS CHOPPED PARSLEY

WHAT TO LOOK FOR WHEN BUYING FARRO   Farro is an ancient grain valued for its high fiber and protein content, nutty flavor, and chewy texture. It is available **whole, semi-pearled,** and **pearled.** Pearling is a process that removes the inedible hull. When part of the germ and bran is also removed, it is semi-pearled, and then it becomes pearled when all the germ and bran is removed. Semi-pearled and pearled farro cook in half the time of whole farro but contain less nutritional value. The process to hull whole grain is gentler and doesn't remove the germ and bran, so it provides the highest amount of fiber and nutrients. Because of this, it requires overnight soaking and an hour to cook. When buying farro, check the label for the type, or the package direction cooking times will indicate the variety.

1. Preheat the oven to 400°F. Lightly coat a 9 x 13-inch ovenproof dish with oil, set aside. Heat the oil and butter in a large sauté pan over medium heat. Sauté the onion until translucent, 5 minutes. Add the garlic and sauté until fragrant, 30 seconds.

2. Sprinkle the onions with the flour and stir with a wooden spoon until light golden brown. Gradually whisk in the milk until incorporated. Whisk in the no-sodium chicken stock and cook until slightly thickened, 3 minutes. Reduce the heat to a low simmer and place kale on top of the sauce and cover the pan. Steam kale until just wilted and bright green, about 2 minutes. Remove from the heat and set aside.

3. Place the chicken in a large bowl, sprinkle with the no-sodium all-purpose seasoning and toss to coat. Add the squash, farro, ¼ cup parmesan, yogurt, and kale mixture, season with pepper, and fold together with a rubber spatula. Place chicken mixture in prepared baking dish and sprinkle with remaining ¼ cup of parmesan and breadcrumbs on top.

4. Bake until chicken is cooked through, squash is tender when pierced with a paring knife, and the top is golden brown, about 20 minutes. Sprinkle with parsley and serve.

NUTRITION SUMMARY & MODIFICATIONS: Low sodium. High potassium. Medium phosphorus. To lower the potassium, use cabbage instead of kale and white rice instead of farro. It will still be a medium-potassium recipe even with these changes. To further lower the potassium and protein, try ½ lb of chicken instead of a full pound.

~~~~~~~~~~~~~~~~~~~~~~ NUTRITION PROFILE ~~~~~~~~~~~~~~~~~~~~~~

YIELD: 8 servings
SERVING SIZE: 1 cup
CALORIES (KCAL): 245
PROTEIN (G): 23
CARBOHYDRATES (G): 27
TOTAL DIETARY FIBER (G): 3

TOTAL SUGARS (G): 5
ADDED SUGAR (G): 0
FAT (G): 6
SATURATED FAT (G): 2
CHOLESTEROL (MG): 43
CALCIUM (MG): 188

MAGNESIUM (MG): 43
PHOSPHORUS (MG): 245
POTASSIUM (MG): 604
SODIUM (MG): 193

~~~~~~~~~~~~ LOWER-POTASSIUM MODIFICATION NUTRITION PROFILE ~~~~~~~~~~~~

YIELD: 8 servings
SERVING SIZE: 1 cup
CALORIES (KCAL): 193
PROTEIN (G): 20
CARBOHYDRATES (G): 16
TOTAL DIETARY FIBER (G): 2

TOTAL SUGARS (G): 5
ADDED SUGAR (G): 0
FAT (G): 5
SATURATED FAT (G): 2
CHOLESTEROL (MG): 43
CALCIUM (MG): 139

MAGNESIUM (MG): 36
PHOSPHORUS (MG): 235
POTASSIUM (MG): 425
SODIUM (MG): 175

ROASTED TOMATO & ZUCCHINI SPAGHETTI WITH VEGAN BASIL-CASHEW PESTO

This pasta dish is all about balance of ingredients and taste. Zucchini "noodles" (also known as "zoodles") combined with whole-wheat spaghetti creates a healthy ratio of vegetables to pasta. Roasting caramelizes natural sugars in the tomato, adding a touch of sweetness, while the acidity cuts the fat and richness of the nuts. Yellow or butternut squash can be used in place of the zucchini with equally delicious results.

1 PINT GRAPE TOMATOES

1/2 CUP EXTRA-VIRGIN OLIVE OIL, DIVIDED

6 TABLESPOONS PINE NUTS, DIVIDED

1 LARGE ZUCCHINI

1 1/2 CUPS FRESH BASIL LEAVES

1/3 CUP UNROASTED, UNSALTED CASHEWS

2 CLOVES GARLIC

1 TABLESPOON LEMON JUICE

8 OUNCES WHOLE-WHEAT SPAGHETTI

VEGAN PARMESAN CHEESE OR NUTRITIONAL YEAST, OPTIONAL, FOR GARNISH

FRESHLY GROUND BLACK PEPPER, TO TASTE

1. Heat the oven to 400°F. Cut the tomatoes in half, place on a baking sheet, and toss with 1 tablespoon oil. Place the pine nuts in one corner of the baking sheet. Roast until pine nuts are golden brown, about 5 minutes. Remove the nuts from the pan, set aside. Return the pan to the oven and continue roasting the tomatoes until blistered, about 10 minutes, set aside.

2. Using a spiralizer, julienne peeler, or mandolin fitted with a julienne blade, julienne the zucchini into long, thin noodle-like strands, set aside.

3. Place ¼ cup toasted pine nuts, basil, cashews, garlic, and lemon juice in a blender or food processor and process until combined. While the machine is running, slowly add the remaining oil through the top feed tube until incorporated. Season with pepper.

4. Bring a large pot of water to boil. Add the spaghetti, cook according to package directions for al dente, and add the zucchini when two minutes remain. Drain the spaghetti and zucchini and return to the pot with the roasted cherry tomatoes over low heat.

5. Gently fold the pesto into the pasta until combined. Season with pepper, if needed. Top with remaining toasted pine nuts and vegan parmesan cheese or nutritional yeast, if desired.

NUTRITION SUMMARY & MODIFICATIONS: Low sodium. High potassium. High phosphorus. For a medium-potassium and medium-phosphorus dish, use regular spaghetti instead of whole wheat and decrease the tomatoes and zucchini to 1 cup each. This also significantly reduces the fiber in the dish, so make this modification only if you need a low-potassium diet.

∼ NUTRITION PROFILE ∼

YIELD: 4 servings	TOTAL SUGARS (G): 6	MAGNESIUM (MG): 176
ANALYSIS PER SERVING	ADDED SUGAR (G): 0	PHOSPHORUS (MG): 379
CALORIES (KCAL): 621	FAT (G): 41	POTASSIUM (MG): 691
PROTEIN (G): 15	SATURATED FAT (G): 5	SODIUM (MG): 19
CARBOHYDRATES (G): 58	CHOLESTEROL (MG): 0	
TOTAL DIETARY FIBER (G): 9	CALCIUM (MG): 76	

∼ LOWER-POTASSIUM MODIFICATION NUTRITION PROFILE ∼

YIELD: 4 servings	TOTAL SUGARS (G): 3	MAGNESIUM (MG): 92
ANALYSIS PER SERVING	ADDED SUGAR (G): 0	PHOSPHORUS (MG): 193
CALORIES (KCAL): 467	FAT (G): 38	POTASSIUM (MG): 384
PROTEIN (G): 8	SATURATED FAT (G): 5	SODIUM (MG): 8
CARBOHYDRATES (G): 26	CHOLESTEROL (MG): 0	
TOTAL DIETARY FIBER (G): 3	CALCIUM (MG): 51	

ROASTED CARROTS, CRANBERRIES & COUSCOUS

Aside from being delicious and nutritious, this festive side dish always finds a place on our holiday tables for its vibrant colors. When possible, search out whole-wheat couscous for higher fiber and protein content. The roasted carrots can also be served on their own as a side dish, tossed with fresh herbs and orange zest.

1 MEDIUM ONION, SLICED 1/4-INCH THICK

4 LARGE CARROTS, SLICED 1/4-INCH THICK ON THE BIAS

2 TABLESPOONS EXTRA-VIRGIN OLIVE OIL

2 CUPS PEARL COUSCOUS, REGULAR OR WHOLE WHEAT

2 1/2–3 CUPS "NO-SODIUM VEGETABLE STOCK" (SEE "SOUPS")

1/2 CUP DRIED CRANBERRIES

1/2 CUP CHOPPED PARSLEY

1/4 CUP "SHERRY VINAIGRETTE" (SEE "DRESSINGS & SPICE BLENDS")

1/8 TEASPOON KOSHER SALT AND FRESHLY GROUND BLACK PEPPER, TO TASTE

1. Heat the oven to 400°F. Place the onions and carrots on a baking sheet, toss with the olive oil, and season with 1/8 teaspoon of salt and freshly ground pepper. Roast the vegetables until tender and just starting to brown, about 20 minutes, stirring halfway through roasting.

2. Heat the couscous in medium saucepan over medium-high heat. Toast the couscous until golden brown and fragrant, stirring frequently, about 10 minutes. Check the package directions for the amount of liquid needed, which varies based on regular or whole-wheat variety. Add the vegetable stock and bring to a boil. Cover the pan with a lid, reduce the heat to low, and simmer until the stock is absorbed, 10 minutes.

3. Transfer the couscous to a large bowl. Add the onions, carrots, cranberries, parsley, and vinaigrette, season with pepper, and toss to combine. Serve warm or at room temperature.

NUTRITION SUMMARY & MODIFICATIONS: Low sodium. Medium potassium. Low phosphorus. To lower the potassium and phosphorus, use regular pearl couscous instead of whole wheat, omit the parsley and use only 2 carrots instead of 4.

continues ➡

ROASTED CARROTS, CRANBERRIES & COUSCOUS continued

~~~~~~~~~~~~ NUTRITION PROFILE ~~~~~~~~~~~~

YIELD: 6 servings

SERVING SIZE: 1 cup

CALORIES (KCAL): 386

PROTEIN (G): 8

CARBOHYDRATES (G): 64

TOTAL DIETARY FIBER (G): 6

TOTAL SUGARS (G): 13

ADDED SUGAR (G): 0

FAT (G): 11

SATURATED FAT (G): 2

CHOLESTEROL (MG): 0

CALCIUM (MG): 62

MAGNESIUM (MG): 40

PHOSPHORUS (MG): 135

POTASSIUM (MG): 422

SODIUM (MG): 131

~~~~~~~~ LOWER-POTASSIUM MODIFICATION NUTRITION PROFILE ~~~~~~~~

YIELD: 6 servings

SERVING SIZE: 1 cup

CALORIES (KCAL): 363

PROTEIN (G): 8

CARBOHYDRATES (G): 59

TOTAL DIETARY FIBER (G): 5

TOTAL SUGARS (G): 10

ADDED SUGAR (G): 5

FAT (G): 10

SATURATED FAT (G): 1

CHOLESTEROL (MG): 0

CALCIUM (MG): 42

MAGNESIUM (MG): 33

PHOSPHORUS (MG): 118

POTASSIUM (MG): 262

SODIUM (MG): 96

Pearl couscous, also known as Israeli couscous, is small balls of toasted semolina flour. Similar to pasta and made without eggs, pearl couscous has a nutty flavor, chewy texture, and requires boiling. Not to be confused with regular couscous, the tiny granules of semolina flour that are dried and prepared by steaming.

LEMON HERB COUSCOUS SALAD

MAKES 4 1-CUP SERVINGS

Inspired by traditional Israeli salads, fresh parsley and mint brightens the dish while the lemony dressing adds a nice tangy note. Toasting the couscous is optional, but I prefer the nuttiness that it adds.

1 CUP PEARL COUSCOUS

1 1/2 CUPS WATER

1 CUP PACKED FLAT LEAF PARSLEY, CHOPPED

1/4 CUP CHOPPED MINT

1 TABLESPOON CHOPPED CHIVES

1 MEDIUM CARROT, DICED

1/2 CUP CORN, FRESH, FROZEN OR LOW-SODIUM CANNED, COOKED, AND COOLED

1/4 CUP "LEMON SHALLOT VINAIGRETTE" (SEE "DRESSINGS & SPICE BLENDS")

1/2 CUP CRUMBLED FETA CHEESE

FRESHLY GROUND BLACK PEPPER, TO TASTE

1. Heat the couscous in a medium saucepan over medium-high heat. Toast the couscous until golden brown and fragrant, stirring frequently, about 10 minutes. Add the water and bring to a boil. Cover the pan with a lid, reduce heat to low, and simmer until water is absorbed, 10 minutes. Spread the cooked couscous on a baking sheet to cool.

2. Combine the couscous, parsley, mint, chives, carrot, and corn in a large bowl. Drizzle with lemon shallot vinaigrette, season with pepper, and toss to combine. Sprinkle with feta cheese and serve.

NUTRITION SUMMARY & MODIFICATIONS: Medium sodium. Low potassium. Medium phosphorus. To lower the potassium content, omit the parsley.

NUTRITION PROFILE

YIELD: 4

SERVING SIZE: 1 cup with lemon shallot vinaigrette

CALORIES (KCAL): 303

PROTEIN (G): 9

CARBOHYDRATES (G): 41

TOTAL DIETARY FIBER (G): 4

TOTAL SUGARS (G): 3

ADDED SUGAR (G): 0

FAT (G): 11

SATURATED FAT (G): 4

CHOLESTEROL (MG): 17

CALCIUM (MG): 139

MAGNESIUM (MG): 34

PHOSPHORUS (MG): 154

POTASSIUM (MG): 285

SODIUM (MG): 254

LOW-POTASSIUM MODIFICATION NUTRITION PROFILE

YIELD: 4

SERVING SIZE: 1 cup with lemon shallot vinaigrette

ANALYSIS PER SERVING

CALORIES (KCAL): 298

PROTEIN (G): 9

CARBOHYDRATES (G): 40

TOTAL DIETARY FIBER (G): 3

TOTAL SUGARS (G): 3

ADDED SUGAR (G): 0

FAT (G): 11

SATURATED FAT (G): 4

CHOLESTEROL (MG): 17

CALCIUM (MG): 118

MAGNESIUM (MG): 27

PHOSPHORUS (MG): 145

POTASSIUM (MG): 201

SODIUM (MG): 245

VEGETARIAN SUMMER PASTA SALAD

When adapting to new healthy eating habits, you are more likely to be successful by adjusting quantities rather than depriving yourself completely. For pasta salad recipes, use one part pasta to two parts vegetables. This increases fiber and nutrients and lowers carbohydrates. Boost the protein by adding baked chicken breast, grilled fish, or low-sodium beans. A general rule for low-potassium diets is to reduce the herbs and vegetables by half, serving one part pasta to one part vegetables.

1 POUND WHOLE-WHEAT ELBOW PASTA, OR NOODLE OF CHOICE

1 HEAD BROCCOLI, CUT INTO SMALL FLORETS

1 PINT CHERRY TOMATOES, HALVED

1 LARGE CARROT, DICED

1 YELLOW, RED, OR GREEN BELL PEPPER, CHOPPED

4 STALKS CELERY, CHOPPED

1/2 SMALL RED ONION, DICED

1/2 CUP CHOPPED FLAT LEAF PARSLEY

1/2 CUP CHOPPED BASIL

6 TBSP "RED WINE VINAIGRETTE" (SEE "DRESSINGS & SPICE BLENDS")

FRESHLY GROUND BLACK PEPPER, TO TASTE

PINCH OF SALT (OPTIONAL—NOT INCLUDED IN NUTRITION PROFILE)

1. Cook the pasta according to package directions, spread out on a baking sheet, and set aside to cool.

2. Prepare an ice bath in a large bowl. Bring a medium saucepan of water to boil, add the broccoli, and blanch for 2 minutes. Drain and place the broccoli in the ice bath to cool; once cooled, drain thoroughly.

3. Combine the pasta, broccoli, tomatoes, carrots, bell pepper, celery, red onion, parsley, and basil in a large bowl. Add the vinaigrette, season with salt and pepper, and toss gently to combine. Allow the salad to rest at least 30 minutes before serving to give the flavors time to meld. Serve at room temperature or chilled.

NUTRITION SUMMARY & MODIFICATIONS: Low sodium. High potassium. High phosphorus. For a low-potassium and low-phosphorus modification, use regular elbow pasta, leave out the broccoli, and use 1/2 the amount of celery, red onion, parsley, and basil. Keep one full pepper and one full carrot.

YIELD: 6 servings

SERVING SIZE: 2 cups

CALORIES (KCAL): 429

PROTEIN (G): 15

CARBOHYDRATES (G): 70

TOTAL DIETARY FIBER (G): 12

TOTAL SUGARS (G): 4

ADDED SUGAR (G): 0

FAT (G): 13

SATURATED FAT (G): 2

CHOLESTEROL (MG): 0

CALCIUM (MG): 125

MAGNESIUM (MG): 148

PHOSPHORUS (MG): 308

POTASSIUM (MG): 625

SODIUM (MG): 42

~~~ LOWER-POTASSIUM MODIFICATION NUTRITION PROFILE ~~~

YIELD: 6 servings

SERVING SIZE: 1 ½ cups

CALORIES (KCAL): 220

PROTEIN (G): 5

CARBOHYDRATES (G): 28

TOTAL DIETARY FIBER (G): 3

TOTAL SUGARS (G): 2

ADDED SUGAR (G): 0

FAT (G): 10

SATURATED FAT (G): 1

CHOLESTEROL (MG): 0

CALCIUM (MG): 49

MAGNESIUM (MG): 29

PHOSPHORUS (MG): 59

POTASSIUM (MG): 221

SODIUM (MG): 17

BALSAMIC ROASTED VEGETABLES

VEGETABLE SIDES

BROCCOLI-CAULIFLOWER MASH WITH ROASTED GARLIC..226

ROASTED GARLIC..227

SAUTEED BROCCOLINI & GARLIC...228

LEMONY CAULIFLOWER RICE...229

BALSAMIC ROASTED VEGETABLES...230

BABY BOK CHOY WITH GINGER & GARLIC..232

ROASTED BRUSSELS SPROUTS...233

MORE RECIPES

FIVE-MINUTE SPINACH
See Part I, "Step 5: Get Potassium Right."

BRAISED PURPLE CABBAGE
See Part I, "Step 5: Get Potassium Right."

SAUTEED RAINBOW CHARD & APPLES
See Part I, "Step 7: Discover Alkaline-Rich Foods."

BROCCOLI-CAULIFLOWER MASH WITH ROASTED GARLIC

MAKES 8 ½-CUP SERVINGS

If your household includes picky eaters who turn their little noses up at vegetables, try serving these low-carbohydrate "green mashed potatoes" in disguise.

1 MEDIUM HEAD CAULIFLOWER, CUT INTO FLORETS

1 MEDIUM HEAD BROCCOLI, CUT INTO FLORETS

3 CLOVES "ROASTED GARLIC"

1 TABLESPOON LEMON JUICE

2 TABLESPOONS OLIVE OIL

FRESHLY GROUND BLACK PEPPER, TO TASTE

1. Bring a large pot of water to a boil. Add the cauliflower and broccoli, cook until tender, 5 minutes. Drain and reserve ½ cup cooking liquid.

2. Place the cauliflower, broccoli, garlic, lemon juice, and oil in a food processor or blender and blend until smooth. Season with pepper. If needed, add a few tablespoons of cooking liquid at a time to adjust the consistency.

NUTRITION SUMMARY & MODIFICATIONS: Low sodium. Low potassium. Low phosphorus. Keep to a ½ cup serving size.

NUTRITION PROFILE

YIELD: 8 servings

SERVING SIZE: ½ cup

CALORIES (KCAL): 54

PROTEIN (G): 2

CARBOHYDRATES (G): 4

TOTAL DIETARY FIBER (G): 2

TOTAL SUGARS (G): 1

ADDED SUGAR (G): 0

FAT (G): 4

SATURATED FAT (G): 0

CHOLESTEROL (MG): 0

CALCIUM (MG): 26

MAGNESIUM (MG): 14

PHOSPHORUS (MG): 40

POTASSIUM (MG): 227

SODIUM (MG): 21

ROASTED GARLIC

Using just two ingredients, oven-roasted garlic goes through a complete transformation in no time—nothing short of culinary magic! Caramelized cloves lose their pungency as the flavor mellows, becoming slightly sweet with a soft, buttery texture. Keep a container on hand to add to dips, salad dressings, sautéed vegetables, sauces, or soups. Or my favorite way, still warm from the oven, spread on a sliced baguette or crackers.

1 WHOLE HEAD GARLIC

1 TEASPOON EXTRA-VIRGIN OLIVE OIL

1. Heat the oven to 400°F. Peel off any loose papery skin, leaving the garlic head whole. Slice off just enough of the top of the head to expose the cloves, about ¼-inch. Place the garlic on a piece of foil, drizzle the cut cloves with olive oil, and wrap with the foil to seal. Bake until tender, about 35–40 minutes depending on the size of the head. The center should be soft when pierced with a paring knife, and the cloves should be golden brown.

2. Remove the foil and set aside until cool enough to handle. Break apart the head of garlic cloves. To remove the roasted garlic, pinch the bottom of the clove until it pops out of the skin. Store refrigerated in an airtight container for up to 4 days or freeze for up to 3 months.

NUTRITION SUMMARY & MODIFICATIONS: Low sodium. Low potassium. Low phosphorus.

~ NUTRITION PROFILE ~

YIELD: 1 garlic head

SERVING SIZE: 1 garlic head

CALORIES (KCAL): 69

PROTEIN (G): 2

CARBOHYDRATES (G): 9

TOTAL DIETARY FIBER (G): 1

TOTAL SUGARS (G): 0

ADDED SUGAR (G): 0

FAT (G): 3

SATURATED FAT (G): 0

CHOLESTEROL (MG): 0

CALCIUM (MG): 51

MAGNESIUM (MG): 7

PHOSPHORUS (MG): 43

POTASSIUM (MG): 114

SODIUM (MG): 5

SAUTEED BROCCOLINI & GARLIC

MAKES 6 SERVINGS

A hybrid between broccoli and Chinese broccoli, broccolini sounds and looks similar to its counterpart but is pleasantly different and may win you over. Compared to regular broccoli, broccolini's bunches and florets are smaller and less compact with long, thin, edible stalks. The taste is more mellow and slightly sweeter.

1 POUND BROCCOLINI, ABOUT 2 BUNCHES

1/2 CUP WATER

2 TEASPOONS EXTRA-VIRGIN OLIVE OIL

2 CLOVES GARLIC, MINCED

ZEST OF 1/2 LEMON

FRESHLY GROUND BLACK PEPPER, TO TASTE

PINCH OF SALT (OPTIONAL—NOT INCLUDED IN NUTRITION PROFILE)

1. Trim the ends of the broccolini stalks ½-inch. Using a large nonstick sauté pan, bring the water to boil. Add the broccolini, cover, and steam 2 minutes. Drain any remaining water and return the pan to the medium-high heat.

2. Drizzle the broccolini with the oil and sauté 2 minutes. Add the garlic and sauté 1 minute. Sprinkle with lemon zest, season with salt and pepper, and toss to combine.

NUTRITION SUMMARY & MODIFICATIONS: Low sodium. Low potassium. Low phosphorus.

NUTRITION PROFILE

YIELD: 6 servings

SERVING SIZE: about ½ cup

CALORIES (KCAL): 31

PROTEIN (G): 2

CARBOHYDRATES (G): 3

TOTAL DIETARY FIBER (G): 1

TOTAL SUGARS (G): 1

ADDED SUGAR (G): 0

FAT (G): 2

SATURATED FAT (G): 0

CHOLESTEROL (MG): 0

CALCIUM (MG): 30

MAGNESIUM (MG): 15

PHOSPHORUS (MG): 41

POTASSIUM (MG): 196

SODIUM (MG): 16

LEMONY CAULIFLOWER RICE

This low-carbohydrate and reduced-calorie alternative to traditional white rice is a great choice for healthy eating plans and for diabetics in search of lower-carbohydrate recipes. Serve as a side dish or as a rice substitute by changing the spices and herbs to complement stir-fried vegetables, burritos, curry dishes, or casseroles. Cauliflower rice is also available frozen, but you will sacrifice flavor for the price for convenience.

1 HEAD CAULIFLOWER

1 TABLESPOON EXTRA-VIRGIN OLIVE OIL

2 SCALLIONS, SLICED

ZEST OF ONE LEMON

1 TABLESPOON LEMON JUICE

1/4 CUP PARSLEY, MINCED

FRESHLY GROUND BLACK PEPPER, TO TASTE

1. Cut the cauliflower head into quarters, trim the core and any green leaves. Using the medium hole of a box grater, grate the cauliflower into rice-size pieces. Alternatively, use a food processor with a grating disc attachment and cauliflower cut into florets.

2. Heat the oil in a large nonstick saucepan over medium heat. Add the cauliflower rice and stir to coat. Cover the pan and steam the cauliflower until tender, about 4 minutes. Add the scallions, lemon zest and juice, and parsley, season with pepper, and toss to combine.

NUTRITION SUMMARY & MODIFICATIONS: Low sodium. Medium potassium. Low phosphorus.

NUTRITION PROFILE

YIELD: 4 servings

SERVING SIZE: 1 cup

CALORIES (KCAL): 61

PROTEIN (G): 2

CARBOHYDRATES (G): 6

TOTAL DIETARY FIBER (G): 3

TOTAL SUGARS (G): 2

ADDED SUGAR (G): 0

FAT (G): 4

SATURATED FAT (G): 1

CHOLESTEROL (MG): 0

CALCIUM (MG): 37

MAGNESIUM (MG): 21

PHOSPHORUS (MG): 53

POTASSIUM (MG): 375

SODIUM (MG): 37

BALSAMIC ROASTED VEGETABLES

Once you learn to roast vegetables, you'll be able to create dozens of new recipes. The technique, with a few tweaks along the way, is transferable to almost any vegetable. Although this is one of my favorite combinations of veggies, I often just use whatever I have on hand. If made ahead of time, roasted vegetables can be added to cooked pasta or fresh salads or used in sandwiches and wraps. (Picture shown with added sliced turnip and black radish. They looked so good at the farmers market that I had to include them.)

2 DAIKON RADISHES, CUT INTO ½-INCH CUBES

2 CARROTS, PEELED, BIAS CUT INTO ½-INCH SLICES

1 LARGE HEAD BROCCOLI, CUT INTO SMALL FLORETS

1 TEASPOON AVOCADO OIL

1 TABLESPOON BALSAMIC VINEGAR, OR TO TASTE

FRESHLY GROUND BLACK PEPPER, TO TASTE

PINCH OF SALT (OPTIONAL—NOT INCLUDED IN NUTRITION PROFILE)

1. Preheat the oven to 400°F. Combine the vegetables, oil, salt, and pepper in a large bowl and toss to coat. Place the vegetables on a baking sheet in a single layer.

2. Roast the vegetables until tender when pierced with a paring knife, about 15–20 minutes, tossing halfway through roasting.

3. Drizzle with balsamic vinegar and serve.

NUTRITION SUMMARY & MODIFICATIONS: Low sodium. Low potassium. Low phosphorus. To create an even lower-potassium side dish, use lower-potassium vegetables such as eggplant, onion, and cabbage. Or, boil or soak your vegetables before roasting.

NUTRITION PROFILE

YIELD: 8 servings

ANALYSIS PER SERVING

CALORIES (KCAL): 24

PROTEIN (G): 1

CARBOHYDRATES (G): 4

TOTAL DIETARY FIBER (G): 1

TOTAL SUGARS (G): 2

ADDED SUGAR (G): 0

FAT (G): 1

SATURATED FAT (G): 0

CHOLESTEROL (MG): 0

CALCIUM (MG): 20

MAGNESIUM (MG): 10

PHOSPHORUS (MG): 26

POTASSIUM (MG): 213

SODIUM (MG): 117

BABY BOK CHOY WITH GINGER & GARLIC

Aromatic ginger, garlic, and sesame burst with flavor while minimizing the need for salt in this simple 10-minutes-to-table vegetable side dish that is sure to rival your neighborhood Asian restaurant. This bok choy recipe easily stands on its own or try pairing with ramen, grain bowls, or stir-fries. To toast sesame seeds, use a dry skillet over medium-high heat and stir frequently with a watchful eye, as they burn quickly. If you like a little heat, add a pinch of crushed red pepper flakes to the sesame oil.

1 POUND BABY BOK CHOY, ABOUT 4 SMALL HEADS OR 1 LARGE HEAD

2 TEASPOONS SESAME OIL

1 1-INCH PIECE FRESH GINGER ROOT, PEELED AND GRATED OR 1/2 TEASPOON POWDERED GINGER

2 CLOVES GARLIC, MINCED

2 TABLESPOONS VEGETABLE BROTH OR WATER

1 TEASPOON TOASTED SESAME SEEDS

1. Trim the ends of the bok choy. Cut small heads in half lengthwise. If using a large head, rough chop.

2. Heat the oil in a large nonstick sauté pan over medium-high heat. Add the bok choy, toss to coat, and sauté 2 minutes. Add the ginger and garlic and cook until fragrant, 30 seconds.

3. Add the broth or water, cover, and steam 2 minutes. Remove the lid and allow any remaining liquid to evaporate. Sprinkle with sesame seeds and serve.

NUTRITION SUMMARY & MODIFICATIONS: Low sodium. Low potassium. Low phosphorus.

Only 1 small head of bok choy is included in each serving.

NUTRITION PROFILE

YIELD: 4 servings	TOTAL SUGARS (G): 1	MAGNESIUM (MG): 20
ANALYSIS PER SERVING	ADDED SUGAR (G): 0	PHOSPHORUS (MG): 41
CALORIES (KCAL): 38	FAT (G): 3	POTASSIUM (MG): 239
PROTEIN (G): 2	SATURATED FAT (G): 0	SODIUM (MG): 60
CARBOHYDRATES (G): 3	CHOLESTEROL (MG): 0	
TOTAL DIETARY FIBER (G): 1	CALCIUM (MG): 99	

ROASTED BRUSSELS SPROUTS

This quick and easy brussels sprouts dish will make you forget about every bitter brussels sprouts dish you've had in the past. If you have extra time on your hands, you can peel off each individual leaf, or slice the brussels sprouts into small leaves for a salad. That's for a special occasion. If you don't have that kind of time, they can be roasted this way into a delicious and healthy side dish. Save any extras for a roasted veggie bowl or salad the next day.

1 POUND BRUSSELS SPROUTS

1 TABLESPOON EXTRA-VIRGIN OLIVE OIL

GRATED PARMESAN CHEESE, OPTIONAL

LEMON JUICE, OPTIONAL

FRESHLY GROUND BLACK PEPPER, TO TASTE

1. Preheat the oven to 400°F. Trim the brown ends of the brussels sprouts and remove any discolored outer leaves. Place the brussels sprouts on a baking sheet with oil, and pepper and toss to coat.

2. Roast until slightly browned and crispy, 15–20 minutes, shaking pan halfway through roasting. Or, leave them in for an additional 10 minutes for a very crispy version.

3. Sprinkle with parmesan cheese and drizzle with lemon juice, if desired.

NUTRITION SUMMARY & MODIFICATIONS: Low sodium. Medium potassium. Low phosphorus.

NUTRITION PROFILE

YIELD: 4 servings

SERVING SIZE: ¾ cup (4.25 ounces)

CALORIES (KCAL): 72

PROTEIN (G): 3

CARBOHYDRATES (G): 8

TOTAL DIETARY FIBER (G): 3

TOTAL SUGARS (G): 2

ADDED SUGAR (G): 0

FAT (G): 4

SATURATED FAT (G): 1

CHOLESTEROL (MG): 0

CALCIUM (MG): 42

MAGNESIUM (MG): 23

PHOSPHORUS (MG): 66

POTASSIUM (MG): 371

SODIUM (MG): 25

CHOCOLATE BARK

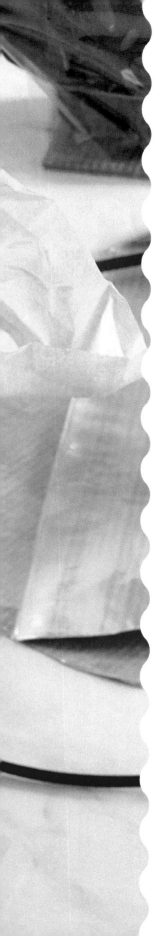

SWEETS

PEACH-RASPBERRY SKILLET BAKE 236

HEALTHIER RICE PUDDING 238

STEWED CINNAMON APPLES 239

ALMOND-PUMPKIN SEED CHOCOLATE BARK 240

PEACH-RASPBERRY SKILLET BAKE

The sweet smell of fresh fruit and cinnamon wafting through the kitchen makes this dessert hard to resist. And there's no reason to! This easy, low-fat recipe comes together quickly and provides a wholesome, satisfying solution for dessert cravings. Pick whatever fruit is in season at peak flavor to eliminate the need for excess added sugar. Plums, apricots, strawberries, blueberries, apples, or pears all work well. Frozen fruit can be used in a pinch; just give it a few minutes to thaw before baking.

1 LARGE PEACH, PITTED AND CHOPPED, ABOUT 1 ¼ CUPS

1 6-OUNCE CONTAINER RASPBERRIES, ABOUT 1 CUP

2 TABLESPOONS SUGAR, DIVIDED

1 ½ CUPS OLD-FASHIONED ROLLED OATS

1 TEASPOON GROUND CINNAMON

3 LARGE EGG WHITES

2 TEASPOONS VANILLA EXTRACT

3 CUPS OAT, RICE, OR 1% MILK

NO-SUGAR SORBET, FOR SERVING, OPTIONAL

1. Heat the oven to 350°F. Place the peaches and raspberries in the bottom of a 9-inch cast-iron skillet, deep-dish pie pan, or casserole dish. Sprinkle with 1 tablespoon sugar and toss to combine.

2. Combine the remaining tablespoon of sugar, oats, and cinnamon in a medium bowl and sprinkle evenly over the fruit.

3. Using the same bowl, whisk together the egg whites, vanilla, and milk and slowly pour over the oats. Bake until the oats are cooked and fruit is bubbling, about 45 minutes. Serve warm, topped with sorbet, if desired.

NUTRITION SUMMARY & MODIFICATIONS: Low sodium. Low potassium. Low phosphorus. Use rice milk for an even lower-phosphorus dessert.

NUTRITION PROFILE

YIELD: 8 servings

ANALYSIS PER SERVING

CALORIES (KCAL): 150

PROTEIN (G): 6

CARBOHYDRATES (G): 28

TOTAL DIETARY FIBER (G): 4

TOTAL SUGARS (G): 8

ADDED SUGAR (G): 3

FAT (G): 2

SATURATED FAT (G): 0

CHOLESTEROL (MG): 0

CALCIUM (MG): 26

MAGNESIUM (MG): 7

PHOSPHORUS (MG): 90

POTASSIUM (MG): 197

SODIUM (MG): 67

HEALTHIER RICE PUDDING

For centuries, cinnamon has been used for its perceived medicinal properties and health benefits. When it comes to sweet and savory foods, it's one of the most popular spices in cultures around the globe. For my lighter version of rice pudding, I use cinnamon sticks to infuse the milk while ground cinnamon adds additional flavor as a garnish. Replacing and eliminating traditional ingredients, such as cream and eggs, allows you to still satisfy sweet cravings and #ChangeYourBuds while reinforcing healthy eating habits.

1 CUP SHORT-GRAIN RICE, COOKED ACCORDING TO PACKAGE DIRECTIONS

4 CUPS OAT OR OTHER NON-DAIRY MILK

1 CINNAMON STICK

PEEL OF 1 LEMON

½ CUP RAISINS

3 TABLESPOONS HONEY

GROUND CINNAMON, FOR SERVING

1. Once the rice has finished cooking, add the milk, cinnamon stick, lemon peel, raisins, and honey and bring to a boil. Reduce the heat to low and simmer until the pudding develops a thick, creamy consistency, stirring occasionally to prevent sticking, about 15 minutes.

2. Remove from the heat, discard the lemon peel and cinnamon stick, set aside to rest 10 minutes. Divide pudding into individual serving bowls and refrigerate to chill. Sprinkle with cinnamon before serving.

NUTRITION SUMMARY & MODIFICATIONS: Low sodium. Low potassium. Low phosphorus.

NUTRITION PROFILE

YIELD: 4 servings	**TOTAL SUGARS (G):** 16	**MAGNESIUM (MG):** 10
ANALYSIS PER SERVING	**ADDED SUGAR (G):** 11	**PHOSPHORUS (MG):** 22
CALORIES (KCAL): 135	**FAT (G):** 1	**POTASSIUM (MG):** 126
PROTEIN (G): 2	**SATURATED FAT (G):** 0	**SODIUM (MG):** 62
CARBOHYDRATES (G): 30	**CHOLESTEROL (MG):** 0	
TOTAL DIETARY FIBER (G): 1	**CALCIUM (MG):** 191	

STEWED CINNAMON APPLES

This is the perfect fall recipe to put those extra apples from the orchard to use. Apples can add fiber to a diet without extra potassium, so this is the perfect dessert if you're on a strict low-potassium diet. The apples are also delicious for breakfast served over oatmeal, pancakes, waffles, or granola.

1 TABLESPOON VEGAN BUTTER

4 MEDIUM APPLES, PEELED, CORED, AND CUT INTO EIGHT WEDGES

1 TEASPOON GROUND CINNAMON

1/4 CUP OF WATER

GREEK OR FROZEN VANILLA YOGURT, FOR SERVING, OPTIONAL

1. Heat the butter in a large sauté pan over medium heat. Add the apples and cinnamon and stir to coat. Add the water and reduce the heat to a low simmer. Cook the apples until tender, 5–7 minutes.

2. Cool slightly and serve warm apples over Greek or frozen yogurt, if desired.

NUTRITION SUMMARY & MODIFICATIONS: This is a low-sodium, low-potassium, and low-phosphorus dessert.

NUTRITION PROFILE

YIELD: 4 servings

ANALYSIS PER SERVING

CALORIES (KCAL): 117

PROTEIN (G): 0.5

CARBOHYDRATES (G): 25

TOTAL DIETARY FIBER (G): 4

TOTAL SUGARS (G): 19

ADDED SUGAR (G): 0

FAT (G): 3

SATURATED FAT (G): 2

CHOLESTEROL (MG): 0

CALCIUM (MG): 12

MAGNESIUM (MG): 9

PHOSPHORUS (MG): 20

POTASSIUM (MG): 195

SODIUM (MG): 19

ALMOND-PUMPKIN SEED CHOCOLATE BARK

Try this delicious recipe as a healthy dessert option when you're craving something sweet and chocolate. This is also a great option for holiday gifts or to bring to an office potluck. If you want to keep it all to yourself, it freezes well and can be stored for up to 30 days in the freezer. Add dried cranberries (as pictured) or a little peppermint extract to change the flavor.

1 POUND DARK CHOCOLATE, CHOPPED

2 CUPS UNSALTED ALMONDS, TOASTED AND CHOPPED IF DESIRED

½ CUPS UNSALTED TOASTED PUMPKIN SEEDS

1. Line a 9 x 12-inch rimmed baking sheet with parchment paper, allowing paper to overhang ends a few inches, and set aside. Place the chocolate in a heatproof bowl over a pan of simmering water, stirring occasionally until melted. Use a candy or instant-read thermometer to keep chocolate below 100°F. Remove the chocolate from the heat and stir until the chocolate reaches 90°F.

2. Add half the almonds and pumpkin seeds (and cranberries if using) and stir to coat. Pour the chocolate mixture onto the prepared baking sheet. Spread evenly with a spatula and sprinkle with the remaining almonds and pumpkin seeds (and cranberries if using), gently pressing into the chocolate. Allow to set 10 minutes. If necessary, refrigerate until chocolate hardens.

3. Lift the ends of the parchment paper and place the bark on a cutting board. Cut the bark into 1-inch squares. Store in an airtight container in a cool place.

NUTRITION SUMMARY & MODIFICATIONS: Low sodium. Low potassium. Low phosphorus. If you keep with small servings and freeze the rest, the dessert can be part of a kidney-healthy diet.

NUTRITION PROFILE

YIELD: 26 servings

SERVING SIZE: 1 ounce

CALORIES (KCAL): 171

PROTEIN (G): 4

CARBOHYDRATES (G): 13

TOTAL DIETARY FIBER (G): 3

TOTAL SUGARS (G): 9

ADDED SUGAR (G): 0

FAT (G): 12

SATURATED FAT (G): 4

CHOLESTEROL (MG): 1

CALCIUM (MG): 39

MAGNESIUM (MG): 68

PHOSPHORUS (MG): 113

POTASSIUM (MG): 191

SODIUM (MG): 5

FROM LEFT TO RIGHT: BLUEBERRY VINAIGRETTE, RED WINE VINAIGRETTE, NO-SODIUM ALL-PURPOSE SEASONING, NO-SODIUM CAJUN SEASONING, AND LEMON SHALLOT VINAIGRETTE.

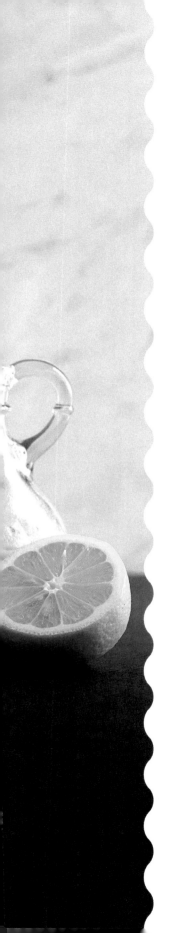

DRESSINGS & SPICE BLENDS

MEDITERRANEAN VINAIGRETTE 244

DIJON VINAIGRETTE 244

LEMON SHALLOT VINAIGRETTE 245

BALSAMIC VINAIGRETTE 245

BLUEBERRY VINAIGRETTE 246

RED WINE VINAIGRETTE 248

SHERRY VINAIGRETTE 248

CUMIN LIME VINAIGRETTE 249

NO-SODIUM ALL-PURPOSE SEASONING 250

NO-SODIUM CAJUN SEASONING 251

MEDITERRANEAN VINAIGRETTE

MAKES ABOUT ⅓ CUP

1 TABLESPOON LEMON JUICE

1 TABLESPOON RED WINE VINEGAR

1 TEASPOON SUMAC

3 TABLESPOONS EXTRA-VIRGIN OLIVE OIL

Whisk the lemon juice, vinegar, and sumac in a small bowl. Gradually whisk in the olive oil. Store refrigerated in glass jar.

NUTRITION SUMMARY & MODIFICATIONS: Low sodium, low potassium, and low phosphorus.

NUTRITION PROFILE

YIELD: ⅓ cup

SERVING SIZE: 1 Tablespoon

CALORIES (KCAL): 73

PROTEIN (G): 0

CARBOHYDRATES (G): 1

TOTAL DIETARY FIBER (G): 0

TOTAL SUGARS (G): 0

ADDED SUGAR (G): 0

FAT (G): 8

SATURATED FAT (G): 1

CHOLESTEROL (MG): 0

CALCIUM (MG): 0

MAGNESIUM (MG): 0

PHOSPHORUS (MG): 0

POTASSIUM (MG): 12

SODIUM (MG): 0

DIJON VINAIGRETTE

MAKES ¾ CUP

1 SMALL SHALLOT

3 TABLESPOONS LEMON JUICE

1 TABLESPOON RED WINE VINEGAR

1 TABLESPOON DIJON MUSTARD

½ CUP EXTRA-VIRGIN OLIVE OIL

FRESHLY GROUND BLACK PEPPER, TO TASTE

Using the small hole on a box grater, grate the shallot into a small bowl. Whisk in the lemon juice, vinegar, and mustard. Gradually whisk in the oil and season with pepper. Store refrigerated in a glass jar.

NUTRITION SUMMARY & MODIFICATIONS: Low sodium, low potassium, and low phosphorus.

NUTRITION PROFILE

YIELD: ¾ cup

SERVING SIZE: 1 Tablespoon

CALORIES (KCAL): 77

PROTEIN (G): 0

CARBOHYDRATES (G): 1

TOTAL DIETARY FIBER (G): 0

TOTAL SUGARS (G): 0

ADDED SUGAR (G): 0

FAT (G): 8

SATURATED FAT (G): 1

CHOLESTEROL (MG): 0

CALCIUM (MG): 1

MAGNESIUM (MG): 1

PHOSPHORUS (MG): 1

POTASSIUM (MG): 9 low potassium

SODIUM (MG): 28 low sodium

LEMON SHALLOT VINAIGRETTE

MAKES 1 CUP

1 SMALL SHALLOT

1/2 CUP LEMON JUICE, ABOUT 2 LARGE LEMONS

1 TABLESPOON DIJON MUSTARD

1/2 CUP EXTRA-VIRGIN OLIVE OIL

FRESHLY GROUND BLACK PEPPER, TO TASTE

Using the small holes on a box grater, grate the shallot into a small bowl. Whisk in the lemon juice and mustard. Gradually whisk in the oil and season with pepper. Store refrigerated in a glass jar.

NUTRITION SUMMARY & MODIFICATIONS: Low sodium, low potassium, and low phosphorus.

NUTRITION PROFILE

YIELD: 1 cup

SERVING SIZE: 1 Tablespoon

CALORIES (KCAL): 63

PROTEIN (G): 0

CARBOHYDRATES (G): 1

TOTAL DIETARY FIBER (G): 0

TOTAL SUGARS (G): 0

ADDED SUGAR (G): 0

FAT (G): 7

SATURATED FAT (G): 1

CHOLESTEROL (MG): 0

CALCIUM (MG): 1

MAGNESIUM (MG): 1

PHOSPHORUS (MG): 1

POTASSIUM (MG): 12

SODIUM (MG): 23

BALSAMIC VINAIGRETTE

MAKES ¾ CUP

2 TABLESPOONS BALSAMIC VINEGAR

2 TABLESPOONS RED WINE VINEGAR

1 SHALLOT, MINCED

1/2 CUP EXTRA-VIRGIN OLIVE OIL

FRESHLY GROUND BLACK PEPPER, TO TASTE

Whisk the vinegars and minced shallot together in a small bowl and let stand 10–15 minutes. Gradually whisk in the oil, season with pepper. Store refrigerated in a glass jar.

NUTRITION SUMMARY & MODIFICATIONS: Low sodium, low potassium, and low phosphorus.

NUTRITION PROFILE

YIELDS: about ¾ cup

SERVING SIZE: 1 Tablespoon

CALORIES (KCAL): 72

PROTEIN (G): 0

CARBOHYDRATES (G): 1

TOTAL DIETARY FIBER (G): 0

TOTAL SUGARS (G): 0

ADDED SUGAR (G): 0

FAT (G): 8

SATURATED FAT (G): 1

CHOLESTEROL (MG): 0

CALCIUM (MG): 1

MAGNESIUM (MG): 1

PHOSPHORUS (MG): 1

POTASSIUM (MG): 8

SODIUM (MG): 1

BLUEBERRY VINAIGRETTE

½ CUP BLUEBERRIES

½ CUP WHITE BALSAMIC VINEGAR OR WHITE WINE VINEGAR

1 TEASPOON DIJON MUSTARD

2 CLOVES GARLIC, SLICED

¾ CUP CANOLA OIL

FRESHLY GROUND BLACK PEPPER, TO TASTE

1. Combine the blueberries, vinegar, mustard, and garlic in a small saucepan and bring to a boil. Reduce to a simmer and cook until the blueberries are very tender, about 5 minutes.

2. Using an immersion or stand blender, purée until smooth. Slowly add the oil, blending until combined. Season with pepper. Transfer to a glass jar and refrigerate until needed.

NUTRITION SUMMARY & MODIFICATIONS: Low sodium, low potassium, and low phosphorus.

NUTRITION PROFILE

YIELD: about 1 ¾ cup

SERVING SIZE: 1 Tablespoon

CALORIES (KCAL): 55

PROTEIN (G): 0

CARBOHYDRATES (G): 1

TOTAL DIETARY FIBER (G): 0

TOTAL SUGARS (G): 0

ADDED SUGAR (G): 0

FAT (G): 6

SATURATED FAT (G): 0

CHOLESTEROL (MG): 0

CALCIUM (MG): 1

MAGNESIUM (MG): 0

PHOSPHORUS (MG): 1

POTASSIUM (MG): 3

SODIUM (MG): 2

RED WINE VINAIGRETTE

1 TEASPOON DRIED OREGANO

1 CLOVE GARLIC, PRESSED

¼ CUP RED WINE VINEGAR

½ CUP EXTRA-VIRGIN OLIVE OIL

FRESHLY GROUND BLACK PEPPER, TO TASTE

Whisk together the oregano, garlic, and vinegar. Gradually whisk in the olive oil until combined, season with pepper. Store refrigerated in a glass jar.

NUTRITION SUMMARY & MODIFICATIONS: Low sodium, low potassium, and low phosphorus.

— NUTRITION PROFILE —

YIELD: ¾ cup

SERVING SIZE: 1 Tablespoon

CALORIES (KCAL): 81

PROTEIN (G): 0

CARBOHYDRATES (G): 0

TOTAL DIETARY FIBER (G): 0

TOTAL SUGARS (G): 0

ADDED SUGAR (G): 0

FAT (G): 9

SATURATED FAT (G): 1

CHOLESTEROL (MG): 0

CALCIUM (MG): 2

MAGNESIUM (MG): 0

PHOSPHORUS (MG): 1

POTASSIUM (MG): 4

SODIUM (MG): 1

SHERRY VINAIGRETTE

2 TABLESPOONS SHERRY VINEGAR

¼ CUP LEMON JUICE

1 CLOVE GARLIC, PRESSED

⅓ CUP OLIVE OIL

FRESHLY GROUND BLACK PEPPER, TO TASTE

Whisk together the vinegar, lemon juice, and garlic. Slowly whisk in olive oil, season with pepper. Store refrigerated in a glass jar.

NUTRITION SUMMARY & MODIFICATIONS: Low sodium, low potassium, and low phosphorus.

— NUTRITION PROFILE —

YIELD: ⅔ cup

SERVING SIZE: 1 Tablespoon

CALORIES (KCAL): 73

PROTEIN (G): 0

CARBOHYDRATES (G): 0

TOTAL DIETARY FIBER (G): 0

TOTAL SUGARS (G): 0

ADDED SUGAR (G): 0

FAT (G): 8

SATURATED FAT (G): 1

CHOLESTEROL (MG): 0

CALCIUM (MG): 1

MAGNESIUM (MG): 1

PHOSPHORUS (MG): 1

POTASSIUM (MG): 8

SODIUM (MG): 1

CUMIN LIME VINAIGRETTE

1/4 CUP FRESH SQUEEZED LIME JUICE, ABOUT 2 LIMES

1/4 CUP RED WINE VINEGAR

1 CLOVE GARLIC, PRESSED

1 TABLESPOON HONEY

1 TEASPOON CUMIN

1/2 CUP EXTRA-VIRGIN OLIVE OIL

FRESHLY GROUND BLACK PEPPER, TO TASTE

Whisk together the lime juice, vinegar, garlic, honey, and cumin in a medium bowl. Slowly whisk in the olive oil, season with pepper. Store refrigerated in a glass jar.

NUTRITION SUMMARY & MODIFICATIONS: Low sodium, low potassium, and low phosphorus.

NUTRITION PROFILE

YIELD: 1 cup

SERVING SIZE: 1 Tablespoon

CALORIES (KCAL): 66

PROTEIN (G): 0

CARBOHYDRATES (G): 1

TOTAL DIETARY FIBER (G): 0

TOTAL SUGARS (G): 1

ADDED SUGAR (G): 1

FAT (G): 7

SATURATED FAT (G): 1

CHOLESTEROL (MG): 0

CALCIUM (MG): 2

MAGNESIUM (MG): 0

PHOSPHORUS (MG): 1

POTASSIUM (MG): 7

SODIUM (MG): 1

NO-SODIUM ALL-PURPOSE SEASONING

As the name suggests, this versatile blend goes with just about everything and is a must-have for spice cabinets. Use it to season a variety of foods from roasted vegetables to grilled meats, sautéed chicken, marinades, dressings, or dips.

2 TABLESPOONS PAPRIKA

1 TABLESPOON ONION POWDER

1 TABLESPOON GARLIC POWDER

1 TEASPOON BLACK PEPPER

1 TABLESPOON DRIED THYME

Combine ingredients and store in an airtight jar away from heat and light.

NUTRITION SUMMARY & MODIFICATIONS: Low sodium, low potassium, and low phosphorus.

~ NUTRITION PROFILE ~

YIELDS: About 5 Tablespoons

SERVING SIZE: 1 teaspoon

CALORIES (KCAL): 7

PROTEIN (G): 0

CARBOHYDRATES (G): 2

TOTAL DIETARY FIBER (G): 1

TOTAL SUGARS (G): 0

ADDED SUGAR (G): 0

FAT (G): 0

SATURATED FAT (G): 0

CHOLESTEROL (MG): 0

CALCIUM (MG): 9

MAGNESIUM (MG): 3

PHOSPHORUS (MG): 8

POTASSIUM (MG): 37

SODIUM (MG): 1

NO-SODIUM CAJUN SEASONING

MAKES ¼ CUP

Use this spice mix to add a flavorful kick to poultry, seafood, oven-roasted French fries, popcorn, or "Crispy Chickpeas" (see "Spreads, Snacks & Sauces"). Around the holidays, add a decorative spice jar, twine, and a hang tag for homemade gift giving.

1 TABLESPOON GARLIC POWDER
1 TABLESPOON ONION POWDER
2 TEASPOONS PAPRIKA
½ TEASPOON CAYENNE PEPPER
½ TEASPOON BLACK PEPPER
½ TEASPOON CHILE POWDER
¼ TEASPOON CELERY SEED

Combine ingredients and store in an airtight jar away from heat and light.

NUTRITION SUMMARY & MODIFICATIONS: Low sodium, low potassium, and low phosphorus.

NUTRITION PROFILE

YIELD: ¼ cup
SERVING SIZE: 1 teaspoon
CALORIES (KCAL): 7
PROTEIN (G): 0
CARBOHYDRATES (G): 1
TOTAL DIETARY FIBER (G): 0

TOTAL SUGARS (G): 0
ADDED SUGAR (G): 0
FAT (G): 0
SATURATED FAT (G): 0
CHOLESTEROL (MG): 0
CALCIUM (MG): 5

MAGNESIUM (MG): 3
PHOSPHORUS (MG): 7
POTASSIUM (MG): 29
SODIUM (MG): 5

ENDNOTES

1 Clark WF, Sontrop JM, Huang SH, et al. Effect of Coaching to Increase Water Intake on Kidney Function Decline in Adults With Chronic Kidney Disease: The CKD WIT Randomized Clinical Trial. *JAMA*. 2018;319(18):1870–1879. doi:10.1001/jama.2018.4930.

2 Rebholz CM, Young BA, Katz R, et al. Patterns of Beverages Consumed and Risk of Incident Kidney Disease. *Clin J Am Soc Nephrol*. 2019;14(1):49–56. doi:10.2215/CJN.06380518.

3 Rebholz CM, Grams ME, Steffen LM, et al. Diet Soda Consumption and Risk of Incident End Stage Renal Disease. *Clin J Am Soc Nephrol*. 2017;12(1):79–86. doi:10.2215/CJN.03390316.

4 Jhee JH, Nam KH, An SY, et al. Effects of Coffee Intake on Incident Chronic Kidney Disease: A Community-Based Prospective Cohort Study. *Am J Med*. 2018;131(12):1482–1490.e3. doi:10.1016/j.amjmed.2018.05.021.

5 Wijarnpreecha K, Thongprayoon C, Thamcharoen N, Panjawatanan P, Cheungpasitporn W. Association of coffee consumption and chronic kidney disease: A meta-analysis. *Int J Clin Pract*. 2017;71(1):10.1111/ijcp.12919. doi:10.1111/ijcp.12919.

6 Lew QJ, Jafar TH, Jin A, Yuan JM, Koh WP. Consumption of Coffee but Not of Other Caffeine-Containing Beverages Reduces the Risk of End-Stage Renal Disease in the Singapore Chinese Health Study. *J Nutr*. 2018;148(8):1315–1322. doi:10.1093/jn/nxy075.

7 One beer contains 100 to 300 calories per drink.

8 Fan AZ, Li Y, Elam-Evans LD, Balluz L. Drinking pattern and blood pressure among non-hypertensive current drinkers: findings from 1999–2004 National Health and Nutrition Examination Survey. *Clin Epidemiol*. 2013;5:21–27. doi:10.2147/CLEP.S12152.

9 He FJ, MacGregor GA. Reducing population salt intake worldwide: from evidence to implementation. *Prog Cardiovasc Dis* 2010; 52:363.

10 Aburto NJ, Hanson S, Gutierrez H, Hooper L, Elliott P, Cappuccio FP. Effect of increased potassium intake on cardiovascular risk factors and disease: systematic review and meta-analyses. *BMJ*. 2013;346:f1378. Published 2013 Apr 3. doi:10.1136/bmj.f1378.

11 Rosique-Esteban N, Guasch-Ferré M, Hernández-Alonso P, Salas-Salvadó J. Dietary Magnesium and Cardiovascular Disease: A Review with Emphasis in Epidemiological Studies. *Nutrients*. 2018;10(2):168. Published 2018 Feb 1. doi:10.3390/nu10020168.

12 Rebholz CM, Tin A, Liu Y, et al. Dietary Magnesium and Kidney Function Decline: The Healthy Aging in Neighborhoods of Diversity across the Life Span Study. *Am J Nephrol*. 2016;44(5):381–387. doi:10.1159/000450861.

13 Ascherio A, Rimm EB, Giovannucci EL, et al. A prospective study of nutritional factors and hypertension among US men. *Circulation*. 1992;86(5):1475–1484. doi:10.1161/01.cir.86.5.1475; Joosten MM, Gansevoort RT, Mukamal KJ, et al. Urinary magnesium excretion and risk of hypertension: the prevention of renal and vascular end-stage disease study. *Hypertension*. 2013;61(6):1161–1167. doi:10.1161/HYPERTENSIONAHA.113.01333; Kass L, Weekes J, Carpenter L. Effect of magnesium supplementation on blood pressure: a meta-analysis. *Eur J Clin Nutr*. 2012;66(4):411–418. doi:10.1038/ejcn.2012.4.

14 Rodríguez-Morán M, Simental-Mendía LE, Gamboa-Gómez CI, Guerrero-Romero F. Oral Magnesium Supplementation and Metabolic Syndrome: A Randomized Double-Blind Placebo-Controlled Clinical Trial. *Adv Chronic Kidney Dis*. 2018;25(3):261–266. doi:10.1053/j.ackd.2018.02.011.

15 Oliveira B, Cunningham J, Walsh SB. Magnesium Balance in Chronic and End-Stage Kidney Disease. *Adv Chronic Kidney Dis*. 2018;25(3):291–295. doi:10.1053/j.ackd.2018.01.004.

16 De Santo NG, Anastasio P, Spitali L, Santoro D, Capodicasa D, Cirillo E, Capasso G. Renal reserve is normal in adults born with unilateral renal agenesis and is not related to hyperfiltration or renal failure. *Miner Electrolyte Metab*. 1997;23(3–6):283–6.

17 Hostetter TH, Meyer TW, Rennke HG, Brenner BM. Chronic effects of dietary protein in the rat with intact and reduced renal mass. *Kidney Int*. 1986 Oct;30(4):509–17.

18 Tovar-Palacio C, Tovar AR, Torres N, Cruz C, Hernández-Pando R, Salas-Garrido G, Pedraza-Chaverri J, Correa-Rotter R. Proinflammatory gene expression and renal lipogenesis are modulated by dietary protein content in obese Zucker fa/fa rats. *Am J Physiol Renal Physiol*. 2011 Jan;300(1):F263–71.

19 Kalantar-Zadeh K, Fouque D. Nutritional Management of Chronic Kidney Disease. *N Engl J Med*. 2018 Feb 8;378(6):584–585.

20 Lew QJ, Jafar TH, Koh HW, Jin A, Chow KY, Yuan JM, Koh WP. Red Meat Intake and Risk of ESRD. *J Am Soc Nephrol*. 2017 Jan;28(1):304–312.

21 Sebastian A, Frassetto LA, Sellmeyer DE, Merriam RL, Morris RC Jr. Estimation of the net acid load of the diet of ancestral preagricultural Homo sapiens and their hominid ancestors. *Am J Clin Nutr*. 2002 Dec;76(6):1308–1.

22 Fulladosa X, Moreso F, Narváez JA, Grinyó JM, Serón D. Estimation of total glomerular number in stable renal transplants. *J Am Soc Nephrol*. 2003;14(10):2662–2668. doi:10.1097/01.asn.0000088025.33462.b0.

23 Tan JC, Busque S, Workeneh B, Ho B, Derby G, Blouch KL, Sommer FG, Edwards B, Myers BD. Effects of aging on glomerular function and number in living kidney donors. *Kidney Int*. 2010 Oct;78(7):686–92.

24 Tan JC, Workeneh B, Busque S, Blouch K, Derby G, Myers BD. Glomerular function, structure, and number in renal allografts from older deceased donors. *J Am Soc Nephrol*. 2009 Jan;20(1):181–8.

25 Passey C. Reducing the Dietary Acid Load: How a More Alkaline Diet Benefits Patients with Chronic Kidney Disease. *J Ren Nutr*. 2017 May;27(3):151–160.

26 Banerjee T, Crews DC, Wesson DE, Tilea AM, Saran R, Ríos-Burrows N, Williams DE, Powe NR; Centers for Disease Control and Prevention Chronic Kidney Disease Surveillance Team. High Dietary Acid Load Predicts ESRD among Adults with CKD. *J Am Soc Nephrol*. 2015 Jul;26(7):1693–700.

27 Goraya N, Simoni J, Jo CH, Wesson DE. A comparison of treating metabolic acidosis in CKD stage 4 hypertensive kidney disease with fruits and vegetables or sodium bicarbonate. *Clin J Am Soc Nephrol*. 2013 Mar;8(3):371–81.

28 Mancini FR, Affret A, Dow C, Balkau B, Clavel-Chapelon F, Bonnet F, Boutron-Ruault MC, Fagherazzi G. High dietary phosphorus intake is associated with an increased risk of type 2 diabetes in the large prospective E3N cohort study. *Clin Nutr.* 2018 Oct;37(5):1625–1630.

29 Chang AR, Lazo M, Appel LJ, Gutiérrez OM, Grams ME. High dietary phosphorus intake is associated with all-cause mortality: results from NHANES III. *Am J Clin Nutr.* 2014 Feb;99(2):320–7. doi: 10.3945/ajcn.113.073148. Epub 2013 Nov 13. Erratum in: *Am J Clin Nutr.* 2017 Apr;105(4):1021.

30 Gutiérrez OM. The connection between dietary phosphorus, cardiovascular disease, and mortality: where we stand and what we need to know. *Adv Nutr.* 2013;4(6):723–729. Published 2013 Nov 6. doi:10.3945/an.113.004812.

31 Fissell RB, Karaboyas A, Bieber BA, Sen A, Li Y, Lopes AA, Akiba T, Bommer J, Ethier J, Jadoul M, Pisoni RL, Robinson BM, Tentori F. Phosphate binder pill burden, patient-reported non-adherence, and mineral bone disorder markers: Findings from the DOPPS. *Hemodial Int.* 2016 Jan;20(1):38–49.

32 Clegg DJ, Hill Gallant KM. Plant-Based Diets in CKD. *Clin J Am Soc Nephrol.* 2019;14(1):141–143. doi:10.2215/CJN.08960718.

33 St-Jules DE, Jagannathan R, Gutekunst L, Kalantar-Zadeh K, Sevick MA. Examining the Proportion of Dietary Phosphorus from Plants, Animals, and Food Additives Excreted in Urine. *J Ren Nutr.* 2017 Mar;27(2):78–8.

34 Sacks FM, Svetkey LP, Vollmer WM, Appel LJ, Bray GA, Harsha D, Obarzanek E, Conlin PR, Miller ER 3rd, Simons-Morton DG, Karanja N, Lin PH; DASH-Sodium Collaborative Research Group. Effects on blood pressure of reduced dietary sodium and the Dietary Approaches to Stop Hypertension (DASH) diet. DASH-Sodium Collaborative Research Group. *N Engl J Med.* 2001 Jan 4;344(1):3–10.

35 Bray GA, Vollmer WM, Sacks FM, Obarzanek E, Svetkey LP, Appel LJ; DASH Collaborative Research Group. A further subgroup analysis of the effects of the DASH diet and three dietary sodium levels on blood pressure: results of the DASH-Sodium Trial. *Am J Cardiol.* 2004 Jul 15;94(2):222–7.

36 Juraschek SP, Miller ER 3rd, Weaver CM, Appel LJ. Effects of Sodium Reduction and the DASH Diet in Relation to Baseline Blood Pressure. *J Am Coll Cardiol.* 2017 Dec 12;70(23):2841–2848.

37 Gomes-Neto AW, Osté MCJ, Sotomayor CG, et al. Mediterranean Style Diet and Kidney Function Loss in Kidney Transplant Recipients. *Clin J Am Soc Nephrol.* 2020;15(2):238–246. doi:10.2215/CJN.06710619.

ACKNOWLEDGMENTS

I am grateful for all the help and support I have had in completing this book. Through the process, I have made connections with some of the most intelligent and competent people I have ever met—and their contributions to this book have been invaluable. First, thanks to my family. My wife and best friend, Michele, for helping me hone my ideas and for giving me the space to write this book in addition to my full-time, busy doctor job. My daughter, Lilly, the most sophisticated 13-year-old food critic around. If she approved of the recipes, you will too. My mom, Lisa, for being the first reader of the book and telling me that I was headed in the right direction. My pop, Alan, for recipe inspiration, cooking techniques, and book editing. Also, thanks to my trio of dietitians. Melanie Betz, MS, RD, for guidance on specific guidelines, recipes, and editing. Lori Huang, RDN, LDN, for her suggestions and friendship. And to Sandra Frank, EdD, RDN, FAND, for helping me compile the nutrition profiles and for putting up with my repeated revisions and recipe changes. I want to thank my first professional editor, Perrin Davis, for her edits and guidance. Thanks to Claire Perez, my recipe tester and food stylist, for elevating the recipes to expert level and giving me the confidence to publish them. I'm also grateful to Dan and Danielle Foster from Scribe Tribe Book Production Services for their outstanding editing and design work, and for getting me to the finish line. Finally, thanks to all the people with kidney disease who I have cared for over the years. Your resilience motivates me every day.

RECIPE INDEX

A

Almond-Pumpkin Seed Chocolate Bark, 240

Avocado Lime Crema, 155

Avocado Toast with Chile Flakes, 165

B

Baby Bok Choy with Ginger & Garlic, 232

Baked Chicken Breasts, 194–195

Balsamic Roasted Vegetables, 224, 230

Balsamic Vinaigrette, 245

Berry-Banana Hemp Smoothie, 40, 131

Blueberry Vinaigrette, 242, 246

Braised Purple Cabbage, 78

Broccoli-Cauliflower Mash with Roasted Garlic, 226

Butter Bean Dip, 153

C

Chicken, Kale & Farro Casserole, 214–215

Chicken Farro Bowls, 187–188

Corn & Black Bean Quesadilla, 170–171

Cranberry, Pepita & Broccoli Salad, 175

Creole Chicken Burgers, 189

Crispy Chickpeas, 142, 146

Cumin Lime Vinaigrette, 249

Curried Sweet Potatoes & Chickpeas, 173–174

D

Deviled Eggs with Pickled Red Onion, 142, 144

Dijon Vinaigrette, 244

E

Edamame Dip, 152

Egg Muffins with Spinach & Artichoke Hearts, 156, 162

F

Five-Minute Spinach, 73

G

Grandma Julie's Chicken Soup, 137

H

Healthier Rice Pudding, 238

Hearty Lentil Vegetable Soup, 132, 139–140

K

Kale & Golden Raisin Salad, 94–95

L

Leek & Yellow Squash Soup, 141

Lemon Caper Roasted Salmon, 198–199

Lemon Herb Couscous Salad, 221

Lemon Shallot Vinaigrette, 242, 245

Lemony Cauliflower Rice, 229

Light Macaroni & Cheese with Peas, 212

M

Maple Cinnamon Chia Pudding, 158–159

Mediterranean Chopped Salad, 178–179

Mediterranean Vinaigrette, 244

N

No-Sodium All-Purpose Seasoning, 242, 250

No-Sodium Cajun Seasoning, 242, 251

No-Sodium Chicken Stock, 134–135

No-Sodium Vegetable Stock, 136

P

Peach-Raspberry Skillet Bake, 236

Pumpkin Pie Smoothie, 41, 131

Q

Quick Pickled Red Onions, 145

R

Red Wine Vinaigrette, 242, 248

Roasted Beet, Goat Cheese & Walnut Salad with Blueberry Vinaigrette, 114–117

Roasted Brussels Sprouts, 233

Roasted Carrots, Cranberries & Couscous, 208, 219–220

Roasted Garlic, 227

Roasted Red Pepper & White Bean Hummus, 149

Roasted Sweet Potatoes, 66

Roasted Tomato & Zucchini Spaghetti with Vegan Basil-Cashew Pesto, 216–217

S

Salmon Burger, 205

Salsa Fresca, 142, 150

Sautéed Broccolini & Garlic, 228

Sautéed Rainbow Chard & Apples, 97–98

Seared Cajun Chicken Thighs, 193

Seared Salmon with Tzatziki Sauce,
      196, 203–204

Sheet Pan Lemon-Lime Chicken & Potatoes,
      182–184

Sherry Vinaigrette, 248

Slow-Cooked Steel-Cut Oats, 160

Smoky Eggplant Spread, 142, 148

Southwest Quinoa Salad, 210–211

Spiced Apricot Walnut Muffins, 161

Spiced Chicken, Orange & Avocado Salad,
      180, 191–192

Stewed Cinnamon Apples, 239

Stuffed Zucchini Boats, 166, 168–169

Sunflower Butter & Blueberry Toast, 164

Sweet Tea Substitute, 33

T

Thai Shrimp Salad, 206–207

Tuna, Cannellini & Dill Salad, 200–201

Tzatziki Sauce, 154

V

Vegan Bolognese Sauce, 176–177

Vegetarian Summer Pasta Salad, 222–223

Z

Za'atar Chicken Salad, 185

INDEX

A

ACE (angiotensin-converting-enzyme) inhibitors, 93

acid

and alkaline numbers, 91

pH measurement, 90

processing by kidneys, 92–93

ADPKD (autosomal dominant polycystic kidney disease), 24. See also CKD (chronic kidney disease)

albuminuria, explained, 20

alcohol, 38–39

alkaline-rich foods

examples of, 68, 91

science of, 90

almond milk

Berry-Banana Hemp Smoothie, 40

Pumpkin Pie Smoothie, 41

almonds, Almond-Pumpkin Seed Chocolate Bark, 240

The American Association of Kidney Patients, 125

American Kidney Fund's Kidney Kitchen, 125

anemia, developing, 19

animal protein, eating less of, 85. See also protein

apples

Sautéed Rainbow Chard & Apples, 97–98

Stewed Cinnamon Apples, 239

apricots, Spiced Apricot Walnut Muffins, 161

ARBs (angiotensin-receptor blockers), 93

aromatics, using to enhance flavor, 184, 232

artichoke hearts, Egg Muffins with Spinach & Artichoke Hearts, 162

arugula, Roasted Beet, Goat Cheese & Walnut Salad with Blueberry Vinaigrette, 116–117

ATP (adenosine triphosphate), 80

autosomal dominant polycystic kidney disease, potassium considerations, 68. See also polycystic kidney disease

avocados

Avocado Lime Crema, 155

Avocado Toast with Chile Flakes, 165

ripening and storing, 192

Spiced Chicken, Orange & Avocado Salad, 191–192

B

bacon, sodium content, 58

bananas, Berry-Banana Hemp Smoothie, 40

basil, Roasted Beet, Goat Cheese & Walnut Salad with Blueberry Vinaigrette, 216–217

beets, Roasted Beet, Goat Cheese & Walnut Salad with Blueberry Vinaigrette, 114–116

beverages

no-sugar options, 34–35

recommendations, 131

schedule, 42

sugar free, 34–35

black beans, Corn & Black Bean Quesadilla, 170–171

blood acid level, 90

blood pressure. *See* high blood pressure

blueberries

Blueberry Vinaigrette, 246

Roasted Beet, Goat Cheese & Walnut Salad with Blueberry Vinaigrette, 116–117

Sunflower Butter & Blueberry Toast, 164

bok choy, Baby Bok Choy with Ginger & Garlic, 232

Bolognese sauce, vegan, 176–177

bottled salad dressings, sodium content, 59

bowls, Chicken Farro Bowls, 187–188

broccoli

amount of protein in, 84

Broccoli-Cauliflower Mash with Roasted Garlic, 226

Cranberry, Pepita & Broccoli Salad, 175

broccolini, Sautéed Broccolini & Garlic, 228

brussels sprouts, Roasted Brussels Sprouts, 233

burgers

Creole Chicken Burgers, 189

Salmon Burger, 205

butter beans, Butter Bean Dip, 153

C

cabbage, Braised Purple Cabbage, 78

Cajun seasoning

No-Sodium Cajun Seasoning, 251

Seared Cajun Chicken Thighs, 193

canned soups, sodium content, 57. *See also* soups; stocks

canned vegetables, sodium content, 58–59. *See also* vegetables

cannellini beans, Tuna, Cannellini & Dill Salad, 200–201

carbohydrates. *See* low-carbohydrate foods

carbonated waters, 29

carrots, Roasted Carrots, Cranberries & Couscous, 208, 219–220

cashews, Roasted Beet, Goat Cheese & Walnut Salad with Blueberry Vinaigrette, 216–217 casserole, Chicken, Kale & Farro Casserole, 214–215

cauliflower

Broccoli-Cauliflower Mash with Roasted Garlic, 226

Lemony Cauliflower Rice, 229

Change Your Buds philosophy, 5–6

#ChangeYourBuds

alternative waters, 28

high-magnesium foods, 80

lowering sodium, 11, 49–51

lower-sugar smoothies, 40

cheddar cheese, amount of protein in, 84

cheeses. *See also* goat cheese

choosing, 87

phosphorous levels of, 105

chia seeds

Berry-Banana Hemp Smoothie, 40

Maple Cinnamon Chia Pudding, 158–159

Pumpkin Pie Smoothie, 41

chicken

Baked Chicken Breasts, 194

Chicken, Kale & Farro Casserole, 214–215

Chicken Farrow Bowls, 187–188

Creole Chicken Burgers, 189

demystifying labels, 195

Seared Cajun Chicken Thighs, 193

Sheet Pan Lemon-Lime Chicken & Potatoes, 182–184

Spiced Chicken, Orange & Avocado Salad, 180, 191–192

chicken breast, amount of protein in, 84

chicken soup, 137

chicken stock, 134–135. *See also* soups; stocks

chickpeas

Crispy Chickpeas, 142, 146

Curried Sweet Potatoes & Chickpeas, 173–174

Roasted Red Pepper & White Bean Hummus, 149

as source of protein, 146

chiffonade, defined, 169

chile flakes, Avocado Toast with Chile Flakes, 165

chips, sodium content, 59

chocolate, phosphorous level of, 105

chocolate bark, Almond-Pumpkin Seed Chocolate Bark, 234, 240

cinnamon

Maple Cinnamon Chia Pudding, 158–159

Stewed Cinnamon Apples, 239

citrus, Sheet Pan Lemon-Lime Chicken & Potatoes, 182–184

CKD (chronic kidney disease), stages of, 21–22. *See also* ADPKD (autosomal dominant polycystic kidney disease)

coffee, 37–38

colds, treating with chicken soup, 137

congestion, easing with chicken soup, 137

cooking, time required and science of, 204

The Cooking Doc®, 4, 6–7

couscous

Lemon Herb Couscous Salad, 221

Roasted Carrots, Cranberries & Couscous, 208, 219–220

Cracker Barrel, sodium content, 53

cranberries, Roasted Carrots, Cranberries & Couscous, 208, 219–220

cranberry juice, 26, 31, 36

creatinine, 18

cucumber-lemon-mint water, 29

D

dairy and milk products, 36–37

DASH (Dietary Approaches to Stop Hypertension) diet, 108–111

DaVita, recipes from, 125

dehydration, causes of, 27

deli meats, sodium content, 57, 194

diabetes

basics of, 118

and heart health, 112–113

dialysis. *See also* hemodialysis; peritoneal dialysis

dietary requirements, 124–125

meeting with dieticians, 125–126

performance of, 19

and protein intake, 88

diet, impact on kidney function, 19

diet diary, keeping for sodium, 52

diet drinks, 36

dieticians, benefits of, 12, 125–126

dips

Butter Bean Dip, 153

Edamame Dip, 152

diuretics, 93

doctors, obtaining numbers from, 23

E

edamame, Edamame Dip, 152

eGFR (estimated glomerular filtration rate), 19, 21

eggplant, Smoky Eggplant Spread, 148

eggs

amount of protein in, 84

Deviled Eggs with Pickled Red Onion, 142, 144

Egg Muffins with Spinach & Artichoke Hearts, 156, 162

electrolyte balance, explained, 19–20

enzyme reactions, relationship to magnesium, 80

erythropoietin, 19

exercise, benefits of, 12–13

expectations, setting, 10–11

F

farro

Chicken Farro Bowls, 187–188

Chicken, Kale & Farro Casserole, 214–215

fast food, sodium content, 58

fiber, Slow-Cooked Steel-Cut Oats, 160

filtration, process of, 19

fish, limiting consumption of, 86

flavor, creating without salt, 50–51, 184

flavored waters, 29

fluid intake, 24

food log, keeping when on dialysis, 125

foods

    components of, 118

    preparing, 54

    taking inventory of, 54–55

freezer bags, using to store vegetable scraps, 135

frozen vegetables, choosing, 59

fruit juices, 29, 42,

fruits, low-potassium content, 77

G

garbanzo beans. See chickpeas

garlic

    Baby Bok Choy with Ginger & Garlic, 232

    Broccoli-Cauliflower Mash with Roasted
      Garlic, 226

    Roasted Garlic, 227

    Sautéed Broccolini & Garlic, 228

ginger

    Baby Bok Choy with Ginger & Garlic, 232

    Grandma Julie's Chicken Soup, 137

glomeruli, defined, 18–19, 92

goat cheese. See also cheeses

    Roasted Beet, Goat Cheese & Walnut Salad
      with Blueberry Vinaigrette, 116

grains. See whole grains

Greek yogurt, Berry-Banana Hemp Smoothie, 40

greens, slicing, 169

H

heart health

    considerations, 121

    and diabetes, 112–113

hemodialysis, potassium considerations, 125.
    See also dialysis

hemp, Berry-Banana Hemp Smoothie, 40

herbs

    extending life of, 207

    using to enhance flavor, 184

high blood pressure

    and diet, 109–111

    lowering with foods, 112

    overview, 108

high-potassium foods. See also low-potassium
    fruits and vegetables; potassium

    adjusting ingredients for, 130

    examples of, 71

homeostasis, maintaining, 21

hormones, production by kidneys, 19

hot dogs, sodium content, 58

hummus, Roasted Red Pepper & White Bean Hummus, 149

hydration of kidneys, 27–28

hyperglycemia, 118

hyperkalemia, 93

I

ice, Berry-Banana Hemp Smoothie, 40

insulin and diabetes, 118

intoxication, impact on kidneys, 19

J

juice, cranberry, 26, 31, 36

K

kale, Chicken, Kale & Farro Casserole, 214–215

kidney cleanses, 42

kidney diet, fundamentals of, 11–12

kidney disease. *See also* single kidney

  causes of, 22

  lack of symptoms, 19, 23

  risk factors, 2, 21

  screening for, 21

  statistic, 20, 30

kidney function

  and dialysis, 125

  and disease, 18–23

  quantifying, 21

kidney stones, 42

kidney transplant, potassium considerations, 70

kidneys

  location and size of, 20

  transplanting, 21

kitchen, stocking based on sodium content, 55–56

L

leafy greens, slicing, 169

leeks, Leak & Yellow Squash Soup, 141

lemon, Lemon Herb Couscous Salad, 221

lemon water, 29

lentils

  amount of protein in, 84

  Hearty Lentil Vegetable Soup, 132, 139–140

low-carbohydrate foods, 119

low-phosphorous diet, following, 103–105. *See also* phosphorous

low-potassium fruits and vegetables, 74, 77. *See also* high-potassium foods; potassium

low-protein diet, following, 87

low-sodium foods, substituting, 66. *See also* salt; sodium

M

macaroni & cheese, Light Macaroni & Cheese with Peas, 212

magnesium, importance of, 79–80

McDonald's, sodium content, 53

meal prep, setting aside time for, 66

meat
    limiting consumption of, 86
    substituting with vegetables, 87

medications, effect on kidneys, 20

Mediterranean diet, 108–111

milk and dairy products, 36–37. *See also*
    whole milk

muffins
    Egg Muffins with Spinach & Artichoke
        Hearts, 162
    Spiced Apricot Walnut Muffins, 161

N

nephrologists, defined, 20

nephrology, defined, 1

nephrons, defined, 20

nephrosclerosis, explained, 20

numbers, obtaining from doctors, 23

Nutrition Facts label, looking at, 52

O

oatmeal, Slow-Cooked Steel-Cut Oats, 160

Olive Garden, sodium content, 53

onions
    Deviled Eggs with Pickled Red Onion, 144
    Quick Pickled Red Onions, 145

orange water, 29

oranges
    Berry-Banana Hemp Smoothie, 40
    Pumpkin Pie Smoothie, 41
    Spiced Chicken, Orange & Avocado Salad,
        191–192

P

pans, preheating, 193

pasta salad, Vegetarian Summer Pasta Salad,
    222–223

peach and raspberry water, 29

peaches, Peach-Raspberry Skillet Bake, 236

peanut butter, amount of protein in, 84

pears, Spiced Chicken, Orange & Avocado
    Salad, 192

peas, Light Macaroni & Cheese with Peas, 212

pepitas, Cranberry, Pepita & Broccoli Salad, 175

peppers, using to enhance flavor, 184

peritoneal dialysis, potassium considerations, 70.
    See also dialysis

pesto, Roasted Tomato & Zucchini Spaghetti
    with Vegan Basil-Cashew Pesto, 216–217

pH scale, 90

phosphorus. *See also* low-phosphorous diet
    amounts in recipes, 130–131
    overview, 100–103
    regulation by kidneys, 20

pickled foods
  Deviled Eggs with Pickled Red Onion, 144
  Quick Pickled Red Onions, 145
pizza, sodium content, 57
plant-based eating
  embracing, 62–65
  Roasted Sweet Potatoes, 66
polycystic kidney disease, 42. *See also* autosomal dominant polycystic kidney disease
pork, limiting consumption of, 86
potassium. *See also* high-potassium foods; low-potassium fruits and vegetables
  amounts in recipes, 130
  CKD Stages 4 and 5 dialysis, 75–76
  daily dietary amounts, 70
  foods high in, 56
  and high blood pressure, 109
  increasing intake of, 72
  pros and cons, 68–69
  Pumpkin Pie Smoothie, 41
  regulation by kidneys, 20
potassium-sparing diuretics, 93
potatoes, Sheet Pan Lemon-Lime Chicken & Potatoes, 182–184
poultry, limiting consumption of, 86
PRAL (potential renal acid load), 91–93
preheating pans, 193
pretzels, sodium content, 59

protein. *See also* animal protein
  amounts in recipes, 130
  avoiding diet high in, 86
  creating restrictive diet for, 85
  in Crispy Chickpeas, 146
  daily dietary amounts, 84
  and dialysis, 88
  in foods, 84
  science of, 82–87
proteinuria, explained, 20
pumpkin seeds, Almond-Pumpkin Seed Chocolate Bark, 240

Q

quesadilla, Corn & Black Bean Quesadilla, 170–171
quinoa
  amount of protein in, 84
  Southwest Quinoa Salad, 210–211

R

rainbow chard, 97–98
raisins
  Kale & Golden Raisin Salad, 94–95
  Pumpkin Pie Smoothie, 41
raspberries, Peach-Raspberry Skillet Bake, 236
raspberry and peach water, 29
recipes, categorization of, 130

red onions

    Deviled Eggs with Pickled Red Onion, 144

    Quick Pickled Red Onions, 145

restaurant foods, sodium content, 58

rice pudding, Healthier Rice Pudding, 238

risk factors, 21

roasting vegetables, 66

S

salad dressings, sodium content, 59

salads

    Cranberry, Pepita & Broccoli Salad, 175

    Kale & Golden Raisin Salad, 94–95

    Lemon Herb Couscous Salad, 221

    Mediterranean Chopped Salad, 178–179

    Roasted Beet, Goat Cheese & Walnut Salad with Blueberry Vinaigrette, 114–116

    Southwest Quinoa Salad, 210–211

    Spiced Chicken, Orange & Avocado Salad, 191–192

    Thai Shrimp Salad, 206–207

    Tuna, Cannellini & Dill Salad, 200–201

    Vegetarian Summer Pasta Salad, 222–223

    Za'atar Chicken Salad, 185

salmon

    amount of protein in, 84

    Lemon Caper Roasted Salmon, 198–199

    Seared Salmon with Tzatziki Sauce, 196, 203–204

salsa, Salsa Fresca, 142, 150

salt. *See also* low-sodium foods; sodium

    creating flavor without, 50–51

    lowering intake and maximizing flavor, 60, 184

    using to elevate flavor, 44–45

salty sweet spot, finding, 48–49

sauces

    Tzatziki Sauce, 154

    Vegan Bolognese Sauce, 176–177

sausages, sodium content, 58

seasonings

    No-Sodium All-Purpose Seasoning, 250

    No-Sodium Cajun Seasoning, 251

seltzer water

    with ice, 29

    recommended intake, 42

shrimp, Thai Shrimp Salad, 206–207

single kidney, potassium considerations, 69. *See also* kidney disease

smoothies

    benefits of, 39

    Berry-Banana Hemp Smoothie, 40, 131

    low-sugar, 35

    Pumpkin Pie Smoothie, 41, 131

snacks, sodium content, 59

soda, giving up, 31–32

sodium. *See also* low-sodium foods; salt
  amounts in recipes, 130–131
  #ChangeYourBuds, 49–51
  finding weakness, 52–53
  and high blood pressure, 109
  keeping diet diary, 52
  lowering intake of, 53, 57–59
  maximum recommendation, 59
  preparing food, 54
  pros and cons of, 45–49
  stocking kitchen, 55–56
  tracking intake of, 59
soups. *See also* canned soups; chicken stock;
    stocks; vegetable stock
  Grandma Julie's Chicken Soup, 137
  Hearty Lentil Vegetable Soup, 139–140
  Leek & Yellow Squash Soup, 141
spaghetti, Roasted Tomato & Zucchini Spaghetti
    with Vegan Basil-Cashew Pesto, 216–217
sparkling orange water with basil, 29
spices, using to enhance flavor, 184
spinach
  Egg Muffins with Spinach & Artichoke
    Hearts, 162
  Five-Minute Spinach, 73
  Roasted Beet, Goat Cheese & Walnut Salad
    with Blueberry Vinaigrette, 116–117
spreads, Smoky Eggplant Spread, 148
squash, Leek & Yellow Squash Soup, 141

stages of CKD (chronic kidney disease), 22
steak, amount of protein in, 84
stocks. *See also* canned soups; soups
  No-Sodium Chicken Stock, 134–135
  No-Sodium Vegetable Stock, 136
stomach upset, easing with ginger, 137
strawberry-lemon-basil water, 29
sugar-free beverages, 34–35
sugary drinks, 29–33
sumac, Mediterranean Chopped Salad, 178–179
sweet potatoes
  Curried Sweet Potatoes & Chickpeas, 173–174
  roasting, 66
sweet tea, 131

T

tea, Sweet Tea Substitute, 33. *See also*
    unsweetened tea
thirst, quenching with water, 26
toast
  Avocado Toast with Chile Flakes, 165
  Sunflower Butter & Blueberry Toast, 164
tomatoes, Roasted Tomato & Zucchini Spaghetti
    with Vegan Basil-Cashew Pesto, 216–217
tubules, explained, 21
tuna (canned)
  amount of protein in, 84
  Tuna, Cannellini & Dill Salad, 200–201

turkey sandwich, sodium in, 47

tzatziki sauce

making, 154

Seared Salmon with Tzatziki Sauce, 203–204

U

unsweetened tea, recommended intake, 42. *See also* tea

uremia, explained, 21

ureter, explained, 21

V

vegetable scraps, storing, 135

vegetable stock, 136. *See also* soups; stocks

vegetables. *See also* canned vegetables

Balsamic Roasted Vegetables, 224, 230

including in meals, 86

low-potassium content, 77

roasting, 66

substituting meat with, 87

vinaigrettes

Balsamic Vinaigrette, 245

Blueberry Vinaigrette, 242, 246

Cumin Lime Vinaigrette, 249

Dijon Vinaigrette, 244

Lemon Shallot Vinaigrette, 242, 245

Mediterranean Vinaigrette, 244

No-Sodium All-Purpose Seasoning, 242

No-Sodium Cajun Seasoning, 242

Red Wine Vinaigrette, 242, 248

Roasted Beet, Goat Cheese & Walnut Salad with Blueberry Vinaigrette, 116

Sherry Vinaigrette, 248

vinegar, using to enhance flavor, 184

W

walnuts

Roasted Beet, Goat Cheese & Walnut Salad with Blueberry Vinaigrette, 116–117

Spiced Apricot Walnut Muffins, 161

water

alternatives, 28–29

amount needed, 27–28

filtering by kidneys, 22

importance of drinking, 24, 26

recommended intake, 42

whole grains, 87, 120–121

whole milk, amount of protein in, 84. *See also* milk and dairy products

whole-food diet. *See* plant-based eating

wildcard beverages, 42

Y

yeast (nutritional), using to enhance flavor, 184

Z

zucchini, Stuffed Zucchini Boats, 166, 168–169

Made in the USA
Las Vegas, NV
18 April 2024

88847601R00169